THE CONSENSUS-CONFLIC
FORM AND CONTENT IN SOCIAL THEORIES

The Consensus-Conflict Debate

Form and Content in Social Theories

Thomas J. Bernard

Columbia University Press
New York—1983

Clothbound editions of Columbia University Press books are Smyth-sewn and printed on permanent and durable acid-free paper.

Library of Congress Cataloging in Publication Data

Bernard, Thomas J.
  The consensus-conflict debate.

  Includes bibliographical references and index.
  1. Sociology—Methodology. 2. Consensus (Social sciences) 3. Conflict (Psychology) 4. Social values.
I. Title
HM24.B414 1983   301'.01   83-2032
ISBN 0-231-05670-2
ISBN 0-231-05671-0 (pbk.)

Columbia University Press
New York   Guildford, Surrey

Contents

Foreword

AT TIMES it seems that sociological theory is still at Auguste Comte's "metaphysical stage" of societal and intellectual evolution. Contrary to Comte's dream of a "social physics," theory is still embroiled in metaphysical debates on questions such as: Are there emergent structural properties of interaction? Are there "deep structures" that explain surface empirical regularities in society? Are social processes determinate or indeterminate? And perhaps most prominently, are societies to be conceptualized as tension-filled, conflict-producing systems or as integrated, consensual systems? In a way that would be highly offensive to Comte, the term "positivism" now appears to legitimate highly standardized and ritualized acts of raw data collection and mindless statistical analysis rather than the testing of formally stated theories.

Indeed, modern positivism is now equated with atheoretical research, whereas a theory is seen as philosophy, history of ideas, moralistic debates, and metaphysical assertions. Accordingly, in the pages of this book, Thomas J. Bernard addresses what is probably the most central metaphysical issue in contemporary sociology: the consensus-conflict debate. Is society a smoldering set of tension-filled relations that periodically erupt into conflict, or is it an integrated and coordinated whole typified by consensus on values and beliefs? When phrased this way, the debate may seem absurd, because both extremes are empirically evident and have been recorded by the atheoretical data collection acts of the "new positivists." Indeed, this fact makes the debate even more fascinating, since it continues despite the recognition that at different historical times in diverse empirical contexts under varying conditions both conflictual and consensual processes are evident in human social systems. So what, then, is the argument about? And why do sociologists spend so much time on it?

This book provides some answers to these questions, and in so doing it can help move sociological theory from the metaphysical to the positivistic stage. As Professor Bernard demonstrates, the consensus-conflict debate is centuries old; it is not just an argument by some contemporary partisans. For this debate to have endured for so long and to be so engrained in Western thinking signals that it touches on social thinkers' most fundamental ways of looking at society. Moreover, the debate rages on to this very day, despite the recognition that each participant's position is true *some of the time* and false *at other times*, signaling again that some much deeper philosophical and moral issues are at stake for the combatants. Bernard exposes these deep, enduring issues by examining the work of selected social thinkers; and by examining these in detail, he exposes the underlying reasons for the debate and its longevity, with the consequence that contemporary social theorists are in a better position to terminate the debate and develop theoretical propositions that can specify the generic conditions under which conflictual or consensual processes occur.

The book examines seven pairs of thinkers who, in terms of their terminological descriptions of the societies of their times, can be classified as "conflict" or "consensus" theorists. Aristotle is compared with Plato, Augustine with Aquinas, Hobbes with Machiavelli, Locke with Rousseau, Comte with Marx, Durkheim with Simmel, and Parsons with Dahrendorf. While their terminological descriptions of society provide the basis for classification, the analysis explores two additional aspects of these scholars' work: their assumptions about human nature and their visions of the "good" or "ideal" society. On the basis of their views on human nature and their descriptions of society, Bernard is able to develop a fourfold typology of conflict and consensus theories. "Conservative consensus theorists," such as Aristotle, Aquinas, and Locke, employ consensus terminology in describing their respective societies and have a basically benign, consensus view of human nature. "Sociological consensus theorists" like Hobbes, Durkheim, and Parsons use consensus terminology in describing society but hold a less benign, more conflictual view of human nature. "Radical conflict theorists," such as Plato, Rousseau, and Marx, develop a conflict terminology for analyzing society but adhere to a benign, consensus position on human nature. And "sociological conflict theorists" like Machiavelli, Simmel, and Dahrendorf maintain a conflict vocabulary in describing society and a conflict vision of human nature.

The failure to recognize the fact that there are two different forms of both conflict and consensus theory has led to considerable confusion in the consensus-conflict debate. In recent decades, the debate has been couched in terms of the sociological consensus theorists on the one side and the radical conflict theorists on the other. For the sociological consensus theorists, the fundamental problem is to reconcile the consensus description of contemporary society with humans' conflictual needs and instincts, creating the "Hobbesian problem of order" as the major theoretical issue. For radical conflict theorists, the intellectual problem is just the reverse and revolves around reconciling humans' benign, cooperative nature with the existence of conflict-producing exploitation and inequality in society. The need to reconcile these contradictory visions of human nature and society creates extreme portrayals of the societal processes that either tame humans' aggressive nature or precipitate their fall from benign grace. It is not surprising, therefore, that large differences between sociological consensus theories and radical conflict theories can be found and that the "debate" can never be resolved when couched in these extreme terms.

In contrast, conservative consensus theories and sociological conflict theories do not reveal such contradictions between the terms used to describe society and the hypothesized view of human nature. As a result, social processes are not expressed in such extremes, since the social order reflects the basic nature of humans. Thus, a debate between these versions of conflict and consensus theory will be less acrimonious. Yet the debate is hardly ever couched in terms of the assumptions and descriptions of conservative consensus theorists and sociological conflict theorists. Even more rare is the joining of sociological and radical conflict theorists, who in holding such different assumptions about human nature have very little in common except their conflict vocabulary. Sociological and conservative consensus theorists rarely debate, primarily because few sociologists adhere to the conservative position. But such a debate—emanating from different conceptions of human nature—would be more productive than the typical arguments between radical conflict and sociological consensus theorists. Indeed, when conflict and disorder are no longer seen as emanating from human nature, the *social* processes systematically producing conflict are more likely to be addressed—thereby providing a basis for reconciling consensus descriptions of society with those of conflict theorists.

Thus, by isolating these types of conflict and consensus theories, Bernard suggests why the debate is never resolved. He also allows us to see why the sociological conflict theories are often considered to have the best chance for reconciling the debate, since they hold a view of human nature that is compatible with sociological consensus theory, yet at the same time they incorporate concepts from the radical conflict tradition without the extremes necessary when society is held to have corrupted human nature. With common assumptions about human nature and with vocabularies describing cooperative and conflictual processes, a more balanced theory of human organization is likely to emerge.

The reconciliation of the debate is confounded, however, by the third dimension by which conflict and consensus theories are compared—namely, their varying views on the "good" or "ideal" society. Much of the debate between conflict and consensus theorists is irreconcilable because advocates adhere to different moral conceptions of the ideal society. And when different moral yardsticks are used to examine contemporary societies, it is not surprising that measurements of what exists should differ. Bernard argues that only the sociological conflict theorists do not implicitly evaluate contemporary society in terms of some hypothetical ideal. Radical conflict theories are the most self-consciously evaluative and judge contemporary social arrangements in terms of a hypothetical society where social arrangements are totally rebuilt so that society and humans' benign nature are in harmony. Conservative and sociological consensus theories do not hold to such an extreme view of the ideal, for the ideal society is simply an extension of the best features of contemporary, consensual society and does not involve a radical reconstruction of the social world. Hence the moral evaluation of contemporary society is less severe than it is in radical conflict theory.

The implications of Bernard's argument for resolving the consensus-conflict debate are important. When social arrangements—whether harmonious or conflictual ones—are defined as undesirable and illegitimate, analyses of society are seriously distorted. Moreover, the chances of reconciling different conceptualizations are very slim, since they follow from varying moralities. Thus, as long as the debate revolves around sociological consensus theories and radical conflict theories, it can never be resolved, because of the contrasting moralities of these two schools. In fact, as long as radical conflict theorists are involved, the debate will rage, even with sociological conflict theorists who use the terminology but not the morality of the radicals.

There is a further implication in Bernard's analysis: once sociological analysis abandons, whether explicitly or implicitly, the hope of value neutrality, debates will never end, since all accounts of social events will be biased by moral commitments. It is one thing to make assumptions about human nature and to let these assumptions direct scientific questions; it is another to let one's morality define these questions. For example, considerably more insight is possible when a consensus theorist like Talcott Parsons examines mechanisms of social control based on his assumptions about human nature than when a radical conflict theorist sees these mechanisms as immoral tools of exploitation by power elites.

But perhaps the most important implication of Bernard's work is the *demonstration* that the consensus-conflict debate is philosophical and ideological. It cannot be resolved when waged at these levels. Only when commitments to "ideal societies" are abandoned and assumptions about human nature are translated into clear theoretical statements about how societies operate will sociology move beyond arguments over whether society is more consensual or conflictual.

Jonathan H. Turner

Acknowledgments

I WOULD like to thank Professor Graeme Newman, who guided this project from its beginnings. He provided detailed comments and trenchant criticisms on a number of occasions, and retained an optimistic faith that the chaotic early drafts I gave him would eventually become a coherent piece of work. I hope his faith has been justified. I would also like to thank Professors Travis Hirschi, David Duffee, Lawrence Sherman, Leslie Wilkins, Walter Freeman, and Darrell Steffensmeier, all of whom read and commented on the manuscript. Finally, I would like to dedicate this book to my wife, Wendy, who has cherished and encouraged me through all the changes of our lives; to our son, Evan, who is a constant reminder to me that the most precious things in life won't get you tenure; and to the memory of my brother, Edward L. Bernard, Jr.

THE CONSENSUS-CONFLICT DEBATE:
FORM AND CONTENT IN SOCIAL THEORIES

CHAPTER 1

INTRODUCTION

THIS BOOK is about theories, not about reality. It is an exploration of patterns of thinking that occur in the context of social theories, and the relationship those patterns have to certain fundamental assumptions (either implicit or explicit) underlying the theories. The pattern of thinking found in a particular theory is referred to as its "form," and the fundamental assumptions are said to be part of its "content," where the content also includes the theory's other assumptions and assertions.[1] It has been argued that social theories are inevitably based on assumptions or assertions that are themselves resistant to empirical verification or falsification but have a substantial impact on the way the theories organize and present empirical data. Gouldner, for example, calls these "background assumptions."[2] This book deals with the relationship between certain of those assumptions (i.e., the content of the theory) and the resulting manner in which empirical data are organized and presented (its form). It argues that such an analysis can be used to explain a persistent controversy in social theory that has been called "the consensus-conflict debate." Because this book argues that the consensus-conflict debate can be resolved through an analysis of the relationship between form and content in social theories, it does not examine the extent to which any of those theories are supported by empirical data.

The phrase "consensus-conflict debate" refers to a controversy based on an uncertain and imprecise method of dividing social theories into two contrasting groups on the basis of their descriptions of broader social processes. Consensus theories are said to include those social theories that emphasize the persistence of shared values and norms as the fundamental characteristics of societies. According to such theories, social order is based on tacit agreements about rules of interaction that are part of the way the world itself is perceived and understood. Social changes occur slowly and "organically" because they reflect large-scale shifts in attitude as community beliefs evolve. In contrast, conflict theories are said to include those social theories that emphasize the dominance of some groups over others. According to these theories, popular attitudes are manipulated by powerful groups through their control of education and the media, and the absence of overt conflict is the result of their control of the mechanisms of physical force. Social changes occur suddenly when new groups arise and successfully challenge the dominant groups.

There are a number of other ways that social theories can be dichotomized—e.g., one can talk about individualism vs. collectivism, or voluntarism vs. determinism. However, dividing theories into "consensus" and "conflict" theories has always been particularly relevant to questions about stratification and inequality. There, the consensus-conflict debate is associated with sharp controversies about the most fundamental views of humanity and society.[3] Consensus and conflict theories are also associated with contrasting views of law and criminality that have strikingly different implications for public policy.[4] The present examination of the consensus-conflict debate is undertaken with an eye to these fundamental academic and public policy questions related to stratification and inequality and to law and criminality.

History of the Consensus-Conflict Debate

The phrase "consensus-conflict debate" seems to be of relatively recent origin and is commonly used to describe a controversy that arose in sociology in the 1950s, reached its peak around 1970, and has been declining since that time. By the mid-1950s, the structural functionalism of Talcott Parsons and his associates had come to dominate sociology to such a degree that Kingsley Davis, in his presidential address to the American Sociological Association in 1959, was able to state that functionalism and academic sociology had become one.[5] But by the time that statement was made, the first challenges to functionalism from what would become known as conflict theory had already been issued.[6] One of the most influential was an article by Ralf Dahrendorf, published in 1958, in which he attacked the consensus model and urged sociologists to turn to the conflict model as a way of addressing certain critical problems.[7] He argued that the consensus model was "utopian" in that it portrayed all normal social change as a process of organic growth. Dahrendorf noted that societies also experience fundamental social changes that can be explained only by assuming that there are individuals in the society who do not agree with the existing consensus and who are ultimately able to modify or replace it. In consensus theory, this type of fundamental change is seen as abnormal and is explained by referring to extraordinary circumstances. But Dahrendorf argued that fundamental change was in fact the normal state of society and that it occurred constantly at all levels, from the seats of governments to the local trade unions and parish houses. Sociologists, he said, should look for factors that interfere with the normal processes of change rather than for the factors that cause it.

Dahrendorf presented a similar argument with the idea of conflict:

> As with change, we have grown accustomed to look for special causes or circumstances whenever we encounter conflict; but again, a complete turn is necessary in our thinking. Not the presence but the absence of conflict is surprising and abnormal, and we have good reason to be suspicious if we find a society or social organization that displays no evidence of conflict. To be sure, we do not have to assume that conflict is always violent and uncontrolled. There is probably a continuum from civil war to parliamentary debate, from strikes and lockouts to joint consultation. Our problems and their explanations will undoubtedly teach us a great deal about the range of variation in forms of conflict. In formulating such explanations, however, we must never lose sight of the underlying assumption that conflict can be temporarily suppressed, regulated, channeled, and controlled, but that neither a philosopher-king nor a modern dictator can abolish it once and for all.[8]

Dahrendorf concluded: "From the point of view of this model, societies and social organizations are held together not by consensus but by constraint, not by universal agreement but by coercion of some by others."[9]

The functional theorists rose to the challenge. One of the most provocative responses was by Edward Shils in the epilogue to a massive collection of readings in sociological theory that was organized around the functionalist framework.[10] He argued that Parsons' *The Structure of Social Action* was the turning point of modern sociology, drawing together the diverse strands of earlier sociological theories into a single theoretical orientation focused on the problem of the formation of a coherent order. Parsons' theory triumphed precisely because it was "consensual sociology," in that it crystallized and expressed what was in fact the modern human experience of affinity with other human beings:

> Modern society, especially in its latest phase, is characteristically a consensual society; it is a society in which personal attachments play a greater part than in most societies in the past, in which the individual person is appreciated, in which there is concern for his well-being. . . . Contemporary Western societies, with all those deficiencies detected by the sensitive moral conscience and the sharpened sociological eye, are probably more decently integrated than any societies that have preceded them in world history or are contemporaneous with them in other parts of the world. They are more integrated in the sense that there is more mutual awareness, more perception of others, more imaginative empathy about the stages of mind and motivations of others, more fellow feeling. . . . These represent a new stage in human existence—a stage in which consensus rests on individuality and on the bonds that can exist between individualities; not a consensus that assumes the absence of individuality and crushes its first manifestations. It is a consensus constructed out of the affectional ties of one individual perceiving the individuality of another, out of a civility that perceives and attaches to the mere humanity of another person, out of a sense of nationality that perceives in the other the element of a shared territoriality.[11]

Consensual sociology does not merely describe this phenomenon but in fact is said to be a part of it. By expressing this fundamental human experience of the modern world, sociology participates in the processes by which societies become even more fully consensual.

But Shils also noted that there was an "alienated tendency" in modern sociology, which he said was derived from the original association of sociological research with studies of the miseries of the poor. The sociologists who were associated with this tendency were said to believe that sociology should be an "oppositional" science that is radically iconoclastic and always directed against authority. He stated that some of those sociologists "are former or quasi-Marxists—who, without giving up their allegiance to Marxism wish nonetheless to retain its original disposition."[12] These were the emerging conflict theorists of the day, and Shils rejected their arguments out of hand, stating that their outlook was "defective intellectually":

> Society is not just "congeries of atomized individuals"; nor has bourgeois society "reduced the family relation to a mere money relation." Contemporary society does consist of anonymous faces in the crowd; political life is not just a scene in which self-interest pressure groups determine every policy.... [These theorists] greatly overestimate the extent to which the Hobbesian state of nature prevails in society; they overestimate correspondingly the role of deception, manipulation, and coercion, and the degree of deliberate concerting of action by the elites against the rest of society. It is not that these observations are entirely without foundation; but they do not merit the preponderance that "oppositional science" accords to them.[13]

Shils concluded: "Sociology can and almost certainly will divest itself of the quasi-Marxist, populistic, rationalistic anti-authoritarianism and the blindness to the nature and working of tradition that it has inherited. It will, on the whole, gain considerably thereby."[14]

So by the early 1960s, the battle between consensus and conflict theorists had been joined. Yet the outcome of that battle was not a clear-cut triumph for either side. The criticisms that conflict theory raised against functionalism have generally been sustained, and now have entered into the mainstream of sociological thinking. Martins, for example, has observed that "functionalism 'dies' every year, every Autumn term, being ritually executed for introductory teaching purposes...."[15] However, conflict theory itself has not assumed a major role in academic sociology; rather, attention has shifted to new topics that are largely unrelated to either consensus or conflict theories—ethnomethodology, phenomenology, exchange theory, and other theories that Martins refers to as a "microscopic reaction."[16] These theories tend to focus on the "microsociological" world of everyday life, rather than on "macrosociological" phenomena such as social structure and process, which were the focus of consensus and conflict theories.

Thus, it is possible to argue that while the consensus-conflict debate was never really resolved, it is no longer relevant because sociology has simply moved on to greener and more fertile pastures. The debate could be said to be associated with a particular episode in the evolution of modern sociology, having no enduring significance. But such an argument would ignore the fact that the consensus-conflict debate has not occurred merely at one specific point in history. It has, rather, been a recurring debate that has taken a variety of different forms throughout the history of Western thought. It had made an earlier appearance in sociology as a debate between the positivistic organicists, such as Comte, Spencer, and Durkheim, and the sociological conflict theorists, such as Bagehot, Glumplowicz, and Small.[17] In addition, a wide variety of theorists who preceded the foundation of sociology have been identified in the secondary literature as either "consensus theorists" or "conflict theorists," despite the fact that these terms did not exist at the time that their theories were written.[18] Such identification seems to be related to the retrospective assessment that the earlier theories were part of a historical tradition that culminated in sociological consensus and conflict theories. But these theorists could also be said to have been part of a "debate" among themselves, independent of whatever influence they had on later theories. For example, Comte cited Aristotle as his "incomparable predecessor," while Popper has argued that Marx's theories grew out of the Platonic tradition and that Marx was an "unconscious Platonist."[19] The works of Plato and Aristotle can be considered relevant to the consensus-conflict debate in the sense that they influenced the later theories of Comte and Marx, but they can also be considered to have engaged in the "consensus-conflict debate" themselves, as it was defined in ancient Greece. In fact, Ossowski has argued that these two types of theories have been found throughout history in almost every kind of society.[20]

The consensus-conflict debate can therefore be viewed much more broadly than merely as a specific confrontation between academic sociologists during the latter part of the twentieth century. Rather, that confrontation is one example of a more general phenomenon that is in some sense bound up with the way we think about our societies. This examination of the consensus-conflict debate focuses on that more general phenomenon, rather than specifically on its most recent incarnation in sociology. The significance of undertaking an examination of the consensus-conflict debate is derived from the fact that its topic is a controversy that has occurred repeatedly throughout history and in a wide variety of cultures, yet no satisfactory resolution of the controversy has been achieved. The movement of modern sociology away from this question therefore does not compromise the significance of the undertaking.

Views of the Consensus-Conflict Debate

One of the reasons the consensus-conflict debate is such a confusing area is that there is literally no agreement about the nature of the debate itself. Opinions about the debate range from the argument that this method of dichotomizing social theories is fundamentally misleading to the argument that one of the two types of theories is "correct" while the other is "wrong." The examination of the consensus-conflict debate therefore begins with an examination of the range of opinions concerning the debate itself.

Perhaps the most common view of the consensus-conflict debate is that the two types of theories represent different aspects of the same reality. For example, Lewis Coser has stated: "It would be a mistake to distinguish a sociology of order from one of disorder, a model of harmony from one of conflict. These are not distinct realities, but only differing formal aspects of one reality."[21] Talcott Parsons has made a similar argument:

> I do not think it is useful to postulate a deep dichotomy between theories which give importance to beliefs and values on the one hand, to allegedly "realistic" interests, e.g., economic, on the other. Beliefs and values are actualized, partially and imperfectly, in realistic situations of social interaction and the outcomes are always codetermined by the values and realistic exigencies; conversely what on concrete levels are called "interests" are by no means independent of the values which have been institutionalized in the relevant groups.[22]

Closely related to this view, although distinct from it, is the argument that consensus and conflict theories represent answers to different questions. Turner, for example, argues that functionalists should focus their attention on "the causal analysis of the antecedents to parts and on the causal relations between parts and social wholes" in order to address the question of what a part "does for" or "contributes to" the society. Conflict theorists should focus on a "careful analysis of the conditions under which different forms of conflict are likely to occur among different types of social units" in order to propose a theory of *conflict*, not a theory of social organization.[23] Dahrendorf takes a similar stance when he argues: "There are sociological problems for the explanation of which the integration theory of society provides adequate assumptions; there are other problems which can be explained only in terms of the coercion theory of society; there are, finally, problems for which both theories appear adequate. For sociological analysis, society is Janus-headed, and its two faces are equivalent aspects of the same reality."[24]

Another view is that the validity of consensus and conflict theories can be evaluated only in the context of specific situations. For example, Williams has stated: "As we have seen, much controversy has raged over the question, which of these doctrines is correct? My own answer is quite direct: all are correct in part, all are partly wrong, none is wholly adequate. Actual societies are held together by consensus, by interdependence, by sociability, and by coercion. This has always been the case, and there is no reason to expect it to be otherwise in any foreseeable future. The real job is to show how actual social structures and processes operating in these ways can be predicted and explained."[25] Robert Merton, a leading exponent of the functionalist school, has made a comment about functionalism that implies a similar point: "It is not enough to refer to the 'institutions' as though they were all uniformly supported by all groups and strata in the society. Unless systematic consideration is given to the *degree* of support of particular 'institutions' by *specific* groups we shall overlook the important place of power in society."[26]

Still another view is that the consensus-conflict debate does not concern empirical matters at all. Horton argued that they express conflicting "value-imperatives," where consensus theories express a transcendent image of society, "greater than and different from the sum of its parts," and a positive attitude toward the maintenance of social institutions, and conflict theories express an immanent conception of society where "men are society, society is the extension of man, the indwelling of man," and a positive attitude toward change.[27] Consensus theories, according to Horton, value "the social good: balance, stability, authority, order, quantitative growth ('moving equilibrium')," while conflict theories value "freedom as autonomy, change, action, qualitative growth." Like Horton, Dahrendorf argues that consensus and conflict theories do not represent assertions of empirical facts, but he goes on to describe them as "heuristic principles."[28]

It has also been suggested that the consensus-conflict debate is the result of oversimplified portrayals of primary theories in the secondary literature. Williams has stated: "It seems clear that many of the debates [between consensus and conflict theorists] have consisted of the demolition of strawmen. Indeed, what sociologist in his right mind ever regarded any empirical society as *only* 'consensus' or *only* conflict? Certainly not Simmel, or Marx, or Weber, or Durkheim, or Parsons."[29] Once these theories are considered in their full complexity, it becomes unclear whether they are opposed to each other at all. It also becomes unclear whether the theories grouped together as "consensus theories" or as "conflict theories" are essentially similar in any way. That is particularly true of conflict theories. Zeitlin notes that "the heading covers several heterogeneous and even contradictory perspectives. Indeed, what do all of these have in common besides the term 'conflict'?"[30] Skidmore states that "conflict theories" are the most obvious example of the mistaken belief that theories grouped under a single category are similar in essentials.[31] Functional theories have in general not been subject to this criticism, since almost all of them have evolved under the strong leadership of Talcott Parsons. But the broader term "consensus theories" would certainly incorporate heterogeneous and even contradictory perspectives, just as "conflict theories" does.

The Present Study

In any scientific investigation, it is necessary to define appropriately the question one is asking. Every way of phrasing a question contains a certain number of assumptions. If other scientists reject those assumptions, they will also reject any findings that the investigation produces. Thus, great care must be taken at the outset to define one's question in a way that will be acceptable to others in the field.

That problem is particularly acute with respect to phenomena such as the consensus-conflict debate, where there is little agreement about any of its aspects. In such a situation, it is appropriate to define one's question so that a minimal number of assumptions are involved. One way to investigate the consensus-conflict debate would be to ask the question Zeitlin asked, as quoted above: What is it that conflict theories have in common besides the term "conflict," and what is it that consensus theories have in common besides the term "consensus"? Such a question assumes that there are a certain number of theories that can be classified as "conflict theories" and a certain number of other theories that can be classified as "consensus theories." That is an assumption that can be challenged and rejected by others in the field, but it seems to be the minimum assumption necessary for any examination of the consensus-conflict debate. In particular, that question makes no assumptions about whether the consensus-conflict dichotomy is a meaningful one. For example, it is possible that the examination would find that conflict theories have nothing in common except the term "conflict," or that some consensus theories have nothing in common with other consensus theories but a great deal in common with some conflict theories. If the findings of the investigation were along those lines, then it would be appropriate to conclude that dichotomizing social theories into consensus and conflict theories is fundamentally misleading. Thus, defining the question in this way allows an examination of the consensus-conflict debate without actually assuming that the consensus-conflict dichotomy is a meaningful one.

An alternative way of defining the question would be to ask about the differences between a series of pairs of theories, where one of each pair of theories was a consensus theory and the other a conflict theory. Again, this question assumes that at least some theories can be classified at the outset as consensus theories and others as conflict theories, but it makes no assumption about the meaningfulness of that classification. This form of the question has the advantage of directly addressing the nature of the consensus-conflict debate. If no consistent differences are found between the pairs of theories, then there is no such thing as a "consensus-conflict debate." If, on the other hand, some consistent differences are found, then the significance of the consensus-conflict dichotomy as a classification for social theories will depend on the significance of those differences.

That, then, is the way the question was framed in the present examination of the consensus-conflict debate. A series of fourteen theorists were selected: eight social philosophers who preceded the foundation of sociology and six major sociologists. The selection of the sociologists was made on the basis of the ease with which they could be classified in the consensus-conflict dichotomy. Thus, Comte, Durkheim, and Parsons were selected because there would be little controversy in describing them as "consensus theorists." Similarly, Marx, Simmel, and Dahrendorf were selected as representative of conflict theorists. Weber was not included in the present analysis because any initial classification of his theory in the consensus-conflict dichotomy would have been subject to considerable controversy. Thus, a comparison between Weber's theory and some other theory would have only limited utility in determining the differences between consensus and conflict theories.

The social philosophers who were selected were Plato, Aristotle, Augustine, Aquinas, Machiavelli, Hobbes, Locke, and Rousseau. The selection of these theorists was somewhat, but not entirely, arbitrary, and was guided by the attempt to describe, if only in rough outline, the theoretical traditions from which consensus and conflict theories in sociology have sprung. It has already been mentioned that the works of Marx and Comte can be traced back to the traditions established by Plato and Aristotle, respectively. Those two traditions were brought into the context of Christianity by Augustine and Aquinas, who therefore are key transitional thinkers from the world of the ancient Greeks to the modern world. Machiavelli is uniformly cited as a predecessor of conflict theorists in sociology, while modern consensus theories (particularly that of Parsons) are in large part a response to the "problem of order" that Hobbes defined. Finally, Locke and Rousseau, as social contract theorists, were generally important in setting the stage for the development of modern sociology. The inclusion of these authors also reflects the broader view that the consensus-conflict debate is a controversy that has occurred throughout history and in a wide variety of cultures, rather than the narrower view that it is strictly a sociological controversy. Thus, these authors are presented not only to portray the historical background of the consensus-conflict debate in sociology, but to portray the forms that the consensus-conflict debate took at other times and places. Presenting the broadest possible range of forms that the consensus-conflict debate has taken increases the likelihood that the exact nature of differences (if any) between the two types of theories will be identified.

Each of these fourteen theorists was extremely prolific, and any attempt to review the entire range of their works would be not only foolish but irrelevant to the present task. Thus, the examination focuses on those aspects of their theories that are relevant to the consensus-conflict debate. In general, that includes the views these theorists had on stratification and inequality and on law and criminality, since those are the areas in which the differences between consensus and conflict theories are most pronounced. Those views, however, can be accurately presented only in their proper theoretical context, so at least a general overview of the theorists' work is also presented. This is particularly true in the presentation of the sociological theories, where individual views tend to be part of a much larger and coherent theory that was developed throughout the entire lifetime of the author. In the presentation of the theories of the social philosophers, views relevant to the consensus-conflict debate are more appropriately presented within the context of a single work. Several of these authors held very different views at different times in their lives, and modern references to them in the context of the consensus-conflict debate tend to focus on a single work and to ignore other works. The present examination focuses on the following works, as they are considered most relevant to the consensus-conflict debate: Plato's *Republic*, Aristotle's *Politics*, Augustine's *City of God*, Aquinas' *Summa Theologica*, Machiavelli's *The Prince*, Hobbes' *Leviathan*, Locke's *Second Treatise on Government*, and Rousseau's *The Social Contract*.

These fourteen theorists are divided into seven pairs for the purposes of comparison. Thus, Plato is paired with Aristotle, Augustine with Aquinas, Machiavelli with Hobbes, Locke with Rousseau, Comte with Marx, Durkheim with Simmel, and Parsons with Dahrendorf. Most of the pairs consist of theorists who lived in the same general period of time and in generally similar societies. Nevertheless, it might be argued that some of the differences between the theories arise because of the different historical situations in which the authors lived. For example, Augustine's fifth-century North Africa was certainly different from Aquinas' thirteenth-century Italy. However, if the terms "consensus theory" and "conflict theory" are to have any meaning as classifications for theories, theories of the same type should contain similarities even though they describe societies at different times. Likewise, if there is such a phenomenon as a "consensus-conflict debate," there should be consistent differences between consensus theories and conflict theories independent of the historical contexts in which those theories appeared. This book searches for those similarities and differences by comparing theories that describe different societies at different times. It concludes that the form of the theory does not depend on the empirical characteristics of the society being described. Thus, the historical context of these theories is not important for the present study, and it is presented only to the extent that it is necessary for understanding the theory itself.

Within each pair, one of the theorists is classified as a consensus theorist, while the other is classified as a conflict theorist. The classification of the sociological theorists is not a problem, since they were selected with that purpose in mind. The classification of the social philosophers, however, is more of an issue. The terms "consensus theory" and "conflict theory" did not exist at the time these theorists wrote, and the consensus-conflict debate, when applied to these theories, is to a certain extent the projection of a modern controversy onto older theories. Nevertheless, the assumption that theories can be classified as either consensus or conflict theories is, as pointed out above, the minimum assumption necessary for any examination of the consensus-conflict debate, and such a classification is made only to determine whether there are any real and consistent differences between the two types of theories. Within that framework, there seems to be no controversy about the classification of at least some of the social philosophers. For example, Aristotle is uniformly classified as a consensus theorist and Machiavelli is uniformly classified as a conflict theorist by those who describe such theorists in terms of the consensus-conflict dichotomy.[32] About other theorists, however, there is considerable disagreement. For example, Hobbes is sometimes described as a conflict theorist and other times as a consensus theorist. In the present study, Hobbes is classified as a consensus theorist, but that classification was made only after the source of the confusion became clear and certain definitional choices were made to insure that the classification of the social philosophers would be consistent with that of the sociologists.

Classifying Theorists in the Consensus-Conflict Dichotomy

The confusion about how to classify certain theorists arises because there are actually three distinct phenomena that may be described in terms of "consensus" or in terms of "conflict." Those are *human nature, the contemporary state of society*, and *the ideal society*. The description of human nature in terms of consensus or of conflict refers to whether humans are said to be naturally cooperative or naturally aggressive. Hobbes' views on this subject are well known, and are summarized by his argument that under the veneer of civilization lies the war of all against all. Aristotle's views on the subject were quite the opposite, and have been summarized by Park and Burgess as follows:

> Aristotle…taught that man was made for life in society just as the bee is made for life in the hive. The relations between the sexes, as well as those between mother and child, are manifestly predetermined in the physiological organization of the individual man and woman. Furthermore, man is, by his instincts and his inherited dispositions, predestined to a social existence beyond the intimate family circle. Society must be conceived, therefore, as a part of nature, like a beaver's dam or the nests of birds.[33]

Park and Burgess remark that the views of human nature held

by Aristotle and Hobbes "measure the range and divergence of the schools upon this topic."

The view found in each of the fourteen theories of whether human nature is essentially consensual or conflictual is presented as part of the present examination. Views of human nature can vary on other dimensions than the consensus-conflict one, but that particular dimension is relevant to the present task. Presenting those views is not a problem for the social philosophers, since they explicitly described human nature and made that description an integral part of their theories. Sociologists, however, have often been uncomfortable with the concept, since it seems to imply biological or psychological explanations of human behavior rather than explanations based on institutional or historical forces. Yet sociological theories necessarily presuppose some view of human nature, even if that view is not made explicit. Wrong has argued: "I do not see how, at the level of theory, sociologists can fail to make assumptions about human nature. If our assumptions are left implicit, we will inevitably presuppose a view of man that fits our special needs...."[34] Gouldner states that views of human nature are one example of "domain assumptions."[35] He argues that all sociological theories contain these assumptions, but that they are usually left implicit in the heart of the theory, rather than being made explicit. While these assumptions are quite resistant to any empirical testing, they are extremely important, because they determine the manner in which empirical data is presented. One of the major arguments of the present study concerns the exact effect that assumptions about human nature (i.e., a part of the theory's content) have on the way the theory is organized (i.e., its form). That argument is summarized in the next section of this chapter.

A second phenomenon that may be described in terms of consensus or in terms of conflict is the contemporary state of society. That phrase refers to the way the theorist described societies that actually existed at the time he was writing his theory. Each theory contains descriptions of contemporary societies, although generally that is not the major focus of the theory. Such descriptions may vary on many dimensions, but it is the consensus-conflict dimension that is of interest here. The key issue, however, is not the *amount* of conflict or of consensus that is said to exist in the society, since that could be the result of differences between societies that existed at different times and places, assuming that the descriptions were accurate. Rather, what is crucial for the examination of the consensus-conflict debate is the *terminology* used as the basis for the descriptions of those societies. Some theorists, such as Comte and Durkheim, described a great deal of conflict in their own societies, but their theoretical descriptions of those societies were based on consensus terminology. Conversely, Dahrendorf's descriptions of contemporary societies could incorporate widespread agreements on many issues, yet those descriptions are based on conflict terminology.

The present examination does not assume that those who describe contemporary societies using consensus terminology are necessarily asserting that there is more "agreement" in those societies than those who describe contemporary societies using conflict terminology, or vice versa. In fact, it treats that as an empirical question. After the presentation of each pair of theories, the "amount" of conflict and consensus that both theories describe in contemporary (i.e., real) societies is compared. No consistent differences have been found between the two types of theories. One of the major arguments of this book, then, is that the selection of consensus or conflict terminology as the basis for describing contemporary societies is not in itself subject to empirical verification or falsification, but rather is the discretionary prerogative of the author of the theory. However, the author's choice in this matter has a substantial impact on the form that the theory must take if it is to be logically consistent and empirically adequate. Accordingly, the book argues that the consensus-conflict debate cannot be resolved through empirical investigations because it is fundamentally a debate about alternative theoretical descriptions rather than about contrasting empirical assertions.

The third phenomenon that may be described in terms of either consensus or conflict is the "ideal" society. Each theory either presents or implies some description of the ideal society, although that description may take one of several different forms. For example, the ideal society may be presented as an amalgamation of the "best" elements from the various societies that existed at the time the theorist was writing, or it may be presented as a society with a totally different socioeconomic or political structure. The ideal society may be said to be the product of inevitable historical forces, or it may be said to be purely hypothetical. Most frequently, ideal societies are described in consensual terms because, within the context of each theory, conflict is considered to be somehow undesirable. However, some theories consider consensual societies to be not only impossible to achieve in practice but inappropriate and misleading even as the description of a hypothetical ideal. These theories present descriptions of the "ideal" society using conflict terminology. As with descriptions of contemporary societies, those who use conflict terminology to describe the ideal society do not necessarily assert that there will be greater amounts of conflict in that society than in an ideal society described in consensus terminology. In fact, many of the "ideal" societies are said to contain considerable amounts of conflict, regardless of the terminology used to describe them.

In the present study, theorists are classified in the consensus-conflict dichotomy on the basis of their descriptions of contemporary societies, rather than on the basis of their descriptions of human nature or of the ideal society. To do otherwise would result in serious problems in the classification of the sociologists. For example, Parsons took his view of human nature from Hobbes, whose theory exemplifies the conflict view on this subject. To classify theorists on the basis of their views of human nature would therefore require that Parsons be classified as a conflict theorist, which is completely unacceptable. Similarly, Marx's description of the ideal society ("communism") was at least as consensual as any consensual society ever described. To classify theorists on the basis of their descriptions of ideal societies would therefore require that Marx be classified as a consensus theorist, which is also unacceptable. The descriptions of human nature and of the ideal society are important in the context of these theories, but they are not relevant to the classification of theorists as consensus or conflict theorists. Rather, the meaning of that classification, as it is commonly used, is derived from the descriptions of contemporary societies.

The specific criterion used to classify theorists in the present study is as follows: *consensus theorists are theorists who use consensus terminology to describe at least some (but not necessarily all) societies that actually existed at the time they were writing, while conflict theorists are theorists who use conflict terminology to describe all societies that actually existed at the time they were writing.* I argue that this criterion successfully distinguishes between consensus and conflict theories in a way that is consistent with common usage and with the content of the theories themselves. In addition, I argue that this criterion produces a meaningful division between social theories, so that certain similarities appear within, and certain differences between, the types of theories. The analysis of those similarities and differences is part of a more general analysis of the way these theories organize and present empirical data—what I have called the relationship between form and content. That analysis represents the major argument of this work, and a summary of that argument is presented in the following section.

The Relation Between Form and Content

I said earlier that the content of a theory includes certain fundamental assumptions or assertions that are either implicit or explicit in the theory. The specific assumptions and assertions that are relevant to my analysis are those related to the descriptions of human nature, contemporary societies, and the ideal society, as described above. There are only a limited number of forms in which those descriptions (the content) can be woven together into a coherent argument. At the broadest level, the description of the ideal society in terms of consensus or conflict appears to be dependent on the descriptions of human nature and the descriptions of contemporary societies, so that there are actually only two independent variables among these three descriptions. Specifically, if a particular theory describes human nature in consensual terms, or describes at least some contemporary societies in consensual terms, then it will also describe the ideal society in consensual terms. To do otherwise would seem to be internally inconsistent for the theory. For example, it would seem quite inconsistent for a theory to describe some real society using consensual terms, and then to describe the ideal society using conflictual terms. In fact, no social theory examined in the course of this study contained such a combination of descriptions. On the other hand, to describe human nature in consensual terms is to argue that, in some sense, "man is made for life in society just as the bee is made for life in the hive." That implies the possibility of a harmonious "consensual" society (i.e., the hive) even if no such society is said to exist at the time the author was writing. Thus, if a particular theory describes human nature in consensual terms, it will also describe the ideal society in consensual terms, regardless of whether it describes contemporary societies in consensual or conflictual terms. To do otherwise would appear to be internally inconsistent for the theory, and no social theory examined in the course of this study combines a description of human nature in consensual terms with a description of the ideal society in conflictual terms. Thus, the only theories that describe the ideal society in conflictual terms are those that also describe human nature and all contemporary societies in conflictual terms. In those theories, a truly "consensual" society is regarded as completely impossible. The "ideal" society would be constituted out of whatever was regarded as "best" about possible societies, but it would not be described in consensual terms.

The criterion formulated above for classifying social theories in the consensus-conflict dichotomy considers only descriptions of contemporary societies. But descriptions of human nature are independent of descriptions of contemporary societies. Thus, there are actually two types of consensus theories—those that describe human nature in consensual terms and those that describe human nature in conflictual terms — and two comparable types of conflict theories. Each of these four types of theories is distinctly different from the others, and the failure to distinguish between the two types of consensus and the two types of conflict theories has led to much of the confusion about the nature of the consensus-conflict debate.

A brief description of these four types of theories is presented below. Within that description, the following points are noted for each type of theory, not necessarily in the following order:

1) the nature and causes of conflict (but not its amount);
2) the definition of the term "consensus"—as full and free agreements, or merely as the absence of overt conflicts;
3) the characteristics of the ideal society—whether it is said to be the "best" of existing societies or an entirely hypothetical society, and whether its socioeconomic system is necessarily different from those in contemporary societies;
4) the evaluation of contemporary societies as implied by their comparison to the ideal society; and
5) the major focus of the theory—whether it primarily describes and analyzes real contemporary societies, or whether it primarily describes ideal societies and analyzes the mechanisms by which real societies can be transformed into ideal ones.

These five points can be considered part of each theory's content, along with its descriptions of human nature, contemporary societies, and the ideal society.

It is important to note that, in a practical sense, neither the above five points nor the three basic descriptions can be empirically verified or falsified. The nature and causes of conflict are empirical issues, but their complexity is such that at present it is not possible to verify or falsify any of the various positions in a conclusive manner. Similarly, the description of human nature as consensual or conflictual represents an empirical but at present untestable assertion. The definition of the term "consensus" is the prerogative of each author, not subject to empirical verification or falsification; and I have already argued that the choice of the terms "consensus" or "conflict" in the description of contemporary societies is similarly the author's prerogative. The ideal society is an inherently speculative concept, so that its nature and characteristics are not verifiable or falsifiable, and the evaluation of contemporary societies by comparing them to that speculative ideal is not an empirical matter either. Finally, the focus of each theory is the choice of its author.

Because none of these points can be empirically verified or falsified, each author is in effect free to choose among the various positions available for each point. Yet each author is constrained in these choices by the need to construct a coherent theory that is logically consistent within itself and is not inconsistent with available empirical data (i.e., those aspects of reality that are empirically testable). I argued above that, because of the need for internal consistency, the description of the ideal society was dependent on the descriptions of human nature and of contemporary societies. In a similar manner, I argue below that the five additional aspects of each theory's content are also dependent on the descriptions of human nature and of contemporary societies. In other words, although none of the above five aspects of a theory's content can be empirically verified or falsified, they can be arranged in only four "packages" in order to form logically consistent and empirically adequate theories. These packages, while not empirically testable themselves, provide the context in which testable empirical data is organized and presented.[36] The logical interrelationships that link aspects of a theory's content into a coherent package are presented in the following summary of the four types of theories, and are also discussed as a part of the comparisons of the seven pairs of theories. These logical interrelationships, generated by the need for internal consistency and empirical adequacy, constitute the theory's form.

Theories that describe both human nature and at least some contemporary societies in consensual terms are referred to as *conservative consensus theories*. They include the theories of Aristotle, Aquinas, and Locke. These theories describe contemporary consensual societies as characterized by full and free agreements based on man's consensual nature. Conflict in those societies must therefore be attributed to "deviant" subgroups who either do not share fully in man's consensual nature (e.g., are "irrational" or "selfish") or who are not fully members of the consensual society (e.g., reside in its territory but are not "citizens"). Contemporary societies that are described in consensual terms are portrayed as having no substantial defects in that nothing in those societies is said to generate any conflict. Consequently, the ideal society is described as being quite similar to contemporary consensual societies, and is said to be comprised of the "best" aspects of each of them.

Theories that describe human nature in conflictual terms but at least some contemporary societies in consensual terms are referred to as *sociological consensus theories* and include the theories of Hobbes, Durkheim, and Parsons. These theories portray the ideal society as one in which man's conflictual nature is fully controlled, so that ideal societies are characterized by the absence of overt conflicts but not by the presence of full and free agreements. The ideal society is therefore hypothetical—it is not simply the "best" of what presently exists, but is a limit point that has not yet been and may never be fully achieved. At least some contemporary societies are described in consensual terms, but those societies are portrayed as having deficient mechanisms for controlling man's conflictual nature. These societies are described in consensual terms despite the presence of large amounts of overt conflict due to these inadequate social control mechanisms.

Theories that describe human nature in consensual terms but all contemporary societies in conflictual terms are referred to as *radical conflict theories* and include the theories of Plato, Rousseau, and Marx. These theories must explain why all contemporary societies are conflictual when human nature is consensual. They respond that the conflict is generated by the socioeconomic organization of the contemporary societies, and focus on methods by which those societies can be reorganized in order to eliminate the conflict. The ideal society in these theories is therefore a hypothetical society which is characterized by full and free agreements among its members, because the causes of the conflict have been eliminated.

Finally, theories that describe both human nature and all contemporary societies in conflictual terms are referred to as *sociological conflict theories*. These include the theories of Machiavelli, Simmel, and Dahrendorf. Such theories argue that conflict is an inevitable part of all human life, and they do not use consensual terminology to describe any societies, even hypothetical ones. The ideal society in these theories is therefore portrayed as being comprised of whatever elements are considered "best" about real societies. That often includes the effective control of all overt expressions of conflict, as is described in the ideal society of the sociological consensus theories. However, such a society would not be described in consensual terminology, since the conflicts still exist.

Sociological conflict and conservative consensus theories

primarily describe and analyze real societies and are not, in the main, concerned with the problem of social reform. That is a consequence of their descriptions of societies as a direct product of human nature—conservative theories describe them as a direct product of man's consensual nature and sociological conflict theories as a direct product of man's conflictual nature. Accordingly, the best possible society (the ideal) cannot be very different from societies that already exist, since it too would directly reflect human nature. In contrast, both sociological consensus and radical conflict theories describe contemporary societies differently from the way they describe human nature. Thus, these theories are able to hypothesize ideal societies that are very different from any real, contemporary societies, which leads to a concern with how to transform real societies into the hypothetical ideal. These theories tend to focus on describing and analyzing the hypothetical ideal society rather than real societies. They concern themselves with real societies only to the extent that they describe the processes by which those societies can or will be transformed into the hypothetical ideal.

Gouldner points out:

> Background assumptions also influence the *social* career of a theory, influencing the responses of those to whom it is communicated. For, in some part, theories are accepted or rejected because of the background assumptions embedded in them. In particular, a social theory is more likely to be accepted by those who share the theory's background assumptions and find them agreeable. Over and above their stipulated connotations, social theories and their component concepts contain a charge of surplus meanings derived in part from their background assumptions, and these may congenially resonate the compatible background assumptions of their hearers or may generate a painful dissonance. [37]

One of the key areas in which social theories either "congenially resonate" or "generate a painful dissonance" is in the inferences one draws from the theory about the evaluation of one's own contemporary societies—i.e., the societies that actually exist at the time one is reading the theory, including one's own society. In general, a positive evaluation is inferred when a society is described in consensual terms, while a negative evaluation is inferred when one is described in conflictual terms. One's receptivity to a social theory depends in part on how these inferences correspond to one's own evaluations. But more specific evaluations of contemporary societies can be derived by comparing one's contemporary societies to the ideal societies proposed in each theory. Societies that are quite similar to the ideal society would then be evaluated positively, while those that are quite different would be evaluated negatively. A major argument of this work is that the actual empirical descriptions of contemporary societies do not vary extensively between consensus and conflict theories. However, the ideal societies proposed by the various types of theories do vary dramatically. Consequently, the evaluations that can be inferred about contemporary societies also vary dramatically, despite the similarity of their empirical descriptions. The closest correspondence between the descriptions of contemporary societies and descriptions of the ideal society can occur in the conservative theories. Because conflict is attributed not to any aspect of the society itself, but to deviant subgroups instead, contemporary societies can be similar in all major respects to the ideal society, and thus can be evaluated very positively. In sociological consensus theories, contemporary societies can be similar to the ideal society in all major respects except their social control mechanisms. Thus, the evaluation of contemporary societies can still be quite positive, even though they are portrayed as deficient in one major respect. In radical theories, however, contemporary societies normally differ from the ideal society in their most fundamental structure—their socioeconomic system—unless those societies have specifically been reformed to conform to the theory. Contemporary societies will therefore normally be evaluated quite negatively, except for the "reformed" societies. With reformed societies, the evaluation is similar to that found in the conservative theories—the social structural causes of conflict have been removed, so the conflict is attributed to deviant subgroups and the society is said to be similar in all major respects to the ideal society and thus is evaluated very positively. Finally, in sociological conflict theories, contemporary societies can be quite similar to the ideal society because, like the conservative ideal, it is merely the "best" of existing societies. Thus, there should be a tendency to infer very positive evaluations about at least some societies. But the ideal society, as well as all contemporary societies, is described as conflictual, so that there should also be a tendency to infer negative evaluations about them. These two opposing tendencies balance, making sociological conflict theories compatible with a nonevaluative, "objective" stance in which contemporary societies are described and analyzed, but not in terms that imply either a positive or a negative evaluation.

A second important evaluation associated with the different types of theories is the evaluation of the actions of ruling groups when they suppress conflict in their own societies. As was pointed out above, no consistent differences were found among the theories in the amounts of conflict said to be present in contemporary societies. However, substantial differences were found in the way that conflict was described. Consensus theories of both types described conflict in such a way that it could legitimately be suppressed by ruling groups in contemporary consensual societies. In conservative consensus theories, it is legitimate for ruling groups to suppress conflict in "consensual" societies because that conflict is attributed to "deviant" subgroups. In sociological consensus theories, it is legitimate for ruling groups to suppress conflict because it is described as the residual expression of conflictual human nature breaking through the bonds of the social control mechanisms. In contrast, neither type of conflict theory describes the suppression of conflict as legitimate. Radical theories portray conflict as the product of the socioeconomic organization of the society, so that its suppression by ruling groups is merely their way of trying to avoid the social reorganizations necessary to resolve the conflict. In sociological conflict theories, the conflict is attributed to human nature, just as it is in sociological consensus theories. However, the ruling groups are not identified with the society itself, but are merely said to be the most powerful groups in the society. Sociological conflict theories may acknowledge that the suppression of conflict by ruling groups is necessary for social life, but it still describes that suppression in terms of the strong dominating the weak. Thus, in spite of its necessity, the suppression of conflict by ruling groups is not described as "legitimate." Rather, it is an expression of the inevitably coercive nature of all societies. The balance between viewing the suppression of conflict as necessary, on the one hand, but not "legitimate," on the other, makes sociological conflict theories tend toward an objective and nonevaluative description of this phenomenon in which the suppression of conflict is not described as being "illegitimate" either.

The term "legitimate" is used here in a general and somewhat imprecise way to refer to an evaluative dimension that can be derived from each social theory, although at least some of those social theories do not use that term. Weber, of course, made the term central to his political theory, arguing:

> Experience shows that in no instance does domination voluntarily limit itself to the appeal to material or affectual or ideal interests as a basis for its continuance. In addition, every such system *attempts to cultivate the belief in its legitimacy.*[38]

Lipset pointed out that legitimacy is an evaluative dimension, stating, "Groups regard a political system as legitimate or illegitimate according to the way in which its values fit with theirs."[39] A similar statement was made by Lane: "A system is regarded as legitimate when the claims to rightful power by its leaders, the procedures which they employ, and the outcomes of their acts are regarded as morally appropriate: to grant legitimacy is to engage in an act of moral evaluation."[40]

The present examination focuses on the moral evaluations of legitimacy made by social theorists themselves. The focus of the analysis is the relationship between the moral evaluation of the legitimacy of a contemporary society and the description of conflict and its suppression in that society. No attempt is made to evaluate the evaluations of legitimacy—to argue that the evaluations of legitimacy found in some theories are in some sense "valid," while those found in other theories are in some sense "false."

Throughout this work, it is argued that assumptions about human nature and contemporary societies logically determine the form that theories take. However, it is not necessary to argue that this also represents the temporal sequence in which theories emerge. The actual processes by which theories are created is not the subject of the present work. For example, a theorist may begin with general attitudes toward the legitimacy of suppressing conflict in a society and work back to the assumptions about human nature and contemporary societies necessary to support that attitude, or may begin with a general evaluation of a society and derive a view of the ideal society necessary to support that evaluation. Any attempt to portray the actual sequences in which theories are created would be purely speculative. This work focuses instead on logical interrelationships that occur within theories. It argues that there is a logical sequence of causation beginning with the assumptions made about human nature and contemporary societies, but it makes no argument about whether theorists actually begin the processes of writing their theories by formulating their views on those two phenomena.

Organization of the Book

In chapters 2 through 8, the fourteen theorists selected for this study are considered. These theorists are presented in pairs, of which one is considered a consensus theorist and the other a conflict theorist. They are also presented in their proper historical sequence, so that the general development of each type of theory, as well as the development of the opposition between them, can be presented. Each chapter presents overviews of the two authors' works but focuses on the elements relevant to the consensus-conflict debate, such as their views on stratification and inequality and on law and criminality. In particular, each authors' descriptions of human nature, contemporary societies, and the ideal society are identified and defined in terms of a consensus-conflict dichotomy. As mentioned above, other elements of the author's descriptions of these phenomena are not relevant to the present examination. Each theory is then classified into one of the four general types described above, and its form is shown to be consistent with the general form of that type of theory. The exact differences between the two theories in their descriptions of consensus and conflict in contemporary societies is then examined. That examination considers whether the two theories make any contrasting assertions that can be empirically tested. It then focuses on theoretical differences between the descriptions of conflict and consensus and analyzes the differing implications those descriptions have for the evaluation of contemporary societies and the legitimacy of suppressing conflict

within those societies. Each chapter concludes that the fundamental difference between the two theories lies in their contrasting evaluative implications rather than in any contrasting empirical assertions.

Chapter 9 addresses the general relationship between consensus and conflict theories. The first part of the chapter generalizes the findings of chapters 2 through 8 and presents them in
a systematic format. It also clarifies and extends the arguments
made in those chapters. The second part of the chapter provides
a discussion of the consensus-conflict debate based on the analysis in the first part of the chapter. Finally, chapter 10 examines
the relevance of the findings of this work for contemporary
theory and research.

Notes

1. The terms "form" and "content" are derived from Simmel's theory (see below,
ch. 7). However, Simmel used those terms as part of the analysis of social relations,
whereas here they are used as part of the analysis of social theories, including Simmel's.

2. Alvin W. Gouldner, *The Coming Crisis of Western Sociology* (New York: Avon, 1970),
pp. 29–35.

3. Gerhard Lenski, *Power and Privilege* (New York: McGraw-Hill, 1966), pp. 22–23.

4. William J. Chambliss, "Functional and Conflict Theories of Crime: The Heritage of
Emile Durkheim and Karl Marx," in William J. Chambliss and Milton Mankoff, eds.,
Whose Law? What Order? (New York: Wiley, 1976), pp. 7–9.

5. Kingsley Davis, "The Myths of Functional Analysis in Sociology and Anthropology," *American Sociological Review* (1959), 24:757–73.

6. For a review of the rise of this challenge, see Robert W. Friedrichs, *A Sociology of
Sociology* (New York: The Free Press, 1970), ch. 2.

7. Ralf Dahrendorf, "Out of Utopia: Toward a Reorientation of Sociological Analysis,"
American Journal of Sociology (September 1958), 64(2):115–27.

8. Ibid., pp. 126–27.

9. Ibid., pp. 127.

10. Edward Shils, "The Calling of Sociology," in Talcott Parsons, Edward Shils, Kaspar
D. Naegele, and Jesse R. Pitts, eds., *Theories of Society*, (New York: The Free Press, 1965),
pp. 1405–48.

11. Ibid., pp. 1410, 1429.

12. Ibid., pp. 1422.

13. Ibid., pp. 1422–23.

14. Ibid., pp. 1425–26.

15. Herminio Martins, "Time and Theory in Sociology," in John Rex, ed., *Approaches
to Sociology* (London: Routledge and Kegan Paul, 1974), p. 247.

16. Ibid.

17. For a complete review of this "debate," see Don Martindale, *The Nature and Types*

of Sociological Theory (Boston: Houghton Mifflin, 1960), pp. 51–207. A summary can be found on pp. 527–34.

18. See, for example, Howard Becker and Harry Elmer Barnes, *Social Thought from Lore to Science*, 3d ed. (New York: Dover, 1961); Martindale, *The Nature and Types of Sociological Theory*; Jonathan H. Turner, *The Structure of Sociological Theory*, rev. ed. (Homewood, Ill.: Dorsey Press, 1978), J. W. Gough, *The Social Contract* (Oxford: Clarendon Press, 1975); P. H. Partridge, *Consent and Consensus* (New York: Praeger, 1971); and Lynn McDonald, *The Sociology of Law and Order* (Boulder, Colo.: Westview Press, 1976).

19. August Comte, *System of Positive Polity* (New York: Burt Franklin, 1968), 2:285–86; and Karl Popper, "Plato," in David L. Sills, ed., *International Encyclopedia of the Social Sciences* (New York: Macmillan, The Free Press, 1968, 12:162). See also Popper, *The Open Society and Its Enemies* (Princeton, N.J.: Princeton University Press, 1966).

20. Stanislaw Ossowski, *Class Structure in the Social Consciousness* (New York: The Free Press, 1963).

21. Lewis A. Coser, *Masters of Sociological Thought* (New York: Harcourt Brace Jovanovich, 1971), p. 185.

22. Talcott Parsons, *Structure and Process in Modern Society* (Glencoe, Ill.: The Free Press, 1960), p. 173.

23. Turner, *The Structure of Sociological Theory*, pp. 116–17, 197.

24. Ralf Dahrendorf, *Class and Class Conflict in Industrial Society* (Stanford, Calif.: Stanford University Press, 1959), p. 161.

25. Robin Williams, "Some Further Comments on Chronic Controversies," *American Journal of Sociology* (May 1966), 71(6):722.

26. Robert K. Merton, *Social Theory And Social Structure* (New York: The Free Press, 1968), p. 176.

27. John Horton, "Order and Conflict Theories of Social Problems as Competing Ideologies," *American Journal of Sociology* (May 1966), 71(6):701.

28. Dahrendorf, *Class and Class Conflict*, p. 158.

29. Williams, "Some Further Comments," p. 718.

30. Irving M. Zeitlin, *Rethinking Sociology* (New York: Appleton-Century-Crofts, 1973), p. 103.

31. William Skidmore, *Theoretical Thinking in Sociology*, 2d ed. (Cambridge: Cambridge University Press, 1979), p. 11.

32. See the works cited in footnote 18.

33. Robert E. Park and Ernest W. Burgess, *Introduction to the Science of Sociology*, 3d ed. rev. (Chicago: University of Chicago Press, 1924), p. 29.

34. Dennis H. Wrong, "The Oversocialized Conception of Man in Modern Sociology," *American Sociological Review* (April 1961), 26:193.

35. Gouldner, *The Coming Crisis*, p. 31.

36. Cf. Thomas S. Kuhn, *The Structure of Scientific Revolutions* (Chicago: University of Chicago Press, 1970).

37. Gouldner, *The Coming Crisis*, p. 29.

38. Max Weber, *Economy and Society* (Totowa, N.J.: Bedminster Press, 1968), p. 213.

39. Seymour M. Lipset, *Political Man* (Garden City, N.Y.: Doubleday, 1960), p. 77.

40. Robert E. Lane, "The Legitimacy Bias," in Bogdan Denitch, ed., *Legitimation of Regimes* (Beverly Hills: Sage, 1979), p. 55.

CHAPTER 2

Plato and Aristotle

EXAMINATIONS OF the consensus-conflict debate often begin with the works of Auguste Comte and Karl Marx. But both of those authors wrote in the context of long theoretical traditions going back to the time of the ancient Greeks. Comte, as mentioned above, cited Aristotle as his "incomparable predecessor," while Marx's theories, argued Popper, grew out of the Platonic tradition.[1] The present chapter examines the works of Plato and Aristotle with a view toward the later development of consensus and conflict theories in sociology. It examines a few specific works that are relevant to that later development—in particular, Plato's *Republic* and Aristotle's *Politics*. The intention of the examination is to compare the two theories on issues relevant to the consensus-conflict debate, as part of an effort to ascertain the nature of the opposition between consensus theories and conflict theories generally. Accordingly, the examination focuses on the descriptions of human nature, contemporary societies, and the ideal society found in those works, since these are the three phenomena that may be described in terms of either consensus or conflict.

Plato's and Aristotle's Descriptions of Human Nature

Both Plato and Aristotle described human nature in consensual terms, arguing that man by nature was a political and social animal and that laws and governments were an outgrowth of that nature rather than an attempt to compensate for its shortcomings. Aristotle held that humans were made for life in society just as bees were made for life in the hive. I presented that view in chapter 1 to illustrate what is meant when a theorist is said to describe human nature in consensual terms. Aristotle's view of human nature had been taken directly from Plato, and the two views can be considered identical.[2] Plato's views were implied in Socrates' description of the origin of societies in the natural cooperation among humans in a division of labor:

> The origin of the city, then, said I, in my opinion, is to be found in the fact that we do not severally suffice for our own needs, but each of us lacks many things.... As a result of this, then, one man calling in another for one service and another for another, we, being in need of many things, gather many into one place of abode as associates and helpers, and to this dwelling together we give the name city or state.... And between one man and another there is an interchange of giving, if it so happens, and taking, because each supposes this to be better for himself.[3]

This illustrates Plato's view that humans are naturally capable of living together in a peaceable and harmonious society. Plato placed the opposing view in a description of the origin of society presented by Glaucon in a dispute with Socrates:

> By nature, they say, to commit injustice is a good and to suffer it is an evil, but that the excess of evil in being wronged is greater than the excess of good in doing wrong, so that when men do wrong and are wronged by one another and taste both, those who lack the power to avoid the one and take the other determine that it is for their profit to make a compact with one another neither to commit nor to suffer injustice, and that this is the beginning of legislation and of covenants between man, and that they name the commandment of the law the lawful and the just, and that this is the genesis and essential nature of justice.[4]

Glaucon's argument combines a conflictual view of human nature with a consensual view of society, which are assumptions found in the later "sociological consensus" theories. In this view, the state is an artificial device designed to compensate for human nature. Aristotle's assertion that "the state belongs to a class of objects which exist in nature, and that man is by nature a political animal" represents a refutation of the position taken by Glaucon and is one of the most famous propositions in the history of political thought.[5]

Plato's Descriptions of Contemporary Societies and the Ideal Society

Despite the fact that he described human nature in consensual terms that were identical to those of Aristotle's later description,

Plato has been identified with the conflict tradition.[6] That identification is based on his descriptions of contemporary societies—i.e., societies that existed in Plato's own time—as found in *The Republic* and other works written during what Popper called Plato's second period. In his first period, Plato presented an apparently accurate portrayal of Socrates as a man, a teacher, and a lover of Athenian democracy. In his second, he retained Socrates as his spokesman in the dialog, but he changed the content of Socrates' teachings rather dramatically:

> Plato now blames democratic Athens—nay, democracy itself, the rule of the many, of the mob—for having murdered Socrates. This mob rule threatens every just man, who is like "a man who has fallen among wild beasts, unwilling to share their misdeeds and unable to hold out singly against the savagery of all."[7]

In his third period, Plato retained his own, antidemocratic, view but no longer used Socrates as the spokesman in the dialogs, apparently in response to the awareness that he had moved far from the teachings of Socrates himself.

In the second period, then, Plato argued that democracy was one of the worst possible forms of government, and sought ways in which governance by the flood of public opinion could be replaced by governance in accordance with the true principles of goodness, righteousness, and justice (the "Forms"). He proposed that this could be accomplished by the "benevolent dictatorship" described in *The Republic*, in which all power would be concentrated in the hands of a small governing class of superior men who were capable of knowing the Good and the other Forms. These men would not own any private property, since the excessive love of material goods was the source of much of the conflict in the community. They also would have wives and children in common, the children having been systematically bred from the mating of those with the best characteristics. These children would be subject to extensive education and training to prepare them to take over their roles as governors of the city. The people would accept and fulfill their roles because they would be taught to believe a "noble lie" that all men are brothers, but some are made with a mingling of gold, still others of silver, and others of iron or brass; each must play his role according to his nature.[8]

Plato's description of the Republic is quite similar to consensus theory descriptions of society in that it is governed in the common interest and all men express their true consensual natures by accepting and fulfilling their particular roles. But the Republic was an ideal society, not a real one. Plato's arguments in *The Republic* imply a conflict view of societies that actually existed at the time he was writing. For example, Plato argues that rulers would own no private property, and goes on to state:

> But whenever they shall acquire for themselves land of their own and houses and coin, they will be householders and farmers instead of guardians, and will be transformed from the helpers of their fellow citizens to their enemies and masters, and so in hating and being hated, plotting and being plotted against, they will pass their days fearing far more and rather the townsmen within than the foeman without—and then even then laying the course of near shipwreck for themselves and the state.[9]

Because the rulers of Plato's own society did own property, he was implying that they were not "helpers" of their fellow citizens, but their "enemies and masters." Plato's major argument in *The Republic* concerns the divisive effects that the ownership of private property has on the unity of the state. Bluhm summarized that argument as follows:

1. Every historical *polis* is in the long run unstable. It becomes disunited and riven by faction.
2. The historical *polis* is therefore evil, because it does not conform to the Form of the *polis*, which is presented to the teleological reason as a united and cooperative commonwealth in which all have a concern for the common good.
3. Conflict in the historical *polis* arises from "a disagreement about the use of the terms 'mine' and 'not mine,' 'his' and 'not his'"; (*Republic* 5.642) i.e., each one is concerned only with his own interests, which he thinks of as distinct from and even opposed to those of his neighbors. The sense of distinct and conflicting interests arises from the distinction of possessions, from the institution of private property.
4. Conversely, harmony and unity in the ideal *polis* derive from the identification by each citizen of his own interest with the interest of all. This identification flows from the institution of common property....
5. Therefore, the institution of common property will produce peace and concord in the historical *polis*.[10]

Some authors have characterized Plato as being in the consensus tradition, but they have not focused on his descriptions of societies that actually existed at the time he wrote. For example, Becker and Barnes focused on Plato's myth of the origin of societies,[11] Martindale on Plato's idealism as a source of organicism,[12] and Gouldner on the similarities between Plato's idealism and functionalism.[13] Wolin attributes to Plato the view that society is a functioning system, stating: "Although Plato may have exaggerated the possibilities of a society's achieving systemic unity, the greatness of his achievement was to point out that in order to think in a truly political way, one had to consider society as a systemic whole."[14] But it is important to note that none of these references are to Plato's descriptions of *existing* societies; rather, Plato stated about existing societies that "each of them, as the saying runs, is no city, but cities upon cities; two at the least, each other's enemies, the city of the poor and the city of the rich; and in either of these is a vast number of cities which you will be entirely wrong to treat as one."[15] The relationship of the real to the ideal in Plato's theory can also be seen in Socrates' response to Thrasymachus when the latter presented a "conflict" view of justice. Thrasymachus argued:

> I affirm that the just is nothing else than the advantage of the stronger.... Each form of government enacts the laws with a view to its own advantage, a democracy democratic laws, and tyranny autocratic and the others likewise, and by so legislating they proclaim that the just for their subjects is that which is for their—the rulers'—advantage and the man who deviates from this law they chastise as a lawbreaker and a wrongdoer. This, then, my good sir, is what I understand as the identical principle of justice that obtains in all states—the advantage of the established government.[16]

Socrates did not dispute Thrasymachus' facts, but argued instead that such a ruler is not acting as a true Ruler (i.e., according to the Form):

> Can we deny, then, said I, that neither does any physician *insofar as he is a physician* seek or enjoin the advantage of the physician but that of the patient? For we have agreed that the physician, "precisely" speaking, is a ruler and governor of bodies and not a money-maker....
>
> Then, said I, Thrasymachus, neither does anyone in any office of rule *insofar as he is a ruler* consider and enjoin his own advantage

but that of the one whom he rules and for whom he exercises his craft, and he keeps his eyes fixed on that and on what is advantageous and suitable to that in all that he says and does. [italics added][17]

Socrates made no comment on those who hold power but do not act as true Rulers of the society, but it can be inferred that they would act as Thrasymachus described. In addition, because all of the rulers of societies that existed in Plato's own time owned property, it can be inferred that, in Plato's view, they all did act as Thrasymachus described. Thus, although Plato described human nature in consensual terms and described the ideal society (the Republic) as a consensual society, he is classified here as a conflict theorist because his views imply that in all contemporary societies (i.e., wherever rulers own property), the rulers act as enemies and masters of their fellow citizens, so that each "is no city, but cities upon cities; two at the least, each other's enemies. . . . "

Aristotle's Descriptions of Contemporary Societies and the Ideal Society

Unlike Plato, there seems to be no controversy about the classification of Aristotle—he is uniformly placed in the consensus tradition. His consensual view of human nature is identical to that of Plato and has already beeen described. But Aristotle is placed in the consensus tradition here because he argued that at least some contemporary societies were consensual, though others were not. Aristotle described six types of states ruled by a single person, by a few persons, or by many people, each ruling in the interests of the common good or in the interests only of those who ruled.[18] He stated that "It is clear then that those constitutions which aim at the common good are *right*, as being in accord with absolute justice; while those which aim only at the good of the rulers are *wrong*." He then considered the various claims in behalf of the rule of the one, the few, and the many (in the name of the common interest) and concluded that all have validity depending on the circumstances. But in general he seemed to prefer the rule of the many in the common interest—

what he called "polity." The polity was to be distinguished from a "democracy" in that the democracy included all groups in the ruling process, whereas the polity included only "citizens," who were a small percentage of the population in Aristotle's time. Aristotle believed that democracy was an inherently bad form of government, since the majority of voters would be poor, and they were incapable of acting in the common interest. Thus, he defined democracy as the rule of the poor (who are always the many) in their own interest, a "wrong" type of state.

Aristotle argued, however, that those who were not citizens and did not participate in the privileges of rule were not necessarily injured by that arrangement. He stated that the teleological end of the city-state is to make men good, and that moral goodness is found for all groups in fulfilling the duties of their roles and statuses.[19] Thus, the social order is not necessarily in the interests only of the governing groups but may be in the "common interests" of all groups in the society, aristocrats to slaves. The concept of common interest was based on a distinction made earlier in the *Ethics* between a person's "interests" and "pleasures."[20] Aristotle did not maintain that slaves or servants desired or approved of their subjugation, or that the nongoverning groups necessarily agreed with the decisions of the ruling groups. However, he argued that such an arrangement may be in the interests of the city-state as a whole, and thus in the interest of each of its groups.

Aristotle's limitation of participation in the processes of governance to citizens, a minority of the population, was based on his rejection of the claim by such philosophers as Antiphon that men are born equal and that the power relations that exist in society are solely the result of force. Antiphon had argued that "the prescriptions of custom-and-law are reached by compact" and that "as a general [proposition] the evidence so far received is in support of the following [conclusion]: what is right, as constituted in terms of custom-and-law, is mostly an enemy to nature."[21] Aristotle argued, on the contrary, that men were born unequal, and that the provisions found in "custom-and-law" reflected that inequality and thus were beneficial to human nature.

Aristotle argued that at least some types of societies could be governed by "consensus," but his use of that term differed substantially from its use by later consensus theorists in sociology. First, Aristotle described "consensus" as a part of "amity" or "friendly feelings," so that "it cannot be congruence of opinion which would be available to men who were mutually unaware of each other. . . . "[22] Later consensus theorists used the term "consensus" to describe just such a congruence of opinion. Second, Aristotle used the term to refer to specific agreements on policy issues: "Examples: unanimous opinion to have the offices elective, or form an alliance with Sparta, or that Pittacus should hold sole office,"[23] whereas later consensus theorists used the term to refer to much more general assumptions. Third, Aristotle argued that consensus was not possible when irrational and selfish groups were included in the consensus formation process:

> Now you get such consensus only in upper classes. . . . They wish for what is morally right, and of interest, and aim in common threat. . . . The inferior classes are incapable of consensus. They aim to grab something selfishly from among the utilities. . . . so that faction is their normal condition since they refuse to do what is right.[24]

Most editions of Aristotle's *Ethics* translate this passage as referring to "good men," rather than to "upper classes." However, the literal translation is "upper classes" or "wealthy," and it is the same term used in Aristotle's discussions of citizens and noncitizens in a democracy.[25] Thus, Aristotle was arguing that a consensus was possible only if the large majority of individuals in the society were excluded from the consensus formation process. Later consensus theorists included all (or nearly all) individuals in the consensus, so that the number of excluded individuals ("deviants") was very small.

Aristotle provided an extensive blueprint for the ideal society, which consisted of a polity small enough for all citizens to know each other well.[26] The body of citizens was not to include any working people, however:

> . . . a state with an ideal constitution—a state which has for its members men who are absolutely just, and not men who are merely just in relation to some particular standard—cannot have its citizens living the life of mechanics or shopkeepers, which is ignoble and inimical to goodness. Nor can it have them engaged

in farming: leisure is a necessity, both for growth in goodness and for the pursuit of political activities.[27]

Aristotle rejected Plato's claim that the elimination of ownership of property by rulers would lead to a consensual society, and insisted that "education is *the* means for making [a *polis*] a community and giving it unity."[28] Thus, a large portion of his discussion of the ideal state is devoted to education. However, he dealt only with the education of the young citizens, emphasizing what might be called the "liberal arts" and excluding "vocational training." Aristotle nowhere stated why he thought noncitizens would consent to this ideal order. However, he stated that the military is necessary, "partly in order to maintain authority and repress disobedience," and that it must be part of the citizen body because "men who have vigour enough to use force (or to prevent it from being used) cannot possibly be expected to remain in permanent subjection."[29] This implies that noncitizens remain in permanent subjection because of coercive force applied by the military.

Aristotle's Theory Compared with Plato's

Aristotle's ideal society did not require any extensive reorganizations, as did Plato's. As Bury remarked:

> The Republic of Aristotle's wish is not quickened like Plato's by strikingly original ideas; it is a commonplace Greek aristocracy, with its claws cut, carefully trimmed and pruned, refined by a punctilious education. . . .[30]

That was related to Aristotle's idea of "telos," a concept that more or less described the "ends" toward which different entities evolved or developed.[31] The ideal state, to be consistent with that concept, was necessarily a projection from the best existing states, since states in general were tending toward that ideal. Thus, Aristotle's ideal society was an "immanent" ideal.[32] Such a conception of the ideal state implied that the "best" existing states "approximated" the ideal state and thus could be said to be "consensual." In contrast, Plato's notion of the Form did not imply that any existing states approximated the ideal. In fact, the

Republic was quite unlike any existing state and was not said to grow naturally out of any of them. Such a conception of the ideal state implied that all existing states were flawed and imperfect— i.e., conflictual. In addition, because the ideal state did not grow naturally (or "organically") out of real states, Plato's theory contained revolutionary implications later associated with conflict theories.

Underlying the distinction between an immanent and transcendent ideal are differing philosophical conceptions about the nature of values and the nature of human rationality. Plato argued that values were real in themselves and thus could be said to be "absolute." His philosophy in the *Republic* revolved around the search for those values, such as the Good or the Just, and for a method by which those values could be incorporated into the lives of men, as well as embodied in the laws and governance of the state. Aristotle, in contrast, argued that what was "good" or "just" could be assessed only by rational and intelligent individuals in particular situations. For example, he argued that there was no single ideal form of government (as Plato had argued in *The Republic*) but that the "best" form depended on the circumstances of the society. Aristotle did provide guidelines for assessing what was "right" or "best" in a particular situation, such as his discussion of the "golden mean." But these were only guidelines, and were to be ignored in cases where they did not apply. Because of these views, Aristotle is generally considered to be the father of "situation ethics," which holds that in every situation there are certain values that are in fact the best ones.[33]

The association of the conflict position with absolute values and of a consensus position with "situational relativism" may be somewhat surprising, since the associations are often perceived to be the opposite way. But on closer examination these associations make a good deal of sense. Plato held that there were absolute values, but he also held that the common people had no awareness of them. Thus, the consensus of the people merely was the "flood of public opinion," and had to be resisted by those who were aware of the true Forms. The people would consent to be governed according to the common interest only if they were taught a "noble lie." This absolute value position is associated with a highly critical view of human rationality, since Plato argued that becoming aware of the Forms was extremely difficult and could be achieved only through the most strenuous efforts. The Socratic dialogs constantly repeat the theme that men have not examined their ideas closely enough and that what they believe to be good, just, and true are not any of those things. Thus, rulers who believe that they act rationally, virtuously, and in the common interest may really be acting irrationally, selfishly, and in their own interest. The human condition is said to be comparable to the condition of men chained in a cave, so that they see only the passing shadows of reality and confuse them with reality itself.[34]

Aristotle, in contrast, linked a less extreme definition of "true values" with a less critical view of human rationality. Thus, he maintained that intelligent, well-meaning people (the citizens) could discern "true values" (those values that are best in a given situation) without great difficulty. These two views are still found in contemporary consensus positions. For example, John Rawls based his consensus theory of justice on the assumption that "each person beyond a certain age and possessed of the requisite intellectual capacity develops a sense of justice under normal circumstances."[35] That is certainly different from Plato's description of the difficulties of becoming aware of Justice as a Form.

In sum, then, Plato held that the ideal society was a consensual one but that, as a transcendent ideal, it required a reorganization of society to achieve and included a prohibition on rulers owning property. Plato's conflictual view of existing societies is derived from his argument that if rulers own property they will invariably pursue their own interests, even if they believe they are pursuing the common interest. Thus, the source of conflict was said to be in property relations and not in human nature, which was said to be consensual. Plato's argument was based on a very high standard of values (the Forms) and on a distrust of human rationality. Aristotle's ideal society was also a consensual one, but as an immanent ideal it required no fundamental reorganization of society. Consistent with his concept of telos, it was a projection from one of several forms of existing societies—the rule of the many in the common interest. The term "consensus" did not refer to a generalized belief system shared by all members of the society but to a process which occurs among a limited portion of the population, through which specific political decisions are made. The decisions that resulted from the process were said to be in the interests of the entire population. Aristotle's view was based on a less strict standard for values (situational relativism) and on a basic trust that intelligent and well-intentioned men can rationally perceive those values without great difficulty.

The Relation Between Form and Content

These two theories have retained their vitality after more than 2,000 years because each forms a coherent argument that can be used to interpret a wide variety of empirical situations. The intention of the present examination is not to challenge the adequacy of either theory; rather, it is to examine the interrelation of form and content in each theory, and on that basis to explore the relationship between the two theories. Plato is classed in the radical conflict tradition because he described human nature as consensual but all contemporary societies as conflictual. The basic form of his argument is directly derived from the content of his assumptions about those two phenomena. He first explained why all contemporary societies were conflictual when human nature was consensual. He then focused on the ideal society, in which man's consensual nature would be expressed, and on the methods by which contemporary societies could be transformed into the consensual ideal. In contrast, Aristotle is classified in the conservative consensus tradition because he considered both human nature and contemporary societies to be consensual. Again, the basic form of his argument is derived from the content of his assumptions about these two phenomena. If contemporary societies reflect man's consensual nature, then they are already about as good as they can be. What remains is to survey the various types of consensual societies and select what is best about each of them. The theory therefore focused on describing and analyzing real societies rather than on hypothesizing ideal ones. Conflict in consensual societies could not be attributed either to human nature or to the societies themselves, so it was attributed instead to individuals who did not share fully in the consensual human nature—the irrational and selfish noncitizens. Aristotle therefore defended social inequality, and described the consensus as a full and free agreement among the citizens.

Consensus and Conflict in Contemporary Societies

Having argued that the form of each theory is substantially derived from the content of its assumptions about human nature and contemporary societies, we now turn to the relationship between the two theories. Plato and Aristotle began with identical assumptions about human nature. The theories diverged in giving differing descriptions of contemporary societies and of the ideal society. It would be quite surprising if Plato and Aristotle gave radically different empirical descriptions of contemporary societies, since they lived only one generation apart and within the context of the same civilization. And in fact the differences between their descriptions of contemporary societies are primarily evaluative rather than empirical. Both described contemporary societies as divided into at least two conflicting groups. Plato described them as "the city of the poor and the city of the rich," while Aristotle described them as the citizens and the noncitizens. While Plato stated that the two cities were "each other's enemies," Aristotle acknowledged the need for the citizens to monopolize force in order to control the noncitizens. The difference between the two theories with respect to their descriptions of contemporary societies is that Aristotle argued that the citizens were rational and virtuous and that they acted in the common interest whereas Plato described them as inevitably irrational and selfish and acting in their own interests because they owned private property. The noncitizen poor were described similarly in both theories—they were said to be irrational and selfish. It might appear that these theories make differing empirical assertions about the behaviors of the ruling groups, but in fact these are evaluative statements. Plato and Aristotle did not disagree on what the ruling groups actually did but rather on the evaluation of those actions. Aristotle trusted in the rationality of virtuous men and described their behaviors as being in the common interest. Plato distrusted the rationality and virtue of all groups except philosophers and described their behaviors as inevitably being in the interests of the rulers only, even if the rulers themselves believed otherwise. The differing descriptions of the ideal society were direct consequences of the differing evaluations of the actions of ruling groups in their own societies. Aristotle's ideal society was necessarily quite similar to the societies he said were already ruled by rational and virtuous men in the common interest, while Plato's ideal society was necessarily very different from any societies that actually existed at the time he was writing, since none were said to be ruled in a truly rational and virtuous manner.

In the last analysis, then, the difference between the theories of Plato and Aristotle with respect to their descriptions of contemporary societies is that they evaluated the "legitimacy" of the actions of the ruling groups of those societies in opposite ways. They did not disagree about the existence or extent of conflict in those societies or about the actual behaviors of the ruling groups. They disagreed on whether those behaviors were rational, virtuous, and in the common interest. Aristotle argued that they were, and therefore maintained that there was a consensus on those actions among rational and virtuous men and a need to suppress any conflict with that consensus by force or other means. Plato argued that they were not, so he described conflict between the ruling group and other groups in the society. The "debate" between Plato and Aristotle with respect to the concepts of consensus and conflict therefore derives from their alternative descriptions of the same empirical phenomena, based on their opposite evaluations of the actions of ruling groups. As such, it is not an empirical debate and cannot be resolved through empirical investigations.

Notes

1. Auguste Comte, *System of Positive Polity*, (New York: Burt Franklin, 1968) 2:285–86; Karl Popper, "Plato," in David L. Sills, ed., *International Encyclopedia of the Social Sciences*,

(New York: Macmillan, The Free Press, 1968), 12:162. See also Popper, *The Open Society and Its Enemies* (Princeton, N.J.: Princeton University Press, 1966).

2. P. H. Partridge, *Consent and Consensus* (New York: Praeger, 1971), p. 11; J. W. Gough, *The Social Contract* (Oxford: Clarendon Press, 1975), pp. 11–13.

3. Plato, *Republic*, 369b–c.

4. Ibid., 358e–359a. See also Plato, *Georgias*, 492c, for a similar theory presented by Callicles. See also Plato, *Crito*, 51d–52a and 52c–53a for Socrates' account of why he will not flee the city to avoid being put to death.

5. Aristotle, *Politics*, 12. See William T. Bluhm, *Theories of the Political System*, 3d ed. (Englewood Cliffs, N.J.: Prentice-Hall, 1978), p. 81, for a discussion of the meaning of this phrase.

6. In addition to Popper's comments about Plato's relationship to Marx, see Lynn McDonald, *The Sociology of Law and Order* (Boulder, Colo.: Westview Press, 1976), pp. 28–29, in which Plato is said to have taken the conflict position in the debate over the economic causes of crime.

7. Popper, "Plato," p. 161. The quotation is from Plato, *Republic*, 496c.

8. Plato, *Republic*, 415a–e.

9. Plato, *Republic*, 417a–b.

10. Bluhm, *Theories of the Political System*, pp. 74–75.

11. Howard Becker and Harry Elmer Barnes, *Social Thought from Lore to Science*, 3d ed. (New York: Dover, 1961), 1:180.

12. Don Martindale, *The Nature and Types of Sociological Theory* (Boston: Houghton Mifflin, 1960), p. 55.

13. Alvin W. Gouldner, *Enter Plato* (New York: Basic Books, 1965); and *The Coming Crisis of Western Sociology* (New York: Avon, 1970), pp. 412–26.

14. Sheldon S. Wolin, *Politics and Vision* (London: Allen and Unwin, 1961), p. 33.

15. Plato, *Republic*, 422e–423a.

16. Ibid., 338c–e.

17. Ibid., 342d–e.

18. Aristotle, *Politics*, 3.6–8.

19. Ibid., 3.5, 7.1–3.

20. Aristotle, *Ethics*, book 7.

21. Quoted in Eric A. Havelock, *The Liberal Temper in Greek Politics* (New Haven: Yale University Press, 1957), p. 271. Although he saw custom-and-law as derived from a compact, Antiphon took a strong stand against it, saying: "It has been by custom-and-law determined for the eye, what it is supposed to see and not see, for the ear, what it is supposed to hear and not hear, for the tongue, what it is supposed to say and not say, for the hand, what it is supposed to do and not do, for the foot, whither it is supposed to proceed and not proceed, for the heart, what it is supposed to want and not want. But verily in terms of what is more *versus* less amicable, more *versus* less proper to nature, there is no difference between what law averts human beings from and what it exhorts them to do" (ibid., p. 275). Antiphon also took a stand directly opposed to Aristotle's distinction between "pleasure" and "interest": "Interests as constituted by law are bonds laid upon nature, but those constituted by nature are liberating. If correct calculation is used, the things which give pain cannot benefit nature more than the things which give pleasure; hence the things which give pain cannot be to our interest either, rather than the things that give pleasure. For things truly to our interest are not supposed to do damage but to benefit" (ibid., pp. 279–80).

22. Aristotle, *Ethics*, 9.6.

23. Ibid.

24. Ibid.

25. J. A. Stewart, *Notes on the Nicomachean Ethics of Aristotle* (New York: Arno, 1973), p. 369.

26. Aristotle, *Politics*, books 6 and 8.

27. Ibid., 3.9.

28. Ibid., 2.5. Emphasis in original.

29. Ibid., 7.8,9.

30. J. B. Bury, *A History of Greece to the Death of Alexander the Great* (New York: Macmillan, 1902), p. 835. quoted in Becker and Barnes, *Social Thought*, 1:192.

31. Bluhm, *Theories of the Political System*, pp. 95–97.

32. See ibid., p. 10, for a discussion of the meanings of the terms "immanent" and "transcendent."

33. Ibid., pp. 110–12.

34. The image of the cave is found in Plato, *Republic*, 514ff and 532ff.

35. John Rawls, *A Theory of Justice* (Cambridge: Harvard University Press, 1971), p. 46.

– CHAPTER 3 –

Augustine and Aquinas

JUST AS the thought of Plato and Aristotle disproportionately influenced the early development of Western social thought, so the thought of Augustine and Aquinas disproportionately influenced its middle development. Augustine is considered a Neoplatonist and Aquinas an Aristotelian. Each carried on the traditions established by their Greek predecessors but applied that tradition within the context of Christianity. When considered from the perspective of the development of the consensus and conflict traditions, one finds that each of these thinkers stayed within the basic framework established by his predecessor. But one also finds that each took significant steps toward the modern consensus and conflict positions, so that they are important as transitional thinkers in the development of these traditions.

Augustine's Description of Human Nature, Contemporary Societies, and the Ideal Society

Plato's philosophy had raised the question of whether those who claim (and even believe) that they rule in the common interest really do so. Augustine, like Plato, believed that they did not. His view was that humans are by nature social animals whose satisfaction and fulfillment is reached in the love of God and the love of fellow humans. But as a consequence of Adam and Eve's sin in the Garden of Eden, humans are overwhelmed by intense drives for material possessions, domination over others, and sexual satisfactions. Because these drives are contrary to human nature, their pursuit leaves people more unsatisfied than they were initially, and is therefore unending.[1]

Augustine's description of people is not very different from the description Aristotle gave of the noncitizens. But in Augustine's view, Aristotle's argument that the citizens could and would act rationally in making political decisions about the common interest was completely unrealistic. Because the drives for possessions, domination, and sexual satisfaction were so intense, people had no rational control over their own behavior, much less their political environment.[2] Thus, Augustine's description of ruling groups was comparable to that of Plato, except that he argued that the source of the conflict was sin, while Plato contended it was the ownership of property.

Augustine provided a long, detailed description of what he called the "City of Man," that is, human society, as being torn by strife, conflict, and unhappiness. In contrast to this is the community of the saints, or the "City of God," in which there is perfect peace, justice, harmony, and satisfaction based on the love of God and the love of fellow humans. His description of the City of God is comparable to Plato's ideal republic, except that it can never be achieved on this earth. Augustine thought that most people were damned and that no form of organized government would change that fact. Therefore, unlike the philosophers who were to run Plato's republic, the saints on earth were not to attempt to take over the earthly government.[3] Rather, they were to obey the laws, whatever they might be, and believe that God in His infinite wisdom and mercy had some overall plan and goal that would ultimately emerge from the seeming chaos.

In spite of this dismal view of the nature of humanity and society, Augustine argued strongly for the necessity of the state:

The state, for Augustine, is an external order; the peace that it maintains is external peace—the absence, or at least the diminution, of overt violence. The state is also a coercive order, maintained by the use of force and relying on the fear of pain as its major sanction for compliance to its commands. It has no weapons by which it can mold the thoughts, desires, and wills of its citizens; nor is it really concerned to exert such influence. It does not seek to make men truly good or virtuous. Rather, it is interested in their outward actions, and it attempts, with some success, to restrain its citizens from performing certain kinds of harmful and criminal acts. . . . The state is a nonnatural, remedial institution; like private property, slavery, and other forms of domination of man over man, it is a consequence of the Fall. It is both a punishment for sin and a remedy for man's sinful condition; without it anarchy would reign, and self-centered, avaricious, power-hungry, lustful men would destroy one another in a fierce struggle for self-aggrandizement.[4]

The necessity of the state and the obligation to obey its commands, however, did not in Augustine's opinion confer any legitimacy on it as an institution. Augustine cited the traditional definition of justice as "giving each man his due," and argued that true justice can exist only in the City of God. No man can truly judge another man because he cannot see into the other's heart to ascertain his true deserts.

Because men do judge one another in the City of Man, all earthly governments are filled with injustice. Augustine used this absence of justice as the basis to reject the consensus view of society which had been presented in Cicero's *De Republica*. In that work, Scipio is portrayed as arguing that a consensual republic can exist only when the people are characterized by a "common acknowledgment of law, and by a community of interests," and that such a situation can never exist unless the state dispenses true justice. But Augustine argued that true justice can never exist in any earthly society, so that there can never be the common acknowledgment of law and community of interests necessary for a consensual society.[5]

Augustine then drew what is perhaps his most controversial analogy by comparing the state to a band of robbers:

> Justice being taken away, then, what are kingdoms but great robberies? For what are robberies themselves, but little kingdoms? The band itself is made up of men; it is knit together by the pact of the confederacy; the booty is divided by the law agreed on. If, by the admittance of abandoned men, this evil increases to such a degree that it holds places, fixes abodes, takes possession of cities, and subdues peoples, it assumes the more plainly the name of a kingdom, because the reality is now manifestly conferred on it, not by the removal of covetousness, but by the addition of impunity. Indeed, that was an apt and true reply which was given to Alexander the Great by a pirate who had been seized. For when that king had asked the man what he meant by keeping hostile possession of the sea, he answered with bold pride, "What thou meanest by seizing the whole earth; but because I do it with a petty ship, I am called a robber, whilst thou who dost it with a great fleet art styled emperor."[6]

Thus, the king is distinguished from the robber, not by the absence of the same covetousness and wickedness in his heart, but merely "by the addition of impunity." Augustine was not arguing, however, that kings and rulers are exceptionally evil—in fact, he said that individual kings and rulers may be good and pious men. Such men, however, rule in full awareness of their own weaknesses, and in humility before the unknowable plans of God. The presence of a good and pious ruler, while certainly to be desired, does not change the coercive and unjust nature of the state itself, while the presence of an evil ruler does not compromise the necessity of his rule.[7]

As a Neoplatonist, Augustine throws Plato's ideas into a sort of relief, so that the meaning of the Forms becomes more clear. The Forms are those values which would, if practiced, result in a society in which true harmony and satisfaction (consensus) would reign. For example, the Form of the Just in Plato would be that justice in which each and every person received his due. The difficulty of achieving such a value is made clear by Augustine, who argued that it could not be achieved in any earthly society. Aristotle's idea of justice, on the other hand, was much more a "this world" view. For him, justice was achievable by rational men of good will who were assessing a particular situation. Thus, there was no "eternal standard" against which their actions could be compared. And if their judgments aroused conflict and dissent among those upon whom they were imposed, that was a reflection of the inherent irrationality and vice of the lower born.

Augustine's work thus contains both the high standard of virtue found in Plato and his critical distrust of human rationality. In fact, Augustine's position is even more extreme than Plato's, since Plato held that it was possible for a small number of truly virtuous men to achieve an awareness of the Forms and to rule in accordance with its dictates. That was because Plato believed the source of human conflict was in the social structural arrangements, especially property relations. Augustine, on the other hand, believed the problem was inherent in the frailties of human nature. True justice was simply beyond human capacity, and men were condemned by the Fall to their lives of trouble and unhappiness. The state could, at best, impose a coercive cap on the more overt forms of violence and conflict, but no social structural arrangement could truly produce consensus.

Augustine's conflict position was similar to Plato's in that he argued that all existing societies were conflictual; but it was stronger than Plato's because of his descriptions of human nature, the origin of society, and the ideal society. Plato had described human nature as consensual, but Augustine introduced conflict into human nature itself, despite the fact that he argued that these conflictual elements were due to sin and were not part of the "true" human nature. Because of the conflictual human nature, Augustine argued, societies originated in conflict—they were a consequence of and a remedy for sin—in contrast to Plato's description of the evolution of societies from man's natural cooperation. Finally, Plato's ideal society (the Republic) was a form of government possible on this earth, although it had never been achieved; while Augustine's ideal society (the City of God) was fully transcendent and could never exist on earth.[8] His ideal "temporal" society—i.e., the best possible society on this earth—was described in conflictual terms, not consensual ones.

Aquinas' Descriptions of Human Nature, Contemporary Societies, and the Ideal Society

Aristotle's philosophy was developed and brought into the realm of Christianity by Thomas Aquinas, just as Plato's philosophy had been by Augustine. Aquinas remained fully within the Aristotelian tradition by asserting that men were able to discern the true and good (what he called "natural law") through reason.[9] He also argued that "natural law" was revealed through man's natural inclinations toward actions and through faith. Aquinas took a very optimistic view of human nature. Gilby described the Thomist view as follows:

> Laws should not seek to suppress natural instincts or to straitlace their functions. Even arbitrary conventions...are primarily means of the enlarging, not the cramping, of human activity....Human emotions which issue from sub-rational depths were not obscene in themselves, but healthy; even jungle law was adapted to the balance of nature and to the preservation of species and individuals.[10]

Thus, Aquinas described human nature in consensual terms, similar to Aristotle's descriptions and in marked contrast to Augustine's conflictual descriptions.

Aquinas also described at least some contemporary societies in consensual terms. He argued that governments must be based on the consent of the governed, although he did not imply that there was an original social contract. Rather, he argued that men would naturally consent to governments that were founded on the natural law. Aquinas carefully considered and rejected two ancient Roman sayings that presented the alternate, conflictual view of contemporary societies: "Whatever the prince wants has the vigor of law," and "The prince is not bound by laws."[11] His answer was that while the law had no coercive power over the prince, the prince still had a moral obligation to establish laws that were in accordance with natural law, and to obey those laws himself. A prince who did not do this should be resisted and overthrown.

Aquinas also presented a consensual description of the ideal society. Like Aristotle, he first reviewed the various types of government, including the rule of the one, the few, and the many, and argued that each could be legitimate if it served the common good rather than only the good of the rulers.[12] But he preferred governments in which power was concentrated in a single individual, arguing that it was consistent with natural law.[13] He also held that there should be various legal restrictions on that individual to prevent tyranny; his "ideal" society is similar to a constitutional monarchy.[14] The people always retained the right of rebellion if those legal restrictions were violated.

By basing the legitimacy of governments on the consent of the governed, and by maintaining that it was morally right to overthrow illegitimate governments, Aquinas acted as a bridge between Aristotle and the later social-contract theorists. But it is important to note precisely what Aquinas meant when he referred to "the consent of the governed." Like Aristotle, Aquinas believed in human inequality. He said that the common people and women were unable to rationally determine the content of natural law.[15] Aquinas believed that it was necessary to coerce those who did not consent to the government, and that those people were concentrated in the poorest groups. Rollin Chambliss has made the following comment with respect to Aquinas' views on this subject:

> Obedience to rightful authority is required of all, especially those whose natures are most imperfect. Coercion is the rule at the bottom of the social scale; it becomes increasingly less necessary as men acquire rational competence.[16]

In addition to natural inequalities, some groups were in error about the natural law, specifically Jews and heretics. Aquinas argued that Jews should be restricted in their activities and forced to wear some special sign to distinguish them from Christians, and that heretics should be forced to recant their errors or be put to death.[17]

Like Aristotle's extensive defense of slavery as reflective of the inherent inequalities in human nature, the statements of Aquinas about Jews and heretics have sometimes been regarded as an unfortunate and unimportant "embarrassment" among the extensive writings of an otherwise noble man. But these arguments were actually essential to Aristotle's and Aquinas' arguments that a consensus existed in society. Aquinas had argued that the consensus was based on a universal and immutable "natural law" that well-intentioned men were able to discern through reason. To the extent that some people in his society disagreed with what he perceived natural law to be, Aquinas had to argue that those people were either not well intentioned or not rational. Aquinas could hardly maintain that a consensus existed in society based on rational perceptions of "natural law" if he had to include the views of Jews and heretics. Similarly, Aristotle could hardly argue that a consensus existed in his society if he had to take account of the views of workingmen and slaves. When they referred to the consensus, then, it is clear that they were referring to consensus among specific groups within the society rather than to a consensus among all groups. For Aristotle, those groups were based on class and sex (male citizens) while for Aquinas, they were based on class, sex, and religion (wealthy Catholic males). Neither of these theorists asserted that there was a "consensus" among a majority of the population.

The Relation Between Form and Content

Aquinas falls in the conservative consensus tradition, as established by Aristotle. Like Aristotle, he assumed that both human nature and contemporary societies were consensual; and the form that his theory took was a consequence of those assumptions. It focused on describing and analyzing real societies, presented the ideal society as one that incorporated the "best" of existing societies, and explained the presence of social conflict by imputing it to those who did not share fully in man's consensual nature. Aquinas' principal contribution to the development of the consensus tradition is that he shifted from a view of consensus as a process which results in specific decisions among people who know each other to a view of consensus as a moral consciousness or awareness of natural law that is shared by all rational, well-intentioned members of the society. That view is more consistent with the modern consensus position than was the view of Aristotle. However, Aquinas was able to assert that a consensus existed only by eliminating from consideration the views of a majority of the population: women, common people, Jews, and heretics, among others. Their views were described as being either irrational or selfish, and thus might legitimately be suppressed by force.

The classification of Augustine is more of a problem. He clearly falls into the conflict tradition, because he described all contemporary societies as conflictual, but his description of human nature was dualistic: man's "true" nature was consensual, but his nature here on earth was inevitably conflictual because it had been corrupted by sin. Thus, Augustine had a foot in both the sociological and the radical conflict traditions. The form that Augustine's theory took reflected the consequences of this dualistic assumption about human nature. To the extent that Augustine assumed that human nature was consensual, his theory falls into the general form of a radical theory. It explained why all contemporary societies were conflictual when human nature was consensual, described the ideal society (the City of God) in which man's consensual nature could fully express itself, and discussed methods by which that ideal society could be achieved. To the extent that Augustine assumed that human nature was conflictual, his theory reflects the form of sociological conflict theories. The theory concentrated on describing and analyzing existing societies (the City of Man), and was not excessively concerned with the problem of social reform. Conflict was assumed to be inevitable because it was attributed to human nature, and the ideal society was described as a conflictual society that combined whatever was seen as "best" about existing societies.

Consensus and Conflict in Contemporary Societies

The form that each theory takes reflects the content of its assumptions about human nature and contemporary societies. We now turn to the question of the relationship between the two theories with respect to their descriptions of contemporary societies. Augustine appears to have described a great deal more conflict in contemporary societies than did Aquinas. That could be attributed to the presence of much more conflict in the particular society in which Augustine lived. But a separate question is whether Augustine's theory asserts that there is more conflict in general than does Aquinas'. That is, are there empirical differences between the two theories concerning the extent of conflict in societies generally? It does not appear that there are. What differs is not the extent of conflict that is alleged, but the way the conflict is described. What is described in Augustine's theory as conflict between rulers and ruled is described in Aquinas' theory as the need for rational and virtuous rulers to use force to control the irrational and selfish behaviors of the ruled. Augustine had described all groups in the society as being irrational and selfish and thus had described each of them as in conflict with the others. Aquinas, in contrast, described one group (upper class Catholic males) as acting rationally, virtuously, and in the common interest, and the actions of other groups in terms of the extent to which they deviated from that norm. Accordingly, Jews and heretics were not described as being in "conflict" with Catholics, and lower class Catholics were not described as being in "conflict" with upper class Catholics; rather, they were described in terms of the extent to which they deviated from the rational and virtuous position. As a consequence, the society was described as consensual despite the necessity to use force to secure the compliance of a variety of groups who were said to be not fully rational and/or virtuous.

As with the theories of Plato and Aristotle, this is an evaluative, not an empirical, difference. Augustine and Aquinas differed primarily in their assessments of the legitimacy of the actions of ruling groups. They did not necessarily differ in their assertions about what the ruling groups actually did. Rather, the same actions that a Thomist would characterize as rational, virtuous, and in the common interest, an Augustinian would characterize as being inevitably corrupted by man's sinful nature, so that they were irrational and selfish. Thus, with respect to their descriptions of contemporary societies, the debate between Augustine and Aquinas was, like the debate between Plato and Aristotle, a debate about the legitimacy of the actions of ruling groups—whether or not these actions are rational, virtuous, and in the common interest. As such, it was not an empirical debate and cannot be resolved through empirical investigations.

Notes

1. Augustine, *The City of God*, bk. 14 and 22.22.
2. P. R. L. Brown, "Political Society," in R. A. Markus, ed., *Augustine* (Garden City, N.J.: Doubleday, 1972), pp. 313–14.
3. Augustine, *The City of God*, 4.3.
4. Herbert A. Deane, *The Political and Social Ideas of St. Augustine* (New York: Columbia University Press, 1963), p. 117.
5. Augustine, *The City of God*, 19.21.
6. Ibid. 4.4. See further analogies to a band of robbers in 4.6 and 19.12.
7. Deane, *Political and Social Ideas*, pp. 130, 134, 147–50.
8. William T. Bluhm, *Theories of the Political System*, 3d ed. (Englewood Cliffs, N.J.: Prentice-Hall, 1978), pp. 131–33.
9. Thomas Aquinas, *Summa Theologica I–II*, question 91, article 2 and question 94.
10. Thomas Gilby, *The Political Thought of Thomas Aquinas* (Chicago: University of Chicago Press, 1958), pp. 120, 140.
11. Aquinas, *Summa*, question 96, article 5.
12. Ibid., question 97.
13. Aquinas, *On Kingship*, 1.2.
14. Ibid., 1.6.

15. Aquinas, *Summa*, question 92, article 1.

16. Rollin Chambliss, *Social Thought from Hammurabi to Comte* (New York: Dryden Press, 1954), p. 272.

17. A. P. D'Entreves, ed., *Aquinas—Selected Political Writings* (Oxford: Basil Blackwell, 1959), p. xxiii.

– CHAPTER 4 –

Machiavelli and Hobbes

PLATO, ARISTOTLE, Aquinas, and, in some ways, Augustine all shared the view that human nature was consensual, although they differed in their descriptions of contemporary societies. The two theorists examined in this section are both known, in contrast, for their deeply pessimistic views of human nature. They differed in their descriptions of contemporary societies, however, Machiavelli describing them in conflictual and Hobbes in consensual terms. Thus, Machiavelli falls into the sociological conflict and Hobbes into the sociological consensus category.

Machiavelli's Description of Human Nature, Contemporary Societies, and the Ideal Society

Machiavelli's Italy was politically fragmented into many small and competing city-states and was the subject of intense maneuvering between the stronger, centralized governments of France, Spain, and the papacy.[1] Machiavelli held an administrative position in a Florentine government that aligned itself with France, and was "exiled" to the countryside when it was overrun by papal and Spanish forces. From "exile," Machiavelli wrote many appeals to Lorenzo de Medici, the new ruler, in vain attempts to get into his good graces. He was also vitally concerned with uniting Italy with a strong, centralized government and driving the foreign powers out. Those two purposes were united in his writing of *The Prince*, which was addressed to Lorenzo and was essentially a "cookbook" of recipes for accomplishing that great task.[2]

Machiavelli's method was to examine the careers of all the great state-builders of history in the attempt to discover the principles which underlay their successes and their failures. He was also heavily influenced by the constant intrigue and conniving that accompanied the maneuvering of the great powers in Italy. He saw that success in this maneuvering went to those who used a shrewd mixture of cunning and force:

> ...a prince...must imitate the fox and the lion, for the lion cannot protect himself from traps, and the fox cannot defend himself from wolves. One must therefore be a fox to recognise traps, and a lion to frighten wolves. Those that wish to be only lions do not understand this.[3]

He also became convinced that statesmen could not afford to operate by conventional rules of morality.

> A man who wishes to make a profession of goodness in everything must necessarily come to grief among so many who are not good. Therefore it is necessary for a prince, who wishes to maintain himself, to learn how not to be good, and to use this knowledge and not use it, according to the necessity of the case.[4]

Thus, Machiavelli proposed to draw up "an original set of rules" about how a prince should govern his conduct, rules that would reflect the realities that the prince faced.

Machiavelli's view of man was essentially Augustinian—he saw him in constant conflict, driven by passions, filled with unhappiness and dissatisfaction. And his image of society was of one divided into interest groups that were in fundamental conflict with each other. The prince acquired and retained power by aligning himself with some of those groups and against others. Machiavelli thought that the most stable base of support for the prince was with the masses and against the elites, but in particular situations other alignments must be chosen. Aristotle and Aquinas had described the masses only in terms of the necessity to coerce them into obedience, while support for the regime was found in a consensus among the elites. Machiavelli, however, argued that the elites were an unstable source of support for the prince because they were constantly conspiring and intriguing to acquire power themselves. The common people, in contrast, seek only "not to be oppressed," and would not challenge the power of the prince if their persons and property were secured. In addition, a strong "consensus" among the masses could be built through the manipulations of the prince. Thus, Machiavelli recommended that, when taking over a state, cruelties should be committed all at once but benefits given out little by little, so that people will eventually forget the one but remember the other; that princes should murder their opponents rather than confiscate their property, since they would then seek revenge; that princes must appear to be liberal and generous but actually be stingy, since to actually be generous would require raising the taxes and that would promote discontent; that they must make themselves feared but avoid being hated, since love is too inconstant to be relied on and cruelty is necessary to prevent disorders and crime from rising, which would be unpopular; that they must appear trustworthy but be willing to break their word to accomplish their goals, since men judge only by appearances and by the outcome of the enterprise, and are always willing to be deceived if the effort was successful. Key to his view was his argument that the mass of men judge by appearances and not by reality:

> It is not, therefore, necessary for a prince to have all the above-named qualities, but it is very necessary to seem to have them. I would even be bold to say that to possess them and always to observe them is dangerous, but to appear to possess them is useful. Thus, it is well to seem merciful, faithful, humane, sincere, religious, and also to be so; but you must have the mind so disposed that when it is needful to be otherwise you may be able to change to the opposite qualities.[5]

Because Machiavelli was concerned primarily with establishing a power base among the masses rather than among the elites, it might be argued that his theories are not inconsistent with those of Aristotle and Aquinas. Certainly he described the masses in the same way these two did—filled with conflict and passions—and Aristotle's arguments against democracy were based on that description. The difference is that Machiavelli described the elite groups in the same terms as the masses, as Plato and Augustine had done, and not in terms of rationality and virtue, as Aristotle and Aquinas had done. He advocated establishing a power base among the poor because the elites were too power hungry to be a constant base of support. He also recognized that in some instances the prince must seek a power base among the elites, but in those cases he must be as cruel and manipulative in order to retain their support as he was when dealing with the masses. Machiavelli regarded consensus descriptions of society as dreams that were dangerous to the health of the prince:

> ...it appears to me more proper to go to the real truth of the matter than to its imagination; and many have imagined republics and principalities which have never been seen or known to exist in reality; for how we live is so far removed from how we ought to live, that he who abandons what is done for what ought to be done, will rather learn to bring about his own ruin than his preservation.[6]

Such views were also dangerous to the health of the state, since a prince who believed these views would not adequately control the destructive conflicts between groups. Machiavelli's ideal state was a stable and prosperous regime in which the prince had firm control of power. For example, he stated: "Cesare Borgia was considered cruel, but his cruelty had brought order to the Romagna, united it, and reduced it to peace and fealty."[7] It was to establish such a stable and prosperous regime in Italy that Machiavelli wrote *The Prince*.

Values in Machiavelli's Theory

Many objections have been raised concerning Machiavelli's ethics. One such objection is that Machiavelli recommended policies in which the ends justified the means, and that therefore he is in some sense responsible for that type of political behavior.[8] But as Lerner has pointed out, "Power politics existed before Machiavelli was ever heard of; it will exist long after his name is only a faint memory. What he did...was to recognize its existence and subject it to scientific study."[9] Machiavelli's primary purpose was not to write an ethical treatise but to describe "things as they are in real truth, rather than as they are imagined." For example, he argued that, in the real world, the general populace will justify the means as long as the ends are accomplished:

> ... in the actions of men, and especially of princes, from which there is no appeal, the end justifies the means. Let a prince therefore aim at conquering and maintaining the state, and the means will always be judged honourable and praised by everyone,

for the mass of mankind is always swayed by appearances and by the outcome of an enterprise... and the few who are not in the mass are isolated when the mass has a rallying point in the prince.[10]

That is not an ethical statement. It is a prediction about the effect of a particular political behavior. The question is not whether these practices are ethical or unethical, but whether these are the standard practices of politics, and whether the results of these practices are as Machiavelli has described them.

Machiavelli described the actions of the prince in terms that conveyed moral illegitimacy—deception, manipulation, cruelty, etc. But modern Machiavellians dispense with such morally loaded terms and focus on objectively describing and analyzing the actions of ruling groups without any implication concerning whether those actions are morally legitimate or morally illegitimate. Burnham described this as the "objective science of politics:"

Such a science will describe and correlate observable social facts and, on the basis of the facts of the past, will state more or less probable hypotheses about the future. Such a science will be neutral with respect to any practical political goal: that is, like any other science, its statements will be tested by facts accessible to any observer, rich or poor, ruler or ruled, and will in no way be dependent upon the acceptance of some particular ethical aim or ideal.[11]

Burnham argues that Machiavelli's "allegiance to objective truth" and his "refusal to pervert or distort political science by doctoring its results in order to bring them into line with 'moral principles'" is itself a moral ideal.[12] He goes on to argue that only by exposing the true processes of politics can individuals protect themselves from abuses of power by political leaders.[13] For this reason he described Machiavellians as "defenders of freedom" in the title of his book.

The objective stance taken by modern Machiavellians is possible because there is no ideal consensual society in the theory on which to base value judgments about contemporary societies. Machiavelli's description of contemporary societies resembled those of Plato and Augustine, but those theorists also described ideal consensual societies (the Republic and the City of God) in which all conflict was resolved. Evaluations of the actions of ruling groups in contemporary societies (e.g., that they were irrational and selfish) were based on implicit comparisons between their actions and the actions of ruling groups in the ideal societies (the "guardians" and the "saints"). But no such ideal society existed in Machiavelli's theory, so that there was no basis for the negative moral evaluation of the actions of the prince. Thus, modern Machiavellians are easily able to stay within Machiavelli's basic framework and yet dispense with the terminology that conveys moral illegitimacy. Such a stance would not be possible for modern Platonists or Augustinians, since it would also require elimination of the description of the ideal consensual society in those theories.

While modern Machiavellians reject negative moral evaluations of the actions of ruling groups in their descriptions of contemporary societies, they do not adopt positive moral evaluations either. Such a positive evaluation can be found in the comments that Jacques Maritain, a modern Thomist, made about Machiavelli's theory:

> Machiavelli... had a somewhat rough and elementary idea of moral science, plainly disregarding its realist, experimental, and existential character.... Accordingly, what he calls vice and evil... may sometimes be only the authentically moral behavior of a just man engaged in the complexities of human life and of true ethics: for instance, justice may call for relentless energy—which is neither vengeance nor cruelty—against wicked and falsehearted enemies. Or the toleration of some existing evil ... may be required for avoiding a greater evil.... Or even dissimulation is not always bad faith and knavery. It would not be moral, but foolish, to open up one's heart and inner thoughts to any dull or mischievous fellow. Stupidity is never moral, it is a vice.[14]

Maritain's evaluation of the actions of the prince is based on an implicit comparison between those actions and the actions of ruling groups in an ideal consensual society. But because the ideal society he uses is Aquinas' and Aristotle's, rather than Augustine's or Plato's, the evaluation is positive rather than negative. This is consistent with the argument in the preceding two chapters that the primary difference between the theories of Plato and Aristotle, and the theories of Augustine and Aquinas, with respect to the descriptions of contemporary societies, concerns the evaluation of the actions of ruling groups in terms of moral legitimacy or moral illegitimacy, rather than any empirical assertions about their actions. Maritain does not argue that the prince behaved any differently from the way Machiavelli described. Nevertheless, he evaluated the behavior of the prince as morally legitimate, where Machiavelli himself evaluated it as morally illegitimate.

Hobbes' Description of Human Nature and Contemporary Societies

Hobbes is probably one of the most confusing cases in the history of the consensus-conflict debate. Those who place him in the conflict tradition have based that classification on his descriptions of human nature as entailing a "war of all against all." That view was an abstraction from the competitive world Hobbes saw around him—not merely an earlier historical state, but what human societies would become whenever the forces of government were lifted. Hobbes believed that the civil peace was a very fragile thing, and that chaos could and did break through the veneer of civilization. People in this natural state greatly resembled what Augustine had described in "the City of Man," especially in the desire to dominate others and in the intense struggle for scarce material goods. Hobbes believed all people were essentially irrational, not merely the masses, as Aristotle and Aquinas did. He argued, for example, that "the Rich, the Potent Subjects of a Kingdome, or those that are accounted the most Learned" are in some ways less capable of rationality than the common people:

> But all men know, that the obstructions to this kind of doctrine, proceed not so much from the difficulty of the matter, as from the interest of them that are to learn. Potent men, digest hardly anything that setteth up a Power to bridle their affections; and Learned men, any thing that discovereth their errours, and thereby lesseneth their Authority: whereas the Common-peoples minds, unless they be tainted with dependence on the Potent, or scribbled over with the opinions of their Doctors, are like clean paper, fit to receive whatsoever by Publique Authority shall be imprinted on them.[15]

He also argued that all people were selfish, as opposed to Aristotle's and Aquinas' arguments that the elite groups were capable of being virtuous. Hobbes believed that to the extent that people were rational, they used their rationality to accomplish selfish ends. Even abstract ideals tended to be merely surreptitious methods of promoting individual interests. Finally, he believed that each individual was isolated from all other individuals in the sense that they did not form into cohesive groups. Every person feared injury and death at the hands of every other person, since even the weakest could kill the strongest if the circumstances were right.

Hobbes argued that people had just enough rationality to recognize their situation, and to come together to form governments in order to (selfishly) protect their own lives. In a "commonwealth by Institution," men "agree amongst themselves, to submit to some Man, or Assembly of men, voluntarily, on confidence to be protected by him against all others."[16] It is as if they say to one another:

> 'I Authorise and give up my Right of Governing myselfe, to this Man or this Assembly of men, on this condition, that thou give up thy Right to him, and Authorise all his Actions in like manner.'[17]

Hobbes argued that there really was not much difference between the "commonwealth by Institution" and what he called the "commonwealth by Acquisition," where power was acquired by force. The only difference between the two forms of government was that "men who choose their Soveraign, do it for fear of one another, and not of him whom they Institute: But in [the commonwealth by Acquisition], they subject themselves to him they are afraid of. In both cases they do it for fear. . . ."[18]

That, according to Hobbes, represents the process by which contemporary societies originated. Thus, although Hobbes described human nature in conflictual terms, he described contemporary societies in consensual terms: people were rational enough to recognize that they had a common interest in self-protection, and therefore they consent to governments to protect that interest. It is important to note, however, that Hobbes posits only a minimal rationality, a minimal common interest, and a minimal consent in his theory. Humans are said to be essentially irrational—not all of them are even rational enough to recognize their situation. The common interest is limited to self-protection—an extremely narrow point—and Hobbes assumes conflicting interests on virtually everything else. Finally, in the context of Hobbes' theory, "consent" implies only that people did not join in overt rebellion against the government, and does not imply any level of substantive agreement. That is why Hobbes said that its motive was always fear of death, and why he did not distinguish between consenting to a government instituted by its subjects and to a government imposed on its subjects by force. Once government was established, said Hobbes, whether by institution or by acquisition, its subjects obeyed the laws not because they agreed with them (i.e., because there was a consensus on the laws) but only because they feared punishment. Even in this minimal sense Hobbes did not argue that the subjects always consented, since they frequently joined in rebellions against their governments. In those rebellions people lost their lives and thus defeated the very purpose for which governments were formed in the first place.

All of the above concerns the way Hobbes described the state of societies as they existed at the time Hobbes wrote. It was in the minimal rationality, the minimal common interest, and the minimal consent that Hobbes' description resembled the descriptions of existing societies found in the earlier theories of Aristotle and Aquinas. Otherwise, his theory was remarkably similar to Augustine's. Like Augustine, he argued that conflict was universal in societies and attributed it to human nature, rather than to socioeconomic elements, as did Plato. Also like Augustine, he argued that governments were absolutely necessary but that they had to rely on force rather than on the consent of their subjects to achieve obedience to laws, and that the best they seemed able to accomplish was to put a coercive cap on the violence.

Hobbes' Description of the Ideal Society

Hobbes, however, went beyond Augustine's position by arguing that governments could accomplish more than suppressing violence, that there was a rational way to organize governments so that they could fulfill their basic purpose of protecting the lives of their citizens. That is, Hobbes not only described existing societies in his theory but also proposed the blueprint for an ideal society. It is his portrait of the ideal society that is more fully in the consensus tradition, since it hypothesized a much broader and stronger consensus than the minimal and unstable one Hobbes found in existing societies.

Hobbes' methodology for deriving this ideal society was consistent with Aristotle's basic methodology—using rationality to discover true values. For Hobbes, true values were based on the need for self-preservation. Thus, he defined a law of nature as "a Precept, or generall Rule, found out by Reason, by which a man is forbidden to do, that, which is destructive of his life, or taketh away the means of preserving the same; and to omit, that, by which he thinketh it may be best preserved."[19] Hobbes delineated a number of laws of nature, including that every man should seek peace although he has the right to defend himself by all means, that he should be content with as much liberty as he is willing to grant all other men, that he should perform all of his covenants, and in general that he should do unto others as he would have done to him. These laws of nature are contrary to man's passions, and are ineffective "without the terrour of some Power, to cause them to be observed."[20] Hobbes argued that the proper function of government was to force men to observe these laws of nature.

The problem with existing governments was that their power was not absolute, so that men's passions would reassert themselves. Hobbes' solution to this problem was Leviathan, the absolute sovereign to whom men irrevocably cede power. The ceding of power had to be irrevocable because, Hobbes maintained, all rebellion was irrational, regardless of the form of government:

> For the prosperity of a People ruled by an Aristocraticall, or Democraticall assembly, commeth not from Aristocracy, nor from Democracy, but from the Obedience, and Concord of the Subjects: nor do the people flourish in a Monarchy, because one man has the right to rule them, but because they obey him. Take away in any kind of State, the Obedience, (and consequently the Concord of the People), and they shall not only not flourish but in short time be dissolved. And they that go about by disobedience, to doe

no more than reforme the Commonwealth, shall find they do thereby destroy it.... [21]

Hobbes' argument here is based on an implicit assumption that there would be the same socioeconomic structure, based on a competitive, free-market economy, regardless of the form of government. [22] Rebellion was irrational because the only thing it accomplished was the shift of power from one group to another, while at the same time people were killed and the economy disrupted. That implicit assumption also underlies Hobbes' argument that the common people can more easily consent to his theory than the "learned" or the "potent." In Hobbes' view, common people did not enter into the competition for power, so they had nothing to gain and much to lose when revolutions occurred.

Hobbes argued that one of the most frequent causes of rebellion in his own time was the reading of the histories of the ancient Greeks and Romans, from which "young men, and all others that are unprovided of the Antidote of solid Reason" receive the idea that prosperity does not proceed "from the aemulation of particular men, but from the vertue of their popular forme of government," as well as the idea that "the Subjects in a Popular Common-wealth enjoy Liberty; but that in a Monarchy they are all Slaves." [23] Hobbes concluded: "I cannot imagine, how anything can be more prejudicial to a Monarchy, than the allowing of such books to be publikely read, without present applying such correctives of discreet Masters, as are fit to take away their Venime."

In place of such "irrational" ideas, Hobbes argued that the people should be taught "the Essentiall Rights (which are the Naturall, and Fundamentall Lawes) of Soveraignty" by "setting a part from their ordinary labour, some certain times, in which they may attend those that are appointed to instruct them." [24] At those times, they would be taught to love their form of government, whatever it is; that they should admire and respect no other person so much as the sovereign; that they should never speak evil of the sovereign or dispute his power; and so on. The sovereign himself was responsible for the "safety of the people," which included not merely preservation of their lives but "also all other Contentments of life, which every man by lawfull Industry, without danger or hurt to the Common-wealth, shall acquire to himselfe."[25] That requires "a general Providence, contained in publique Instruction, both of Doctrine, and Example; and in the making, and executing of good Lawes, to which individuall persons may apply their own cases." He must also administer justice equally to "all degrees of People"; care for those who "become unable to maintain themselves by their labour"; choose good counselors who "have least hope of benefit by giving evill Counsell, and most knowledge of those things that conduce to the Peace, and Defence of the Common-wealth"; and be receptive to "the generall informations, and complaints of the people of each Province, who are best acquainted with their own wants, and ought therefore, when they demand nothing in derogation of the essentiall Rights of Soveraignty to be diligently taken notice of."[26] But in these duties, the sovereign is accountable to God "and to none but him," so that his failure to fulfill these duties is no justification for rebellion. It is through the combination of absolute power, heavy indoctrination, and a virtuous sovereign that the ultimate purpose of government—the safety of the people—can be achieved.

Hobbes compared his proposals for the ideal society with those of Plato in *The Republic*, stating, "I am at the point of believing this my labour, as useless, as the Common-wealth of Plato; For he also is of opinion that it is impossible for the disorders of State, and change of Governments by Civill Warre, ever to be taken away, till Soveraigns be Philosophers."[27] But Hobbes then pointed out two differences: Plato believed that rulers would have to understand all of the sciences, while Hobbes argued that they needed only the "Science of Naturall Justice"; and Hobbes believed that he was the first to lay out and prove the "theorums" of that science, "that men may learn thereby, both how to govern, and how to obey." Accordingly, Hobbes stated: "I recover some hope, that one time or other, this writing of mine may fall into the hands of a sovereign, who will consider it himselfe (for it is short, and I think clear), without the help of any interested, or envious Interpreter; and by the exercise of entire Soveraignty, in protecting the Publique teaching of it, convert this Truth of Speculation into the Utility of Practice."

Other differences between the two proposals can be found. For example, Hobbes seemed to believe that the acquisition of absolute power would eliminate the need for the sovereign to be greedy, since in a monarchy

> the private interest is the same with the publique. The riches, power, and honour of a Monarch arise only from the riches, strength and reputation of his Subjects. For no King can be rich, nor glorious, nor secure; whose Subjects are either poore, or contemptible, or too weak through want or dissention to maintain a war against their enemies.[28]

Plato, in contrast, attributed social conflict in his own society to the greed generated by the ownership of property by the rulers. Hobbes also stated that the absolute sovereign could never commit injustice, though he could work "iniquite," since justice was defined by the will of the sovereign. Plato, of course, defined Justice as a Form, independent of the will of the rulers, and accordingly was quite concerned with how to insure that their behavior was just. Plato addressed both problems by proposing an entire regimen beginning even before birth in order to train the guardians to fulfill their roles as rulers of the society. He also argued that they should not be allowed to own private property; thus, The Republic required a socioeconomic as well as a political reorganization. Hobbes' proposals, on the other hand, required only political reorganization. Although he believed that humans were essentially irrational, he believed that at least some of them (including, he hoped, the sovereign) were sufficiently rational to understand the arguments presented in Leviathan and that most others could be taught to believe the essential points, even if they could not fully understand the arguments. In contrast, Plato had assumed that only philosophers could understand the teachings in The Republic; others would have to be taught a "noble lie." Finally, the most fundamental difference is that Hobbes attributed the conflict to human nature, so that even in the ideal society force would be necessary as the foundation of government; whereas Plato attributed conflict to social structural arrangements, so that once those arrangements were changed, force would no longer be necessary for the maintenance of order.

In terms of its structure, Hobbes' ideal society is more similar to Aquinas' ideal society than it is to Plato's. Both maintained that the consensus in the ideal society was based on natural law, which was accessible to rational men through their rationality. Like Aquinas, Hobbes assumed that there were a limited number

of people in the society who would fully understand and agree
with the consensus but that most of the rest could be taught to
believe in it. Force would be necessary among the less rational
groups in the society, but those in the more rational groups,
including the sovereign, would be expected to act in the common
interest—executing good laws, administering justice equally,
caring for the helpless, etc. Neither the ideal society of Aquinas
nor that of Hobbes required any socioeconomic reorganization.
The major difference between the two ideal societies lay in what
the consensus was about—i.e., what the people agreed on or
believed in. For Aquinas, the consensus was on the doctrines of
Catholicism; for Hobbes it was on the doctrines contained in
Leviathan. What Hobbes had done was to offer his own ideas as
the basis for a consensus in society. Like Aquinas, he maintained
that his ideas were rational in themselves and that those who
fully understood them would agree with them. Later consensus
theorists, especially Comte and, to a lesser extent, Durkheim,
would similarly offer their own ideas as the basis for a consensus
in society (see chs. 6 and 7).

The Relation Between Form and Content

Hobbes falls into the sociological consensus category because he
described human nature as conflictual, as expressed in the hypothetical "war of all against all," but contemporary societies as
consensual, even if it was only a minimal and unstable consensus. The form that his theory took is logically derived from the
content of these two assumptions. First, he had to explain why
contemporary societies were consensual when human nature
itself was conflictual. He then hypothesized an ideal consensual
society in which man's conflictual nature was fully controlled,
and discussed methods by which contemporary societies could
be transformed into the hypothetical ideal. Such transformation
would be effected solely through changes in the mechanisms of
social control, while changes in other social structures, such as
the socioeconomic system, were described as irrelevant. Accordingly, his theory defended whatever socioeconomic system happened to be in place at the time. Machiavelli described both

human nature and contemporary societies in conflictual terms, so his theory falls into the sociological conflict category. It describes conflict as being inevitable in every society, so that no consensual society—even a hypothetical ideal one—is possible. His theory therefore focuses on describing and analyzing real societies and describes the "ideal" society as being the "best" of the real societies.

Consensus and Conflict in Contemporary Societies

The form that each theory took therefore follows from the content of its assumptions about human nature and contemporary societies. The next issue to be examined concerns the exact difference between Hobbes' description of contemporary and ideal societies in consensual terms and Machiavelli's description of them in conflictual terms. Certainly there is an evaluative difference concerning the legitimacy of the actions of the rulers similar to the difference found between the theories of Plato and Aristotle and of Augustine and Aquinas. Machiavelli described the actions of the prince in terms that conveyed moral illegitimacy—lying, manipulating, killing—whereas Hobbes described the actions of the sovereign in terms that conveyed moral legitimacy—natural law, rationality, common interest. The question is whether this is the primary difference between the two theories or whether there is some other, more fundamental, difference.

In fact, Hobbes' descriptions of contemporary societies and the ideal society as consensual do not appear to differ significantly with respect to their empirical assertions from Machiavelli's comparable descriptions of contemporary and ideal societies as conflictual. Both Machiavelli and Hobbes described the societies that actually existed at the time they were writing as being filled with conflicts, and their empirical descriptions of those societies do not appear to differ substantially in spite of their use of opposite terms. Hobbes is sometimes portrayed as attributing a minimal consensus to all members of the society on the desirability of having a government per se, but in fact he merely argued that it was *rational* for all of them to so consent. He did not argue that they all actually did consent, even in the ideal society. Both Machiavelli and Hobbes called for strong centralized regimes to suppress all conflict as a means of achieving a stable and prosperous society. Hobbes described such a society as "consensual" because he said that all the members of the society would "consent" to it, if only to avoid losing their own lives. Machiavelli described such a society as conflictual because various groups in the society would oppose the prince, even if they did not overtly express that conflict for fear of losing their lives. The difference between the two descriptions appears to turn on whether a coercive order in which there is neither overt conflict nor substantive agreement should be described as "consensus" or "conflict."

Hobbes went even further, though, and argued that there would be some level of substantive agreement in the ideal society, as described in *Leviathan*. Such a regime would be rational, and therefore rational people would recognize its rationality and consent to it. The remainder of the population would not substantively agree with the rule of the sovereign because of their irrationality, but they would not overtly enter into conflict with it because of his absolute control of power. But Machiavelli also expected that a certain portion of the population would recognize the benefits of the stable and prosperous regime instituted by the prince, and thus be in substantive agreement with it, while the remainder of the population would not overtly be in conflict with it due to the prince's firm control of power. The difference between the two descriptions is that Hobbes attributed rationality and virtue to the sovereign and to those who agreed with him and irrationality and selfishness to those who disagreed with him. Machiavelli attributed irrationality and selfishness to all members of the society, including the prince and his followers, and he described the way to establish a stable and prosperous regime within the context of that assumption. Accordingly, Hobbes described *Leviathan*'s society as consensual because there was a consensus among rational people, but he described the need to use force and other means to suppress conflict with irrational groups. Machiavelli described the regime of the prince as conflictual because there was conflict between the various equally irrational and selfish groups in the society.

The debate between Machiavelli and Hobbes with respect to the concepts of conflict and consensus comes down to whether the actions required to produce a stable and prosperous regime should be described as morally legitimate or morally illegitimate. There is no substantial disagreement between the two theorists on the specific actions required or on the effect that they have. The two theories differ in some respects on those points, but that is not the core of the difference between them. Rather, the core of the difference is that Hobbes described those actions as rational and consistent with natural law and Machiavelli described them as necessary and beneficial but morally blameworthy nonetheless. This difference is purely evaluative, not empirical. Thus, the debate between Machiavelli and Hobbes with respect to the concepts of conflict and consensus is not an empirical debate and cannot be resolved through empirical investigations.

Notes

1. For brief accounts of Machiavelli's life, see Max Lerner, Introduction to Niccolo Machiavelli, *The Prince and The Discourses* (New York: Modern Library, 1950), pp. xxv–xxix; and J.R. Hale, "Machiavelli and the Self Sufficient State," in David Thomson, ed., *Political Ideas* (Baltimore: Penguin, 1966), pp. 22–33.

2. James Burnham, *The Machiavellians: Defenders of Freedom* (New York: Day, 1943), pp. 31–33.

3. Machiavelli, *The Prince*, ch. 18, p. 64.

4. Ibid., ch. 15, p. 56.

5. Ibid., ch. 18, p. 65.

6. Ibid., ch. 15, p. 56.

7. Ibid., ch. 17, p. 60.

8. See Leo Strauss, *Thoughts on Machiavelli* (New York: The Free Press, 1958). Strauss views Machiavelli as a "teacher of evil."

9. Lerner, Introduction to *The Prince*, p. xliii.

10. Machiavelli, *The Prince*, ch. 18, p. 66.

11. Burnham, *The Machiavellians*, p. 223.

12. Ibid., p. 38.

13. Ibid., especially pp. 223–54.

14. Jacques Maritain, *The Range of Reason* (New York: Scribner's, 1953), p. 138.

15. Thomas Hobbes, *Leviathan* (New York: E.P. Dutton, 1950), ch. 30, pp. 290–91.

16. Ibid., ch. 17, p. 144.

17. Ibid., ch. 17, p. 143.

18. Ibid., ch. 20, p. 167.

19. Ibid., ch. 14, p. 107.

20. Ibid., ch. 17, p. 139.

21. Ibid., ch. 30, p. 291–92.

22. C.B. Macpherson, *The Political Theory of Possessive Individualism* (New York: Oxford University Press, 1962), pp. 61–68.

23. Hobbes, *Leviathan*, ch. 20, p. 281.

24. Ibid., ch. 30, pp. 291, 293.

25. Ibid., p. 288.

26. Ibid., pp. 296–304.

27. Ibid., ch. 31, pp. 318–19.

28. Ibid., ch. 19, p. 157.

– CHAPTER 5 –

Locke and Rousseau

IT IS sometimes argued that the social-contract theorists, as a group, laid the foundations for consensus theories in sociology. But on closer examination, it can be seen that they took widely different positions on human nature, contemporary societies, and the ideal society. Hobbes has already been classified as a sociological consensus theorist because he described human nature in conflictual terms but contemporary societies in consensual terms. Locke, in contrast, returned to the conservative consensus tradition established by Aristotle and continued by Aquinas, and described both human nature and contemporary societies in consensual terms. Rousseau described human nature in consensual terms but contemporary societies in conflictual terms, so he falls into the radical tradition established by Plato.

Locke's Description of Human Nature, Contemporary Societies, and the Ideal Society

Like Aristotle and Aquinas, Locke hypothesized a consensual "state of nature," arguing that men there were perfectly free and equal.[1] In that state, there was originally no private property, but each man appropriated by his labor that portion of the natural resources, particularly the land, needed to support his family. Because land was plentiful, there was no reason for a man to covet the land of another man, and because money had not been invented, it made no sense for any man to appropriate more land than he and his family could actually use. But with the invention of money, individuals were enabled to appropriate more of the land than they could personally use. Because money has no intrinsic value, but attains its value only through the common consent of mankind, mankind also consented, albeit tacitly, to the unequal distribution of land:

> But since Gold and Silver, being little useful to the Life of Man in proportion to Food, Rayment, and Carriage, had its *value* only from the consent of Men, ... it is plain, that Men have agreed to disproportionate and unequal Possession of the Earth, they having by a tacit and voluntary consent found a way, how man may fairly possess more land than he himself can use the product of.... [2]

This consent to a money system and to the unequal distribution of the land occurred prior to the formation of civil societies:

> This partage of things, in an inequality of private possessions, men have made practicable out of the bounds of Societie, and without compact, only by putting a value on gold and silver and tacitly agreeing in the use of Money. [3]

The formation of civil societies, according to Locke's theory, took place when any number of individuals decided to join together to form a community. It did not require that all the people of a given locality join together:

> The only way whereby any one devests himself of his Natural Liberty and *puts on the bonds of Civil Society* is by agreeing with other Men to joyn and unite into a Community, for their comfortable, safe, and peaceable living one amongst another, in a secure Enjoyment of their Properties, and a greater Security against any that are not of it. This any number of Men may do, because it injures not the freedom of the rest; they are left as they were in the Liberty of the State of Nature. [4]

The key characteristic of a civil society is the establishment of impartial rules which all members agree to abide by and the appointment of an impartial judge or magistrate to mediate disputes. The chief purpose, Locke stated repeatedly, is the preservation of the "property" of each man, by which he meant at some points the lives, liberties and estates and at other points apparently just the estates—i.e., the land and goods. The state of nature continues to exist wherever men are not bound among themselves to civil society—for example, he stated that the rulers of independent commonwealths are in the state of nature with respect to each other and that absolute monarchs are in the state of nature with respect to their subjects, "For where-ever any two Men are, who have no standing Rule, and common Judge to Appeal to on earth for the determination of Controversies of Right betwixt them, there they are still *in the state of Nature....*"[5]

Of crucial importance to understanding Locke's theory is to note that when these men join together, their land is also joined together to form the territory of the commonwealth. Once having joined the commonwealth, one cannot withdraw from it, nor can the lands be taken out of it.[6] However, an individual who acquires property within the bounds of the commonwealth is not thereby made a member of that commonwealth—only his *express* consent can make him so. But he must accept that property only on the condition that he submit to the government of the commonwealth.[7] This is Locke's famous theory of *tacit consent:*

> ... every Man, that hath any Possession, or Enjoyment, of any part of the Dominions of any Government, doth hereby give his *tacit Consent,* and is as far forth obliged to Obedience to the Laws of that Government, during such Enjoyment, as any one under it; whether this his Possession be of land, to him and his Heirs for ever, or a Lodging only for a Week; or whether it be barely travelling freely on the Highway; and in Effect, it reaches as far as the very being of any one within the Territories of that Government.[8]

Tacit consent conveys no rights, only the obligation to obey the laws of the government. It "makes not a Man a Member of that Society," Locke argued strongly and forcefully; "nothing can make any Man so, but his actually entering into it by positive Engagement, and express Promise and Compact."[9] One who has only tacitly consented to the commonwealth is free to sell his lands and leave, while a member of the society is not free to do so. Even inheritance cannot bind a man to a commonwealth, for a father "cannot by any *Compact* whatsoever, bind *his Children* or Posterity."[10] The son, by inheriting the lands of the father, is bound by tacit consent to obey the laws of the commonwealth, but only by his express consent can he himself become a full member of it.

The significance of becoming a member of the society is twofold: one binds oneself irrevocably to the commonwealth, and one thereby attains voting rights. Because of the nature of the compact, it necessarily entails universal, express agreement—every person in it has necessarily joined it voluntarily at some point in time. However, each person also joins with the understanding that all decisions will be made by majority vote. Locke gave various practical reasons for the fact that there cannot be universal consent for anything except the actual joining of the commonwealth.[11] It is in this body of full members that Locke rested the sovereignty of the commonwealth.[12] He said they had the supreme power to establish the form of the government, to alter it at any time they wished, or to overturn it and establish a new form of government on the vote of the majority.

Up to this point Locke's theory was intended to be descriptive of the actual historical development of all real societies, rather than a prescription about what would be the best type of society. Even his arguments about majority rule were descriptive, not prescriptive: "It is necessary the Body should move that way whither the greater force carries it, which is the *consent of the majority:* or else it is impossible it should act or continue one Body, *one Community....*"[13] It was after this point that Locke began to make prescriptive assessments about the better forms of government. Like Aristotle and Aquinas before him, Locke first reviewed the various "forms of a Commonwealth"[14] and then recommended such things as division of powers with final authority resting in a representative assembly.[15] These prescriptive assessments constitute Locke's description of the ideal society.

The Commonwealth as an Association of Landowners

Locke's arguments about majority rule are usually considered prescriptive rather than descriptive, especially since England at the time limited voting rights to landowners. The process of relaxing these restrictions did not begin until 1832, at which point only 4.4 percent of the adult population of England was enfranchised.[16] Yet Locke's theory makes a great deal of sense if one considers that it essentially describes an association of landowners. The ownership of the land preceded the formation of the association (civil society). Each owner freely consents to join with the other owners in a compact, and the total territory owned by the members collectively is then governed by their decisions. Collectively, these owners represent the ultimate authority of the association, and any other person who is in the territory, because it is private property, tacitly consents to obey whatever rules the association makes. Any person who does not wish to conform to the rules is free to leave the territory.

Locke himself did not expressly limit membership in the commonwealth to landowners, but he simply did not deal with the case of nonlandowners. Macpherson examined Locke's writings and concluded that nonlandowning people could not become full members of the commonwealth.[17] It would seem to be irrational within the context of Locke's theory for the landowners to allow nonlandowners to join. When a landowner joined the commonwealth, both he and the commonwealth experienced benefit: he became a voting member of the decision-making structure, and his property was annexed to its territory. But if a nonlandowner joined the commonwealth, he would benefit but the commonwealth would not. A nonlandowner could not logically join the commonwealth unless he was already within its territory, but then he would already be obliged to obey its laws by tacit consent. By allowing the nonlandowner to become a full member, the landowners allow him to have a vote in the decision-making structure in which the majority rules, but they receive absolutely nothing in return. The absurdity of such an arrangement can be seen by considering the case of a single landowner who makes a commonwealth with the nonlandowners on his property. He would gain nothing but would bind himself to obey the rule of the majority. That would be tantamount to deeding the property to his peasants. In the context of Locke's theory, that would be irrational behavior, since the primary purpose of the commonwealth is the protection of the landowners' property. In addition, an association of nonlandowners is a contradiction in terms within Locke's theory. Those people must already be on someone else's property and thus, by tacit consent, subject to the rules of whatever commonwealth the landowner belongs to. The only option they have, within the context of the theory, is to go to a new place, "*in vacuis locis*, in any part of the World they can find free and unpossessed."[18] There, they can set up their own commonwealth because they can take possession of the land.

Rousseau's Description of Human Nature, Contemporary Societies, and the Ideal Society

Locke's theory attributed a consensus only to a small portion of the population (the full citizens) and argued that agreement among them could be achieved only on the issue of joining the commonwealth; on all other issues the majority would have to rule. Rousseau's theory addressed a much broader issue: how to attain consensus on all issues, not merely on the desirability of joining the commonwealth, and among all people, not merely among the propertied class. In *The Social Contract,* he proposed that the sovereignty of the state represented the "general will" of the people and that a government was legitimate only if it acted in accord with this general will. That conception was incorporated into the sociology of Auguste Comte and Emile Durkheim, and became the forerunner of modern sociological conceptions of consensus.[19]

But Rousseau did not see this type of society as easily achieved. He argued that for a "general will" to exist, there must be a true "community of interest" among the people of the society.[20] Such a community of interest can exist only in very small societies, where the members have roughly the same social and economic statuses within a simple economic organization with a minimum of specialization. The "general will" is then expressed in assemblies of the entire people, such as New England town meetings. Rousseau went to great lengths discussing how to avoid particular interests' being expressed at these meetings—for example, he argued that citizens should not be allowed to discuss matters with each other before the assembly lest they form factions and groups.[21] Like Plato's Republic, Rousseau's extremely complex mechanism for achieving the "general will" implied that in real societies such a will did not exist and that those societies were characterized, rather, by factions and groups expressing particular interests.

Underlying this view of society was a complex view of human nature. Rousseau argued that in the state of nature man is reduced to sensations and his desires to purely physical ones. That was the source of what Rousseau believed was man's natural consensuality. Durkheim summarized Rousseau's argument as follows:

> What characterizes man in this [natural] state—whether real or ideal is of no importance—is a perfect balance between his needs and the resources at his disposal. Why? Because natural man is reduced exclusively to sensations.... Our natural man can desire only the things to be found in his immediate physical environment, for he cannot imagine any other. Hence his desires will be purely physical and extremely simple.... But such needs are easily satisfied. Nature has provided for them. It is very unusual for the things he needs to be lacking. Harmony is achieved spontaneously. Man has all he desires because he desires only what he has.[22]

Rousseau rejected Hobbes' view that man in a state of nature was involved in a war of all against all. Rather, he argued that human desires (except those that are purely physical) arise as society arises and are generated in the process of association with other men. Man in the state of nature is seen as naturally isolated from other men, but enviromental conditions can disrupt the balance between his needs and resources and create the necessity for cooperation with other men. This, in turn, leads to the division of labor, to the accumulation of property, and to the unequal distribution of resources. At this point, the war of all against all develops, and "the rich man, who was the most severely affected because he had the most to lose,... proposed to his fellows that they institute rules of peace and justice to which everyone would have to conform, that all individual forces be united into one supreme power which would protect and defend all the members of the association."[23]

Although Rousseau rejected Hobbes' view of man in the state of nature, the similarity of their views on the origin of civil society is obvious. The difference is that Rousseau proposed a consensual, harmonious state that was the truly natural state of man and had existed prior to the war of all against all. This difference in assumptions about the natural state of man led to differences in their attitudes about how the war of all against all could be resolved. Because Hobbes saw this conflict as inherent in man's nature, he contended that it was necessary to repress it through the use of overt force. Rousseau, on the other hand, believed that man was naturally harmonious and that conflict was socially generated. Thus, conflict could also be resolved socially and man's natural harmony reestablished.

The Relation Between Form and Content

Locke's theory returned to the mainstream of the consensus tradition established by Aristotle and continued by Aquinas. The consensus he described occurred among the propertied class and did not include the propertyless, except that because of their presence on private property they tacitly consented to the decisions of the propertied class. Those in the propertied class were portrayed as capable of being rational and virtuous, making decisions that would represent their own common interest. Locke, however, maintained that the decisions were not in the common interest of all the people, but merely of those who were full members of the commonwealth—i.e., those who owned property. Locke also perceived a limited irrationality and selfishness among those in the propertied class, a problem he resolved through his doctrine of the separation of powers. Locke recognized as well that his doctrine of "majority rule" did not adequately protect the rights of minorities:

> ... though they have a right to defend themselves, and to recover by force, what by unlawful force is taken from them; yet the Right to do so, will not easily ingage them in a Contest, wherein they are sure to perish; it being as impossible for one or a few oppressed Men to *disturb the Government*, where the Body of the People do not think themselves concerned in it, as for a raving mad Man, or a heady Malecontent to overturn a well-settled State; the People being as little apt to follow the one, as the other.[24]

Of course, the "minority" described in the above quotation referred to those who were full members of the Commonwealth—i.e., property owners—as opposed to those who merely gave their tacit consent. Locke did not deal with what government oppression of the latter might entail.

One difference between the theories of Aristotle and Aquinas and the theory of Locke is the ways these different theories described conflict in consensual societies. Aristotle and Aquinas had attributed such conflict to irrational and selfish individuals who did not share fully in man's consensual nature. Locke, in contrast, did not attribute conflict to such a "defective" subgroup in the society. He argued instead that no groups had the right to oppose the will of the majority of full citizens. Those full citizens who were in the minority had expressly and irrevocably agreed to abide by the will of the majority at the time they joined the commonwealth. Those who were noncitizen residents of the commonwealth had no rights to agree or disagree. Thus, all conflict could be characterized as "illegitimate" within the context of Locke's theory. Locke's formulation is different from the formulation found in the theories of Aristotle and Aquinas, but it has the same effect: societies are described in a totally positive way, and no aspect of society is described as flawed or responsible in any way for conflict. Rather, conflict is attributed to "deviant" subgroups who are described as being in some sense external to the society itself.

Rousseau is sometimes considered a consensus theorist because of his ideas in *The Social Contract*, but in fact the structure of his argument is identical to that in Plato's *Republic*. Like Plato, Rousseau argued that humans in the state of nature were consensual—he described a "noble savage" in a virtual Garden of Eden[25]—and that societies evolved from the natural need for cooperative association with other people.[26] But Rousseau also argued, as did Plato, that all contemporary societies were conflictual. Perhaps the most famous statement of these two contrasting ideas is at the beginning of *The Social Contract:* "Man is born free, but everywhere he is in chains."[27] Like Plato, Rousseau associated the loss of freedom and the generation of conflict in contemporary societies with the development of private property and the unequal distribution of resources: "Usurpations by the rich, robbery by the poor, and the unbridled passions of both suppressed the cries of natural compassion and the still feeble voice of justice, and filled men with avarice, ambition, and vice."[28] There is also a critical distrust of human rationality in Rousseau's theory. He described contemporary societies as the result of a deception by the rich, who had convinced the poor that governments were in their interests.[29] Thus, the rational arguments of the rich were described as self-interested fabrications, while the poor were described as not rational enough to be able to see through those fabrications. There is also a very high standard of values in Rousseau's theory, just as there is in Plato's. Rousseau's "social contract," he said, was based on justice, duty, and right, while contemporary societies were based on appetite, impulse, and instinct.[30] Such an ideal society required, as did Plato's, a total reorganization of the socioeconomic structure, with the elimination of property differentials.[31] Rousseau ultimately had to hypothesize a "legislator," comparable to Plato's "guardians," who was able to rise above his passions to true rationality in order to discern the true values. The legislator had a "superior intelligence which can survey all the passions of mankind, though itself exposed to none; an intelligence having no contact with our nature, yet knowing it to the full; an intelligence, the well-being of which is independent of our own, yet willing to be concerned with it."[32] The absoluteness of the values which Rousseau believed would underpin his society was finally made clear when he stated that "only Gods can give laws to men."[33]

Consensus and Conflict in Contemporary Societies

Both theories, then, took forms that are consistent with the content of their assumptions about human nature and contemporary societies. The principal difference between them with respect to the concepts of consensus and conflict lies in their opposite descriptions of contemporary societies, since both described human nature and the ideal society as consensual. As with the comparisons between other theorists, the question raised here is whether the difference between those descriptions entailed any contrasting empirical assertions that could be tested.

There appear to be no such empirical differences. Rather, these are alternative ways of describing the same empirical phenomena, based on opposite evaluations of the actions of ruling groups. Locke did not claim that there was a consensus among all the people of the society. He claimed only that there was a consensus among a majority of the full citizens, making no assertion about the proportion of the population that were full citizens. He described societies as consensual because within the context of his theory the majority of full citizens had the "right" to make all rules in the commonwealth, and no group had the "right" to oppose them. Thus, a society could be described as consensual despite the existence of conflict and the need to suppress that conflict by force or other means. Where Locke's theory could be said to attribute an inherent "legitimacy" to the actions of ruling groups, Rousseau attributed the same "illegitimacy" to the actions of ruling groups that he did to the actions of other groups. All groups were said to be irrational and selfish due to the conflict-generating properties of the society. Consensus was defined as being full agreements among all the groups in the society, not merely among a majority of the full citizens. Thus, Rousseau described conflict between the ruling group and the other groups in the society, where Locke had described consensus in the ruling group and the need to use force and other means to insure the compliance of the other groups.

Both theorists based their descriptions of contemporary societies on a myth about the origin of societies. In both myths, the division of property occurs prior to the foundation of the society and societies were founded so that those with substantial amounts of property would be able to protect it. The two myths differ primarily in the moral evaluations attached to the descriptions, rather than in the descriptions themselves. Locke attached positive moral evaluations to his myth of the origin of society, defending the "natural law" of unlimited accumulation of property. Rousseau described the same accumulation as "usurpations by the rich." Both agreed that contemporary societies did not represent the interests of the poor—Locke argued that there was no obligation (and, in fact, no mechanism) for governments to represent the interests of the poor because the latter were not full members of the Commonwealth, and Rousseau argued that the poor were deceived by the rich if they believed that governments represented their interests.

Locke's theory of tacit consent is sometimes portrayed as attributing some minimal level of consensus to all members of the population, which would then constitute an empirically testable difference from any theory, such as Rousseau's, that described only conflict in contemporary societies. But "tacit consent" was evidenced solely by physical presence on the territory of the commonwealth—no other behavioral or psychological manifestations were asserted. A group of people could be in full-scale rebellion against the government, and yet according to Locke's theory they would be "tacitly consenting" to it as long as they were within its territory. Thus, Locke's doctrine of tacit consent does not empirically contradict Rousseau's description of societies as conflictual.

The primary difference between these two theories with respect to the concepts of consensus and conflict concerns their evaluation of the legitimacy of the actions of ruling groups in contemporary societies. Locke evaluated those actions as rational and consistent with natural law. Thus, he described the societies as consensual and argued that any conflict in them was "illegitimate," and so could be suppressed by force and other means. Rousseau evaluated those actions as irrational and selfish, no different from the actions of other groups in the society. Thus, he described conflicts among the various groups in the society. That is not an empirical difference, because the two theories did not argue that the ruling groups actually behaved differently. Rather, they incorporated opposite moral evaluations of the behavior of the ruling groups. The debate between Locke and Rousseau with respect to their descriptions of contemporary societies, then, is not an empirical debate and cannot be resolved through empirical investigations.

Notes

1. John Locke, "The Second Treatise of Government," in Peter Laslett, ed., *Two Treatises of Government* (Cambridge: Cambridge University Press, 1960), ch. 2, secs. 4–15, pp. 287–96. An alternative interpretation is that Locke engaged in "secret writing," and that his position was actually identical to Hobbes'. See Richard H. Cox, *Locke on War and Peace* (Oxford: Clarendon Press, 1960). For a defense of the present interpretation, see Richard Ashcraft, "Locke's State of Nature: Historical Fact or Moral Fiction?" *American Political Science Review* (September 1968), 62(3):898–915.

2. Locke, "Second Treatise," ch. 5, sec. 50, pp. 319-20.

3. Ibid., p. 320.

4. Ibid., ch. 8, sec. 95, pp. 348-49.

5. Ibid., ch. 7, sec. 91, p. 344.

6. Ibid., ch. 8, sec. 120, p. 366.

7. Ibid., ch. 8, secs. 120, 121, pp. 366-67.

8. Ibid., ch. 8, sec. 119, p. 366.

9. Ibid., ch. 8, sec. 122, p. 367.

10. Ibid., ch. 8, sec. 116, p. 364.

11. Ibid., ch.8, secs. 96, 97, 98, pp. 349-51.

12. Ibid., ch. 13, sec. 149, pp. 384-85.

13. Ibid., ch. 8, sec. 96, p. 350.

14. Ibid., ch. 10, secs. 132-33, pp. 372-73.

15. Ibid., chs. 11–14, secs. 134-68, pp. 373-98.

16. *Encyclopedia Brittanica* (Chicago: William Benton, 1973), p. 384.

17. C.B. Macpherson, *The Political Theory of Possessive Individualism* (New York: Oxford University Press, 1962), pp. 221–38.

18. Locke, "Second Treatise," ch. 8, sec. 121, p. 367.

19. Jonathan H. Turner, *The Structure of Sociological Theory*, rev. ed. (Homewood, Ill: Dorsey Press, 1978), p. 20; Emile Durkheim, *Montesquieu and Rousseau* (Ann Arbor: University of Michigan Press, 1960), pp. 69–70.

20. Jean Jacques Rousseau, *The Social Contract*, in Ernest Barker, ed., *The Social Contract: Essays by Locke, Hume, and Rousseau* (London: Oxford University Press, 1947), p. 269.

21. Ibid., p. 275.

22. Durkheim, *Montesquieu and Rousseau*, pp. 69–70.

23. Ibid., p. 79.

24. Locke, "Second Treatise," ch. 18, sec. 208, p. 422.

25. Jean Jacques Rousseau, "A Discourse on the Origin of Inequality," *The Social Contract and Discourses* G.D.H. Cole, ed., (New York: E.P. Dutton), 1946.

26. Ibid., pp. 193–94.

27. Rousseau, *The Social Contract*, p. 240.

28. Rousseau, "A Discourse," p. 203.

29. Ibid., p. 205.

30. *The Social Contract*, p. 262.

31. Ibid., p. 268.

32. Ibid., p. 290.

33. Ibid., p. 291.

– CHAPTER 6 –

Comte and Marx

AUGUSTE COMTE and Karl Marx are generally regarded as the first consensus and conflict theorists, respectively, in sociology. The present chapter reviews their theories in the context of the historical traditions from which they sprang. It focuses on those elements in the theories that have led to their being classified in the consensus-conflict dichotomy, and compares the theories as part of the effort to specify the nature of the opposition between consensus theories and conflict theories generally.

These two theorists are clearly classified in the consensus-conflict dichotomy, so there is no need to rely on an explicit criterion for differentiating consensus from conflict theorists. However, the criterion used in the preceding chapters is shown in this and the two following chapters to be appripriate for making the distinction between consensus theorists and conflict theorists in sociology. That criterion is as follows: consensus theorists are theorists who use consensus terminology to describe at least some (but not necessarily all) societies that actually exist at the time they write; conflict theorists are those who use conflict terminology to describe all societies that actually exist at the time they write.

It should be noted, however, that with the founding of sociology, the context of the descriptions of existing societies changed fundamentally. Earlier theories were part of "social philosophy," so that descriptions of societies that actually existed were couched primarily in philosophical terms. But sociology originated as the historical analysis of the development of societies. It was founded in the turmoil generated by the French and Industrial Revolutions and was concerned with the reestablishment of social order in the chaos that was nineteenth-century Europe. Sociologists attempted to provide a rational, scientific analysis of the monumental social changes that were occurring in order to "mastermind the political course of social regeneration."[1] In early sociological analysis, that meant that the description of the present state of society was only a small part of an overall theory of social development—i.e., where society had come from and where it was going. These descriptions of historical development were based on the Enlightenment idea that progress was an inevitable process in human history. The significance of the description of the present state of society was limited to the illustration of a particular society at a particular point in that process.

Both Comte and Marx phrased their theories in terms of the historical development of societies,[2] so that societies that actually existed at the time they wrote could be at different stages of development within the context of their theories. Thus, Marx, for example, did not necessarily describe in conflictual terms all of the societies that existed at the time he wrote, since it was possible that there were some societies in remote corners of the world that were still in states of primitive communism. However, he described all advanced capitalist societies in conflictual terms. That, for practical purposes, meets the criterion specified above for conflict theorists. Similarly, Comte described a great deal of conflict in his own and other contemporary societies, but he argued that the *normal* state of society was consensual. That argument can be interpreted to mean that most societies at most times are consensual, which meets the above criterion for consensus theorists.

Comte's Descriptions of Contemporary Societies and the Ideal Society

Comte is generally considered a consensus theorist because of his analogy between the biological organism and what he called the "Social Organism":

> We have thus established a true correspondence between the Statical Analysis of the Social Organism in Sociology, and that of the Individual organism in Biology.... I shall treat the Social Organism as definitely composed of the Families which are the true elements or cells, next the Classes or Castes which are its

proper tissues, and lastly of the Cities and Communes which are its real organs.[3]

Extending this biological analogy, he divided sociology into the study of social structures, which he called Social Statics and defined as "the study of Order," and the study of the laws of the development of societies, which he called Social Dynamics and defined as "the study of Progress."[4] Comte recognized the existence of disorder and conflict but saw them as temporary aberrations from the true state of society. In fact, he saw the disorder of his own society, following the chaos of the French and Industrial Revolutions, as one such aberration:

> The great political and moral crisis that societies are now undergoing is shown by a rigid analysis to arise out of intellectual anarchy. While stability in fundamental maxims is the first condition of genuine social order, we are suffering under an utter disagreement which may be called universal.[5]

Comte argued that social order was not possible unless there was a communality of ideas in the minds of all the members of the society, and it was the absence of such a communality that was the source of the disorder in his own society. His model for this communality of ideas was that found in Medieval Europe, under the intellectual domination of the Catholic Church. He saw a great flowering of art, science, and industry during that period and attributed it to the remarkable consensus of ideas which provided the base for a religious and political stability. Comte's ideal society was to be similarly based on his doctrine of "positivism," which in some ways resembled Catholicism stripped of its theological and metaphysical beliefs. For example, Comte argued against "liberty of conscience," saying that the "most important conceptions" cannot be abandoned to "the least competent minds" without the dissolution of the entire society.[6] He believed that the doctrine of liberty of conscience was useful in breaking up the old regime, but must be abandoned in the positivist reorganization of society. He argued similarly about the idea of equality among people.[7] The imposition of the Positive philosophy on society would contribute to order by resolving conflicts about difficult questions, abating unreasonable expectations from political institutions, teaching that political change is unimportant while the perturbation attending change is supremely mischievous, and developing a "wise resignation to incurable political evils."[8]

Comte's Description of Human Nature

Comte believed that the organization of society was based on the natural tendency for people to organize themselves into cooperative, hierarchical groups, beginning with the family as the basic unit. That was a truly remarkable phenomenon in Comte's eyes:

> We cannot, of course, fully appreciate a phenomenon which is for ever proceeding before our eyes, and in which we bear a part; but if we withdraw ourselves in thought from the social system, and contemplate it as from afar, can we conceive of a more marvellous spectacle, in the whole range of natural phenomena, than the regular and constant convergence of an innumerable multitude of human beings, each possessing a distinct and, in a certain degree, independent existence, and yet incessantly disposed, amidst all their discordance of talent and character, to concur in many ways in the same general development, without concert, and even consciousness on the part of most of them, who believe that they are merely following their personal impulses? This is the scientific picture of the phenomenon: and no temporary disturbances can prevent its being, under all circumstances, essentially true.[9]

This natural order springs out of inherent human inequalities and the inherent predispositions of some to govern and others to obey.[10] In the modern world, those tendencies result in the natural organization of industry, and government springs from the natural organization of the chiefs of industry. The inculcation of a spirit of obedience and discipline thus takes place in the industrial setting and is extended to the general society, just as in the ancient world that discipline and obedience was inculcated through war. Comte saw two serious problems in this situation, however. The first was that "the desire to command is almost always stronger than the willingness to obey."

> [The desire to command] can only meet satisfaction in certain families, and thus the rest are urged to a state of chronic revolt against all and any control. The whole history of the past is an illustration of this, notwithstanding the spirit of submission in-

culcated by the long ages of theological and military discipline. The tendency towards insurrection would be fatal to humanity, and distract all progress, unless a vigorous use of material force were always at hand to restrain it. Our own stormy times show us the need of this check....[11]

Thus, Comte argued that Hobbes, with his doctrine that government is the natural result of force, was the only philosopher since Aristotle to contribute to the Positive theory of power. He argued that "force is essential as the basis of every human society" and that "social science would remain for ever in the cloud-land of metaphysics, if we hesitate to adopt the principle of Force as the basis of Government."[12]

The second problem Comte recognized was that those in power sometimes did not rule correctly. He stated that "the spirit of command... becomes a true benefaction to society, where families have been disciplined, educated, and so placed as to have the means and the responsibilities of exercising power rightly."[13] But it was also necessary to "control the dangerous tendencies" of political power, since the abuse of force might not only check the progress of society but threaten it with actual destruction.[14] The regulation of political power could be accomplished through intellectual guidance and moral sanctions, but the true social control of political power was to be found in religion. Comte provided an extended discussion of the role of the priests in his Religion of Humanity. These priests must be free from temporal power and wealth, in order to "foster and preserve the generality of Thought and the generosity of Feeling which are required for its social work."[15] Their principal work is "to check and direct the Government, though without ever overstepping the limits of advice."[16]

Comte's Theory Compared with Earlier Consensus Theories

Comte cited Aristotle as his "incomparable predecessor," and a number of similarities can be found between the two systems of thought. Both are based on logical rationality as the ultimate method of discerning truth. In each case, the view of rationality is founded on a view of the inherent inequalities among men, this being necessary to explain why the views of one particular set of people were correct, while the views of all others were wrong. Comte in general argued for the superior rationality of the white race over other races, of men over women, and of the upper class over the working class.[17] While Aristotle simply excluded the common people as incapable of consensus, Comte advocated an aggressive program to mold their thinking patterns into the true beliefs. Without such molding, he saw nothing but chaos and the dissolution of society. Comte believed that the less rational groups in society would never fully understand positivism but could be taught to accept it in much the same way peasants had been taught to accept Catholicism in the Middle Ages. That position was similar to the position taken by Hobbes, who also had argued that common people should be taught to believe the doctrines of his theory.

Hobbes, of course, was the other major influence on Comte's thinking, although Comte only partially accepted Hobbes' description of human nature as conflictual. Comte divided human emotions into the "egoistic" tendencies and the "altruistic" ones.[18] The purely egoistic emotions, in Comte's theory, were the nutritive, the sexual, and the maternal instincts. Emotions that were primarily egoistic, but had elements of altruism in them included the instincts to overcome obstacles, to produce goods, to dominate or command, and to seek the approval of others. Emotions that were purely altruistic were friendship, veneration, and kindness. With the exception of the instinct to dominate or command, none of the egoistic instincts are necessarily associated with social conflict, although they may be incidentally related to it. All these emotions, in fact, are generally better fulfilled within the context of a peaceful community than within a war of all against all. Thus, with the exception of the instinct to dominate, Comte's description of human nature was essentially consensual. But it was the instinct to dominate that led Comte to believe, with Hobbes, that force was the necessary basis for all governments.

Despite this disagreement, Comte's theory was similar in a number of respects to Hobbes' theory. Hobbes had argued that men were not rational enough to figure out a rational way to govern themselves, but that at least some of them were rational enough to recognize one if it were explained to them. Comte took the same position, but added the idea of progress: he argued that individuals were inevitably developing toward positivism as a way of thinking, so that societies were inevitably developing toward the consensus that was both normal and necessary for their unity. But Comte also argued that rational and intelligent men would more quickly recognize the rationality of positivism if it were explained to them. Thus, the function of Comte's books, in his own view, was to advance the course of what was otherwise an inevitable development in human history.[19] Comte's ideal society also required only a minimal political and no socioeconomic reorganization, which was identical to the position taken by Hobbes and other consensus theorists. Comte believed that the "natural" organization of man was that of industrial capitalism, and nowhere in his description of "order" and "progress" was there any indication that such an organization could be expected to change. On the contrary, Comte held, like Aristotle and Aquinas, that the inequalities of the socioeconomic order reflected the natural inequalities of man.

Comte was also supportive of the existing political authorities, stating, for example, "These governing persons usually even deserve the respect they receive; and they ultimately often justify the general readiness to accept them as models."[20] That support was related to Comte's position on the distribution of rationality in society. He held that the highest degree of rationality was to be found in the dominant power group—upperclass white males—and that decreasing degrees of rationality were found in other groups, a position that was consistent with the general consensus tradition although inconsistent with the position of Hobbes. Finally, like Hobbes, Comte described a great deal of conflict in his own and other contemporary societies, although he used consensus terminology to describe those societies. By arguing that the "normal" state of society throughout history was "consensual," Comte took a stronger stance than had earlier consensus theorists, most of whom had described only the "best" societies as consensual. Comte's argument was that most societies at most times were consensual, something that earlier consensus theorists had not claimed.

One difference between Comte's theory and the theories of earlier consensus theorists was his focus on the possibility that rulers might abuse their power. Aristotle had argued that those who ruled in their own interests were "wrong," but he did not explore how such rule could be avoided. Hobbes had rather generally argued that the sovereign would be virtuous once he achieved absolute power, but this was clearly a weakness in his theory. In contrast, Comte's description of the priests in the Positive society is reminiscent in many ways of the guardians in Plato's Republic, except that they were to be advisors with no political power. That was evidently because Comte saw something that Plato had missed—that power itself could corrupt, even if it was not used to acquire property. Comte also advocated that a workingman be installed as a dictator in the transition period, since workingmen in general have broader views and a better sense of duty, and "as yet, the wealthy classes have shown themselves too debased in thought and feeling for an office of such importance."[21] The wealthy would be required to administer the government, however, since they are the only ones with sufficient skills to do so. Comte expressed the hope that "unworthy as they seem of it at the present they will gradually become less so as spiritual reorganization proceeds...."[22] Comte had also argued elsewhere that, as men accumulated capital, they would be freed from their egoistic desires and would become altruistic, so that these captains of industry would become so rich that they would feel no greed.[23] But ultimately this problem would be resolved through the sense of resignation inculcated in the working class by the positivist religion—"a sense of dignified submission to the necessary inequalities of society, inequalities which in so complex an organism may involve severe abuse."[24]

Marx's Theory: Human Nature, Contemporary Societies, and the Ideal Society

One who was most concerned with such inequalities and abuses of power was, of course, Karl Marx. Marx's theory was essentially an economic interpretation of history, rather than a theory of individual or group behavior.[25] The principal conflict that Marx presented in his theory, and on which the theory is based, was the conflict between the material forces of production and social relations of production.[26] The material forces of production can generally be considered to be society's capacity to produce, which includes both technological equipment and the knowledge, skill, and organization to use that equipment. The social relations of production refer primarily to property relations, and consequently to the distribution of the income generated by the material forces of production. The development of the material forces of production is relatively continuous throughout history, whereas the social relations of production tend to freeze into particular patterns. Social relations tend to change only abruptly and violently in revolutions when they have become so inconsistent with the material forces that they substantially impede the further development of production. Thus, for example, the social relations of feudalism gave way to bourgeois capitalism with the advent of industrialized society. The social relations of capitalism initially acted as a stimulant to industrial production, but, Marx argued, were becoming an impediment to the further development of the material forces of production due to certain inherent contradictions in the capitalist system. In particular, Marx argued that the system would inevitably concentrate the ownership of the means of production into fewer and fewer hands. Because of increasing mechanization, there would also be a growing pool of unemployed and underemployed workers, and those workers who were employed would be paid subsistence wages because of the labor surplus and the competition for jobs. Thus, the capitalist system would inevitably tend toward a polarization of society into two classes, one of which was both shrinking and becoming grotesquely wealthy and the other of which was large and growing and was barely able to survive. Here the contradiction between the forces of production and the relations of production is quite clear, as is the necessity for a revolutionary restructuring of the relations of production. That restructuring would consist, according to Marx, of establishing collective ownership of the means of production and instituting centralized planning to end the cycles of overproduction and depression that plagued capitalism. It would also mean the end of classes and class conflict, and the establishment of a nonanta-gonistic society.

Marx did not describe in detail the nature of the nonantago-nistic society that would emerge with the advent of communism. But he did provide some general information about it in the *Critique of the Gotha Programme*.[27] Initially, the proletariat would have to defend itself against its enemies by assuming dictatorial control of the state mechanisms. But as full communism devel-oped, the proletariat would form the "immense majority" of the population, and their enemies would become fewer and fewer. The state itself would then begin to wither away, and men would cease to govern men but would only administer things. There would be no exploited class who would want to revolt and no state to revolt against. Communism, as envisaged by Marx, would be characterized by a full, free, and spontaneous consen-sus among the vast majority of the population on the fundamen-tal structures of society.

Marx had described all contemporary societies in terms of conflict, with the possible exception of any primitive communist societies still in existence in remote corners of the world. But conflict for Marx was an analytical category central to his theory of history and his theory of social change—it was not necessarily descriptive of specific events. Marx's theory was based on the argument that, in general and in the long run, individuals act and think in ways that are consistent with their economic inter-ests. He argued that although there were many conflicts in soci-ety, the most fundamental conflict was the conflict of economic interests generated by private ownership of the means of pro-duction. The owners of the means of production could be de-scribed as a class (the "ruling class") because their similar posi-tion in the social structure would result in similarities in their beliefs and actions. Marx's term "ruling class" did not imply that the owners of the means of production had organized them-selves into a cohesive group. Marx made a similar argument about the nature of the "working class." The conflict between the two classes was thus a long-range, structurally determined con-flict that would inevitably result in fundamental social change.

As Marx described it, the communist society was at least as consensual as any consensual society described in a consensus theory. But he did not argue that communism would be characterized by a total absence of conflict. The normal conflicts between individuals and groups would continue in that society as in any other. However, the communist society would be free from the basic structural conflicts that generate fundamental social change. Thus, the normal conflicts between individuals and groups would occur within the context of a stable social structure.

Despite the fact that Marx did not describe the communist society as totally conflict free, he expected that the level of conflict within it would decrease dramatically. That was because conflicts were attributed to social structural arrangements, not to human nature. Marx wrote: "Every alienation of man from himself and from nature appears in the relations which he postulates between other men and himself."[28] It was because he did not attribute conflict to human nature that Marx was able to hypothesize an ideal society in which people were not alienated either from themselves or from nature. Thus, Marx's theory implied a consensual view of human nature. As Atkinson stated, "For Marx, the question became: How is conflict possible when man is rational and cooperative?"[29]

The Relation Between Form and Content

The above description of Marx's theory is extremely brief, but it is sufficient to support the argument that the theory falls into the radical conflict tradition established by Plato and continued by Rousseau. Like them, he described all contemporary societies as conflictual. But he described human nature itself in consensual terms, and attributed conflict to social structural arrangements. The thrust of his theory therefore concerned how contemporary societies could be transformed into ideal consensual societies by changing their social structural arrangements. Marx also displayed the same critical distrust of human rationality found in the theories of Plato and Rousseau. Where Plato had described commonly held beliefs as the "flood of public opinion," Marx described them as "false consciousness." The difference between the two was that Marx argued that when social and economic conditions were right, all people would be able to discern the true state of affairs, while Plato argued that even in the ideal society most people would have to be taught a "noble lie," as only philosophers would be able to discern the true state of affairs. That critical distrust of rationality was associated with a very high or "absolute" standard of truth. Where Plato had discussed the "Forms," Marx talked about the "objective" conditions in societies.

The classification of Comte is somewhat more complex because he derived his theories both from Aristotle (who described human nature as consensual) and from Hobbes (who described human nature as conflictual). The form that Comte's theory took reflected the influence of this dualistic portrayal of human nature. To the extent that Comte assumed that humans were naturally consensual, his theory took the form of a conservative consensus theory. The "normal" state of society was described as one in which there were full and free agreements among its members in the cooperative hierarchies that Comte found so remarkable. These societies were characterized by broad commonalities of ideas, and their governments sprang naturally from the hierarchical organizations at the subsocietal level. Conflict simply does not enter into this description, so that when it appeared in the society it would have to be attributed to some "deviant" subgroup that did not share fully in the consensual human nature. The ideal society that Comte described was quite similar to the above description of contemporary societies, both of which were characterized by the absence of conflict rather than by its control. But Comte also argued that human nature had a flaw in that the desire to command was greater than the willingness to obey. That led to a natural tendency for people to enter into conflict with each other. To the extent that Comte described humans as naturally conflictual, he argued that societies were characterized not by the absence of conflict but by its control. Thus, he said, force was at the base of all governments. He therefore described the ideal society as one in which man's conflictual nature was fully controlled, and which was therefore quite different from contemporary societies, in which the control mechanism were deficient. His theory therefore focused on methods by which contemporary societies could be transformed into the hypothetical ideal.

Consensus and Conflict in Contemporary Societies: Evaluations and Predictions

Both theories take general forms that are consistent with the content of their assumptions about human nature and contemporary societies. Our attention now turns to the similarities and differences between the two theories with respect to their descriptions of consensus and conflict. Both Comte and Marx described human nature and the ideal society in consensual terms, and despite the differences between them on those two descriptions it would appear that the major difference lay in their opposite descriptions of contemporary societies. Certainly, those opposite descriptions contained the same contradictory moral evaluations of the actions of ruling groups that were found in the theories of the philosophers. Comte described the ruling groups as the most rational groups, who were the only ones capable of running the government or industry. Marx described those same groups as being caught in a historical contradiction so that their actions would ultimately lead to the destruction of the capitalist system. Comte described ruling groups as generally deserving the respect they received and becoming altruistic as they became wealthier, while Marx described them as compulsively accumulating wealth to the point that everyone else was impoverished. Thus, Comte described the actions of the groups that ruled his own and other contemporary societies in terms that conveyed moral legitimacy, while Marx described them in terms that conveyed moral illegitimacy. The question is whether these opposite evaluations are themselves the heart of the difference between the two theories or whether there are other, more fundamental differences.

One basic difference between the two theories lies in their differing predictions about the future. Comte argued that contemporary societies were inevitably developing toward "Positive" societies, in which the social structural arrangements and ruling groups would remain fundamentally the same. Marx argued that contemporary societies were inevitably developing toward "communism," in which the social structural arrangements and ruling groups would be fundamentally changed. These predictions constitute empirical assertions that, in the long run, can be tested in order to verify or falsify each theory. Thus, in contrast to the earlier social theories of the philosophers, there do appear to be some empirical differences between consensus and conflict theories as represented by the theories of Comte and Marx.

But predictions about the future must be based on assessments made about the past and present. One can therefore ask what it was in contemporary societies that led Comte and Marx to hypothesize such totally different ideal societies. Both Comte and Marx based their predictions on the idea of progress—i.e., that societies were inevitably moving toward the "better." Their very different predictions about the future were based on very different ideas about what constituted a better society. Those ideas, in turn, were based on the evaluations each made about contemporary societies and the actions of groups who ruled contemporary societies. Comte had described the actions of those groups in terms that conveyed moral legitimacy. He therefore argued that those same groups would rule in the ideal societies. Marx had described the actions of the same groups in terms that conveyed moral illegitimacy, and he therefore argued that they must be overthrown in order to establish the ideal society. Thus, the differing predictions about the future course of societies were ultimately based on differing assessments of the moral legitimacy of the actions of ruling groups in contemporary societies, combined with the idea that societies were inevitably progressing toward the "better."

Consensus and Conflict in Contemporary Societies: Empirical Descriptions

In the preceding chapters, it was argued that theorists who described contemporary (as opposed to ideal) societies in consensual terms did not make any substantive empirical assertions

that contradicted theorists who described contemporary societies in conflictual terms. The two descriptions were said to be
alternative methods of describing the same empirical phenomena, based on opposite moral evaluations of the actions of the
rulers of that society. That argument also holds for the theories
of Comte and Marx. If one ignores the moral evaluations of the
actions of ruling groups, as well as the predictions about the
future course of societies that are based on the combination of
those evaluations with the idea of progress, then there are a
number of similarities in the descriptions found in the two theories. For example, Comte wrote that "government springs from
agreement between the natural chiefs of the various types of
industry, who gather round their best representative."[30] Marx
wrote that "the modern state is but an association that adminis-
trates the common business of the whole bourgeois class."[31]
Except for the value judgment, these statements are virtually
identical. In addition, both Comte and Marx argued that governments ultimately rested on force. Comte saw this as inevitable
because of the predominance of the natural inclinations to command over those to obey, and argued that order could be maintained only if this rebelliousness on the part of subjects were
continuously repressed. Marx saw it as a function of the class
struggle between the oppressors and the oppressed at each stage
of history. Again, the difference between the two theorists is not
one of empirical descriptions of existing societies, but rather one
of value judgments about what is described and predictions
about the future course of society—Comte quite evidently believed that the use of force would and should succeed in retain-
ing the existing power structure, while Marx believed that it
ultimately and inevitably would fail, so that the "ins" would be
replaced in power by the "outs."

There is also a similarity in the works of Comte and Marx on
the role of ideas in the maintenance of social order. Comte argued
that disorder was due to the breakdown of the unity of ideas
among the people, and proposed his positivist philosophy to be
imposed by the dominant groups in the society on the lower
classes as a method of reestablishing order. Marx described the
same breakdown of order in terms of the rejection of the "false
consciousness" in the lower class and the establishment of "class

consciousness" based on the awareness of their true interests. Comte would probably have agreed with Marx's statement that "the thoughts of the ruling class are the ruling thoughts."[32] The difference between the two on this subject did not concern the function of ideas in the maintenance of social order, but rather the validity or truth content of the ideas themselves. Comte believed that the ruling ideas were valid, while Marx believed that they were false and intended only to maintain the advantages of the ruling class. That difference led to differences in value judgments about the use of those ideas and in predictions about whether such use would ultimately succeed or fail. Comte approved entirely of the use of ideas by the ruling class to support their own rule—in fact, this is absolutely central to his whole philosophy. He believed not only that such use was right and inevitable but that social order could not be maintained without it. Thus, he believed that the assertion of those ideas would ultimately triumph, despite the obvious problems with which it was faced. Marx, on the contrary, believed that the ideology would ultimately fail as it confronted the inevitable processes of the organization of the working classes in defense of their own interests.

There were also similarities in their descriptions of the behavior of the upper class. Both Comte and Marx saw them as acting in pursuit of their own individual interests. But Comte believed, along with the classical economists, that ultimately the pursuit of private interests by each individual is in the interests of all and thus contributes to the general consensus of the society. Marx believed that the pursuit of individual interests contributed to the functioning of the capitalist system in the short run but in the long run would lead to the destruction of that system as the contradictions of capitalism work themselves out.[33] In addition, both Comte and Marx agreed that under the capitalist system the upper class naturally accumulates vast amounts of wealth. Comte argued that such accumulation would ultimately lead to the satisfaction of egoistic drives in its members, so that they would then rule society according to altruistic motives.[34] Marx's contention, similar to Durkheim's later argument, was that the egoistic desires were never satisfied, so that accumulation would continue indefinitely, resulting inevitably in the polarization of society and the overthrow of capitalism. Again, Comte and Marx are in substantial agreement concerning the descriptions of the behavior of the upper class, although they make radically different evaluations of that behavior and different predictions about its final effect.

Both theorists also described their own societies as filled with conflicts. Comte is considered a consensus theorist because he argued that the *normal* state of society was consensual, but he also argued that his own society was in an abnormal state associated with the breakdown of theological and metaphysical thinking patterns and the incomplete establishment of positivist thinking patterns. This resulted in intellectual anarchy and the consequent social disorder. Comte argued that an example of the normal state of society was the general consensus in medieval times when all ideas were under the domination of the Catholic church. Marx interpreted such an absence of overt conflict as the convergence of the forces and the relations of production at a particular historical point, but he saw in that convergence the seeds of its own destruction as the two progressively diverged. During such periods the conflicts were latent but still present, so that the "normal" state of society (except during periods of primitive and advanced communism) was one of conflict.[35]

Although Comte and Marx agreed that their own societies were filled with conflict, their interpretations of that conflict differed profoundly. That difference in interpretation extended to the interpretation of specific events. Marx was a member of the generation that succeeded Comte's, so that the revolutionary upheavals of 1848 that occasioned the ending of Comte's career marked the true beginning of Marx's. Comte was appalled by the bloody events of the revolutions, and aligned himself with the powerful of the world, founding the Société Positiviste to preach the gospel of order and progress.[36] Marx, on the other hand, produced his most famous tract, *The Communist Manifesto*, in response to the same revolutions, in which he urged the workers of the world to unite and revolt. These opposite political positions were based on opposite evaluations of the actions of ruling groups together with opposite predictions about the future course of societies.

One final and rather remarkable convergence between the theories of Comte and Marx is that perhaps the best illustrations of the actual workings of Comte's theories can be found in present-day communist societies. These societies, of course, bear little resemblance to what Marx described as "communism." In official communist literature, they are said to be "socialist" societies in the process of creating the material and technical basis, and the social conditions and social consciousness, that are all preconditions for the transition to communist relations of production.[37] The structure of these societies is actually quite similar to the structure that Comte proposed for his "Positive" societies. They are elaborate structural hierarchies in which the leadership of the state is combined and unified with the leadership of business and industry and holds absolute power. A broad and general "social consensus" is generated by propounding an official ideology (communism instead of positivism), and that ideology is supported, in the last analysis, by the force of the state. Social unity is based on the unity of thinking patterns, and there is no liberty of conscience. All of this is precisely what Comte prescribed. In addition, Communist party members represent a small group in these societies and, officially at least, play the role that Comte assigned to his "priests." They are the ones who are ideologically pure, and they officially act only as advisors to the government, insuring its fidelity to Communist principles.[38] They do not hold any office as members of the party per se, although of course in the real world leadership of party and state are practically the same.

The substitution of communism for positivism as the official ideology in these societies actually may reinforce one of the weakest points in Comte's theory. The function of the ideology was to be not only to resolve conflicts about difficult questions but also to abate unreasonable expectations from political institutions. Comte's ideology did this by teaching that political change is unimportant, while the disruptions associated with change are harmful, and that the people must develop "a wise resignation to incurable evils." Such reasoning was bound to be quite unsatisfying to all those who had deeply felt grievances. But in communism, the people are taught that they must make long-term, heavy sacrifices in order to build the blissful communist society of the future. As a rationale for abating unrealistic expectations, that attitude can be seen to have a much greater chance of success. At least the people are given some reason to sacrifice that relates to their own future well-being and that of their children, whereas Comte's theory merely tells them, "That's the way it is."

Using the example of present-day communist societies to illustrate Comte's theory is important because consensus theories are often associated with freedom and democracy, while conflict theories are associated with ideological rigidity and dictatorship.[39] But in theory at least, Comte's Positive society was more of an ideological dictatorship than was Marx's communism, since it ultimately had to rely on force as the basis for its "consensus," while communism (theoretically) did not.

Why Are the Theories Considered Mutually Contradictory?

Given all the similarities in their empirical descriptions of existing societies, it needs to be asked why these two theories are considered to be in some sense mutually contradictory. That question is especially provocative given the fact that both theorists made the same general assumptions that man is naturally consensual, but there was no consensus in societies that actually existed at the time they were writing; that the course of human history consisted of the inevitable progress toward an ultimate state of consensus; and that theories describing that progress merely help move it along faster. One usually gets the impression from reading descriptions of their work in the secondary literature that Comte described existing societies as essentially consensual and that Marx described them as essentially conflictual. But in fact Comte stated that his own society was characterized by "an utter disagreement which may be called universal," as well as by widespread conflict and strife. The societies he described as consensual were past societies associated with the theological and metaphysical ways of thinking and the future, Positive society. But Marx also described periods of stability in the historical development of societies, when there was a convergence of the forces and relations of production. During such periods, there was also a consensus of ideas, since the thoughts of the ruling class were unchallenged as the ruling thoughts. In addition, Marx's description of the future communist society is even more "consensual" than Comte's description of the future Positive society.

Certainly these are two very different theories, and it might be simply stated that Comte's is considered a consensus theory because it is *about* consensus, while Marx's is considered a conflict theory because it is *about* conflict. But again, the question is why these two theories are often considered in some sense mutually contradictory. Comte's theory is about consensus, but it also describes the dissensus that inevitably arose in the process of the development of the human mind and the conflict that resulted from it. Marx's theory is about conflict, but it also describes the periods of stability when the forces and relations of production converged, and the consensuses of ideas that were associated with those periods. Both argued that conflict was the source of social change and consensus the source of social stability, although one was talking about consensus and conflict in human thinking and the other about consensus and conflict in economic relations. Perhaps it could be argued that the two theories simply have different intentions, the one emphasizing and explaining social stability and the other emphasizing and explaining social change. But such a statement would not explain why the two theories are often viewed as mutually contradictory instead of mutually complementary, or at least roughly parallel.

One point at which the two theories are directly contradictory, and also highly visible, has to do with the political implications that can be derived from them. Comte's theory supports the existing socioeconomic and political structures and justifies the use of force to maintain them, while Marx's theory opposes those same structures and justifies the use of force to overthrow them. The view that these two theories are mutually contradictory derives primarily from this specific contradiction. This contradiction is not based on empirical assertions about existing societies, since those assertions, as described above, are relatively similar. Rather, it is based on the descriptions of the hypo-

thetical ideal society, which in turn are based on the moral evaluations of the actions of ruling groups in societies that actually
existed when these theorists were writing, combined with the
idea that societies were inevitably progressing toward the "better." Comte evaluated the actions of ruling groups very positively,
and predicted that societies would inevitably progress toward an
ideal society organized around them. He also described the need
to use force and other means to suppress conflict against the
ruling groups and prevent it from impeding the progress toward
the ideal state. Marx evaluated the actions of the ruling groups
very negatively, and predicted that societies would inevitably
progress toward a point at which those groups could be overthrown and the ideal society established. He also described the
need to use force and other means against the ruling groups in
order to advance that progress. Thus, Marx viewed conflict in
societies favorably for precisely the same reason that Comte
viewed it unfavorably—because it was part of the process of
destroying the existing socioeconomic and political structures.
The difference between the two theories with respect to descriptions of contemporary societies is not that one alleges that there
is more consensus and the other that there is more conflict in
those societies, but rather that consensus and conflict are alleged
to play opposite roles in the progress toward the ideal state. The
one theory argues that the future ideal state will arise out of the
consensus that presently exists in society, the other that it will
arise out of the conflict. But there is no specific disagreement
between the two theories on the existence or extent of conflict in
their own societies—both agreed that their societies were characterized primarily by conflict and dissensus.

Despite the fact that Comte described contemporary societies in terms of consensus and Marx described them in terms of
conflict, they did not make contradictory empirical assertions
about those societies. Rather, they interpreted the same empirical phenomena in very different ways and made very different
predictions about the future course of societies. Those differing
interpretations and predictions were based on opposite moral
evaluations of the actions of ruling groups in those societies. The
heart of the difference between the two theories lies in these
opposite moral evaluations. To the extent that the two theories

did make contrasting empirical assertions and predictions, they can be tested to empirically verify or falsify the theories. But in practice, such testing has not convinced the adherents of either view that the other view is correct. That is because it is possible to adjust each theory to incorporate contradictory empirical findings without changing the basic assumptions.[40] Such a process is particularly apparent in the case of Marxism, since that is a living ideology, whereas Comte's positivism has few adherents in the modern world. Thus, the empirical assertions these two theories make are not the focus of the opposition between them. Rather, the focus of that opposition lies in their opposite moral evaluations of the actions of ruling groups in contemporary societies. Those evaluations, of course, are not empirical and cannot be resolved through empirical investigations.

Notes

1. Dominick LaCapra, *Emile Durkheim, Sociologist and Philosopher* (Ithaca: Cornell University Press, 1972), p. 41.

2. Others whose theories were similarly constructed included Durkheim, Von Gierke, Maine, Fustel de Coulanges, Tönnies, and Weber. See Robert A. Nisbet, *The Sociological Tradition* (New York: Basic Books, 1966), pp. 71–82.

3. August Comte, *System of Positive Polity* (New York: Burt Franklin, 1968), 2:239, 242.

4. Ibid., 2:1.

5. August Comte, *The Positive Philosophy*, Harriet Martineau, trans. (London: George Bell, 1896), 1:3. See also 2:139–42.

6. Comte, *The Positive Philosophy*, 2:153.

7. Ibid., p. 155.

8. Ibid., pp. 185–86.

9. Ibid., p. 289.

10. Comte, *System of Positive Polity*, 2:244.

11. Ibid., pp. 244, 247.

12. Ibid., pp. 246–47.

13. Ibid., p. 244.

14. Ibid., p. 249.

15. Ibid., p. 262. See also p. 271.

16. Ibid., p. 253.

17. See ibid., 1:104; 2:163, 378. In each case, Comte argued that the group which is inferior in rationality is superior in affection.

18. See Raymond Aron, *Main Currents in Sociological Thought* (New York: Basic Books, 1965), 1:88–89, for a summary of Comte's ideas.

19. See ibid., pp. 80–85 for a discussion of Comte's views of the subject.

20. Comte, *System of Positive Polity*, 2:245.

21. Ibid., p. 161.

22. Ibid., p. 160.

23. Ibid., vol. 1, ch. 2.

24. Ibid., 2:269.

25. Alexander Balinky, *Marx's Economics: Origin and Development* (Lexington, Mass.: Heath, 1970), p. 8.

26. Karl Marx, *A Contribution to the Critique of Political Economy* (New York: International Publishers, 1970), pp. 20–22.

27. Karl Marx, *Critique of the Gotha Programme* (New York: International Publishers, 1970). See also the discussion in D. Ross Gandy, *Marx and History: From Primitive Society to the Communist Future* (Austin: University of Texas Press, 1979), pp. 72–95.

28. T. B. Bottomore and Maximilien Rubel, eds., *Karl Marx: Selected Writings in Sociology and Social Philosophy* (London: C. A. Watts, 1961), p. 169.

29. Dick Atkinson, *Orthodox Consensus and Radical Alternative* (London: Heineman, 1971), p. 109.

30. Comte, *System of Positive Polity*, 2:246.

31. Quoted in Ralf Dahrendorf, *Class and Class Conflict in Industrial Society* (Stanford, Calif.: Stanford University Press, 1959), p. 13.

32. Ibid., p. 14.

33. Aron, *Main Currents*, pp. 70–71, 134–35.

34. Comte, *System of Positive Polity*, vol. 1, ch. 2.

35. Cf. Gandy, *Marx and History*, pp. 109–17; and Dahrendorf, *Class and Class Conflict*, pp. 179–81.

36. Lewis A. Coser, *Masters of Sociological Thought* (New York: Harcourt Brace Jovanovich, 1971), p. 20.

37. Y. Polyakov, ed., *A Short History of Soviet Society* (Moscow: Progress, 1971), pp. 431–32.

38. See V. M. Chkhikvadze, ed., *The Soviet Form of Popular Government* (Moscow: Progress, 1972), pp. 69–73. It states, for example, "Party leadership is based exclusively on persuasion, ideological influence and moral authority" (p. 71).

39. Seymour M. Lipset, *Political Man* (Garden City, N.Y.: Doubleday, 1960), pp. 26–28, 65–66.

40. Cf. the discussion of "normal science" in Thomas S. Kuhn, *The Structure of Scientific Revolutions* (Chicago: University of Chicago Press, 1970), pp. 23–42.

CHAPTER 7

Durkheim and Simmel

SIMMEL'S AND Durkheim's life-spans almost exactly matched each other, both having been born in 1858 and each dying within a year of the other at the height of the First World War. Like Comte and Marx, Durkheim reacted to the disorders and conflicts that were generated in the wake of the French and Industrial Revolutions, and his primary purpose was to explain the disintegration of order in French society and to propose methods of reestablishing it. Also like Comte and Marx, he phrased his theory in terms of the inevitable historical development of society from a primitive stage to an advanced one. In marked contrast, Simmel did not display any particular interest in social change or in the reorganization of society, and his theory was not framed in the context of the historical process of social development. His was the more strictly academic endeavor: to reflect upon, understand, and describe societies. This difference in orientation had far-reaching consequences for their respective theories.

Durkheim's Description of Contemporary Societies

Durkheim argued that in the primitive, "mechanical" form of societies, each social group is relatively isolated from other groups and is basically self-sufficient.[1] Within these social groups, individuals live under largely identical circumstances, do identical work, and hold identical values. There is little division of labor, with only a few persons in the clan or village having specialized functions. Thus, there is little need for individual talents, and the solidarity of the society is based on the uniformity of its members. In contrast to this is the advanced, "organic" form of society, with a highly developed division of labor. Social solidarity is no longer based on the uniformity of the individuals but on the diversity of functions of the different parts of the society. Durkheim argued that all societies were at some stage of the progression between the mechanical and the organic forms, with no society being totally one or the other. Even the most primitive societies had some forms of division of labor, while even the most advanced societies required some degree of uniformity among their members.

Durkheim rejected Comte's position that the source of social order was a consensus of moral beliefs.[2] Comte had recognized that the division of labor could itself be a source of social solidarity, but he saw it as only a minor source and generally believed that both the moral consensus and the social solidarity would be inevitably weakened as the division of labor became more complex.[3] Durkheim argued that the division of labor itself would become the primary source of social solidarity in advanced societies, and that the moral consensus, or "collective conscience," as Durkheim called it, would play "only a very restricted part."[4] The "organic" solidarity generated by the division of labor was based on the functional interdependence of the widely differentiated social roles, rather than on the uniformity of ideas or beliefs. But Durkheim argued that the functional interdependence of the various parts of society was not in itself sufficient for the resolution of social conflicts and the establishment of social solidarity. There must also be a regulation of the interaction between these parts, rules of conduct which originate in habits of interaction and which form the "network of links which little by little have been woven and which makes something permanent of organic solidarity."[5] The absence of this regulation, which Durkheim called "anomie," was the source of the conflict which existed in his own society.

Durkheim expanded his conception of anomie in his most famous work, *Suicide*.[6] There he argued that society regulated not only the economic interactions of its various parts but also the individual's perceptions of desires and needs. Durkheim stated that in times of rapid economic change society loses its ability to regulate human desires, which results in increases in suicides. Later in his career, Durkheim examined the role of cognitive thought and religious beliefs in the establishment of social solidarity, and at the time of his death he was beginning a work on the role of moral beliefs and ideals. While Comte had held that society was possible only if a moral consensus of beliefs existed, Durkheim argued the opposite: that moral beliefs, religious beliefs, and even cognitive thoughts were derived from the social relations of the society. This position was consistent with, although more general than, that of Marx, who had argued that beliefs were derived from economic relations.[7] Because Comte believed that the moral consensus was causally prior to social order, his solution to the problem of disorder was to impose a moral consensus—i.e., positivism—on the society. Durkheim believed that such a solution could never work and that, instead, social relations had to be changed to promote the natural evolution of new moral beliefs. As part of these new social relations he proposed that inheritance be abolished[8] and that a network of professional and occupational groups be established that would act as buffers between the individual and the state.[9] These groups would both act to facilitate communications so that the state's organization reflected the beliefs of the people and serve as a check on the power of the state, to insure individual freedom.

Durkheim's Description of Human Nature

Underlying this theory was a view of human nature that had been principally derived from the ideas of Rousseau, although with a significant change.[10] Rousseau had argued that in the state of nature human desires are reduced to physical needs. People are naturally consensual because those needs are fully satisfied by the environment. Conflict arises as the result of human association, which generates desires beyond the purely physical. That leads to the unequal distribution of resources and the founding of the civil state in order to protect the resources of the wealthy.

Durkheim admired the "dialectical ingenuity" of Rousseau's conception of the origin of the civil state and pointed out that its central concept was the inherent instability of the original balance of nature. People in the state of nature are harmonious, but they can remain so only as long as environmental conditions correspond exactly to the organization of human nature:

> Once the balance is upset, it cannot be restored. One disorder follows from another. Once the natural limit is crossed, there is no turning back. Passions beget passions and stimulate the intelligence, which offers them new objectives that rouse them to a fever pitch. The very satisfactions they obtain make them more demanding. "Superfluity awakens cupidity. The more one has, the more one wants."[11]

Rousseau's concept that "the more one has, the more one wants" was adopted in its entirety by Durkheim, but with one important change. Rousseau had argued that this condition arose as an effect of society and that humans in the state of nature were consensual. Durkheim argued that humans are inherently social and that the essence of being human is precisely that one can never be reduced to sensations. Thus, Rousseau's description of people in the state of nature was directly comparable to Durkheim's description of animals:

> In the animal, at least in a normal condition, this equilibrium (between needs and means) is established with automatic spontaneity because the animal depends on purely material conditions.... When the void created by existence in its own resources is filled, the animal, satisfied, asks nothing further. Its power of reflection is not sufficiently developed to imagine other ends than those implicit in its physical nature.[12]

And Durkheim's description of human nature is directly comparable to Rousseau's description of people in society:

> This is not the case with man, because most of his needs are not dependent on his body or not to the same degree... for beyond the indispensable minimum which satisfies nature when instinctive, a more awakened reflection suggests better conditions, seemingly desirable ends craving fulfillment.... Nothing appears in man's organic nor in his psychological constitution which sets a limit to such tendencies.... In no society are they equally satisfied in the different stages of the social hierarchy. Yet human nature is substantially the same among all men, in its essential qualities. It is not human nature which can assign the variable limits necessary to our needs. They are thus unlimited so far as they depend on the individual alone. Irrespective of any external regulatory force, our capacity for feeling is in itself an insatiable and bottomless abyss.[13]

This description of human nature was in some ways even more conflictual than was that of Hobbes. Although Hobbes believed that humans were essentially irrational, selfish, and isolated from others, he also believed that they did have a limited rationality. For example, he argued that a monarch could be satisfied with his power and possessions, or that individuals could understand the doctrine of *Leviathan* and be satisfied with their place in society. But Durkheim described every person as possessing unlimited and insatiable desires, so that no one would ever be really satisfied with his place or possessions, be he absolute sovereign or the poorest peasant. Each possessed an irrational and unceasing drive for more of everything and anything, a drive that would generate massive social conflict unless it were checked.

But, unlike Hobbes, Durkheim argued that there was another side to human nature. That was the social side (much as it had been described in the writings of Comte), so that human nature was actually dualistic:

> It is not without reason, therefore, that man feels himself to be double: he actually is double. There are in him two classes of states of consciousness that differ from each other in origin and nature, and in the ends toward which they aim. One class merely expresses our organisms and the objects to which they are most directly related. Strictly individual, the states of consciousness of this class connect us only with ourselves, and we can no more detach them from us than we can detach ourselves from our bodies. The states of consciousness of the other class, on the contrary, come to us from society; they transfer society into us and connect us with something that surpasses us. Being collective, they are impersonal; they turn us toward ends that we hold in common with other men; it is through them and them alone that we can communicate with others.[14]

It is society, through the social side of human nature, that limits the desires of the individual side of human nature. It does this through the "dim perception, in the moral consciousness of societies, of the respective value of different social services, the relative reward due to each, and the consequent degree of comfort appropriate on the average to workers in each occupation."[15] Each person then recognizes his own place in society and "aspires to nothing beyond.... Thus, an end and goal are set to the passions."[16]

Durkheim's dualistic view of human nature led him to a different perspective from those of his predecessors on how social conflict could be addressed. Hobbes believed human nature was essentially conflictual, so he argued that the primary social control mechanism would have to be coercive force. Rousseau, in contrast, believed that human nature was essentially consensual, and therefore he believed that in the proper social structure conflict would be almost entirely eliminated and force would be necessary only for a small, residual group. Durkheim believed that conflicts could be socially resolved because of the social side of human nature, but because of the individual side, he also recognized that this would be associated with painful tensions within each person, a problem that could only be expected to grow worse as society evolved:

> The painful character of the dualism of human nature is explained by this hypothesis. There is no doubt that if society were only the natural and spontaneous development of the individual, these two parts of ourselves would harmonize and adjust to each other without clashing and without friction. . . . In fact, however, society has its own nature, and, consequently, its requirements are quite different from those of our nature as individuals: the interests of the whole are not necessarily those of the part. Therefore, society cannot be formed or maintained without our being required to make perpetual and costly sacrifices. . . . We must, in a word, do violence to certain of our strongest inclinations. Therefore, since the role of the social being in our single selves will grow ever more important as history moves ahead, it is wholly improbable that there will ever be an era in which man is required to resist himself to a lesser degree, an era in which he can live a life that is easier and less full of tension. To the contrary, all evidence compels us to expect our effort in the struggle between the two beings within us to increase with the growth of civilization.[17]

Durkheim's Description of the Ideal Society

Durkheim's theory described the tension between the individual and social forces in human nature. The individual forces were described as constant—i.e., they were said to be essentially similar in different individuals and at different times and places. As Durkheim said, "Human nature is substantially the same among all men, in its essential qualities."[18] What Durkheim believed varied were the social forces, which at different times and places might be stronger or weaker.[19] In his own society, Durkheim believed, the social forces were quite weak, resulting in all the undesirable phenomena he called anomie. The ideal society, on the other hand, was not one in which the social forces were totally victorious over the individual forces, since in such a society there would be no individual freedom and no possibility of beneficial social change. Rather, in the ideal society, the social forces would predominate but would also allow sufficient individuality to permit freedom and change. Such a society would necessarily also have a certain level of criminality as a result of the individuality, but that level was considered "normal" and was to be distinguished from the much higher, "pathological" level of criminality that resulted from the breakdown of the social forces.[20]

Durkheim believed that the ideal state of society, in which there was only the minimal and necessary level of conflict, was also the "normal" state of societies throughout history. That view clearly was derived from the theories of Comte. He also believed, like Comte, that the present state of conflict in society would inevitably develop into the normal state of consensus. Durkheim's description of the consensus was also similar to that portrayed in Comte's and Hobbes' theories in that it required continuous and pervasive social forces to maintain it. While Comte and Hobbes had described those social forces in terms of propaganda and force, Durkheim described them in terms of the "social side of human nature" limiting the "individual side." Those social forces range from the mildest forms of ridicule and social isolation up to the most severe forms of criminal sanctions, and they were applied to almost all people at almost all times.[21] That was quite different from the consensus described by Rousseau, where social forces were required to come into play only when specific individuals refused to abide by the "general will." In all other cases, the members of the society were portrayed as being in a full, free, and spontaneous consensus among themselves, so that the social forces described by Hobbes, Comte, and Durkheim would be quite unnecessary.

The differences between Rousseau's and Durkheim's theories on the need for social forces to maintain a consensus was related to the differences in the way they described the sources of social conflict. Rousseau attributed the conflict to inequalities in the distribution of resources, while Durkheim attributed it to rapid changes in economic growth.[22] The significance of that difference was that Durkheim saw absolutely nothing wrong with the existence of the socioeconomic hierarchy itself, whereas Rousseau believed that it would have to be abolished in order to establish a consensual society. Durkheim believed, like Aristotle and Aquinas, that the socioeconomic hierarchy itself was reflective (albeit somewhat imperfectly so) of the natural inequalities of humanity.[23] He also believed that once individuals had found their own true level in the hierarchy, they would be satisfied with their lot if the social forces were operating properly. Consequently, Durkheim's ideal or "normal" society was a projection from the society in which he lived. It required only a relatively minor adjustment to the socioeconomic structure—the abolition of inheritance—and a relatively minor adjustment to the political structure—the institution of professional organizations. But it did not require the nearly total political and socioeconomic reorganization that Rousseau's theory did.

The "Normal" Society as Common or General

Durkheim's use of the term "normal" to describe a society in which there was only a minimal and necessary amount of conflict has been the subject of some debate. The term was defined by Durkheim as follows:

> A social fact is normal in relation to a given social type, at a given phase of its development, when it is present in the average of the societies of that type at the corresponding phase of their evolution.[24]

Pathological phenomena were identified by their unusualness, their divergence from the common or average. Durkheim identified such phenomena as planning and organization, normative regulation, and social justice as normal in modern industrial types of societies and economic anarchy, exploitation, and rising levels of crime, suicide, and divorce as pathological. Yet he also recognized that the "normal" phenomena were not present in his own society and that, in fact, it was the pathological phenomena that were general throughout all existing societies.[25] For example, he stated:

> Indeed, history records no crisis as serious as that in which European societies have been involved for more than a century. Collective discipline in its traditional form has lost its authority, as the divergent tendencies troubling the public conscience and the resulting general anxiety demonstrate.[26]

These divergent tendencies in the public conscience resulted in a crisis in which governments could no longer act as the "organ of social thought," representing the collective conscience of the people:

> [The crisis results] above all from the disarray in which men's consciences find themselves and in the extreme confusion of ideas. The most diverse and the most contradictory conceptions clash with one another in men's minds, cancelling one another out. How could our legislators fail to be impotent when the country is to this degree uncertain about what it should aim at?[27]

The disarray in men's consciences was a consequence of the fact that the society was in a state of crisis and anomie that was "constant and, so to speak, normal":

> From top to bottom of the ladder, greed is aroused without knowing where to find ultimate foothold. Nothing can calm it, since its goal is far beyond all it can attain. Reality seems valueless by comparison with the dreams of fevered imaginations; reality is therefore abandoned, but so too is possibility abandoned when it in turn becomes reality. A thirst arises for novelties, unfamiliar pleasures, nameless sensations, all of which lose their savor once known. Henceforth one has no strength to endure the least reverse.[28]

Men in the state of anomie will pursue their own interests to the exclusion of all else. Yet Durkheim also argued:

> Where interest is the only ruling force, each individual finds himself in a state of war with every other since nothing comes to mollify the egos, and any truce would not be of long duration. There is nothing less constant than interest. Today it unites me to you; tomorrow it will make me your enemy. Such a cause can only give rise to transient relations and passing associations.[29]

These quotations all represent various aspects of Durkheim's description of the anomic society, but it also was his description of his own and other European societies. That description certainly had more in common with what is usually considered to be conflict theory, with its emphasis on instability, disintegration, and dissensus, than with what is usually considered to be consensus theory, with its emphasis on stability, integration, and functional coordination.[30] Durkheim, of course, had insisted that this condition was pathological in the sense of being temporary and abnormal, while the normal and usual state of society was the consensual one.

The "Normal" Society as Ideal

Durkheim's description of the "normal" society as the common or usual one has been challenged by several scholars who argue that it is more closely related to the ideal than to the general. For example, Lukes argued that the "normal" society as described by Durkheim was really a hypothetical description of the ideally integrated state and that all deviations from that state were called pathological.[31] Richter focused on the operative nature of the ideals in Durkheim's theory, in that they are beliefs which affect men's behavior in the real world.[32] Quoting Lord Lindsay, Richter described Durkheim's focus as the study

> of what is actually operative; of the operative ideals which at any time inspire men in their relations to law; of the authorities and obligations from their belief in those ideals men actually recognize, even though they act only imperfectly in such recognition and the authorities they respect are not all that they are supposed to be.[33]

Durkheim maintained that these "normal" societies were general or common over the course of history—that is, in the past and future—even though they were extremely uncommon or even totally absent in his own time. But the ideal character of what he describes as a "normal" society becomes clear in his discussion of democracy. Durkheim described a continuum of governments ranging from those where governmental consciousness is as isolated as possible from the rest of society and has a minimum range to those where the degree of communication between government and society is maximized.[34] He defined democracy as the latter, stating that it is

> the political form by which society arrives at the purest consciousness of itself. A people is more democratic insofar as deliberation, reflection and the critical spirit play a more considerable role in the conduct of public affairs. It is less democratic insofar as unawareness, unconsidered practices, obscure sentiments and, in brief, unexamined prejudices are predominant.[35]

Durkheim argued that democracy is a superior form of government and that it is "the political system that conforms best to our present-day notion of the individual."[36] That, he asserted, is why democracies are becoming the typical form of government among advanced, industrial societies. In contrast, he argued that the militaristic government of Kaiser Wilhelm in Germany was an abnormal case of hypertrophy of the will.[37] In addition, he described the bureaucracy that had accumulated great power in France as an abnormal form caused by inadequate communication between the state administrative mechanism and the people.[38] Thus, Durkheim argued that superior forms of government will become typical or common because of their superiority, and that inferior forms will become unusual or infrequent precisely because they are inferior.

In the years since Durkheim wrote, his optimism about the evolution of governments toward superior forms has not been validated. Whether or not it will be in the long run is unknown. But at the present it seems best to think of what he described as "normal" societies not as common or general, but as ideal in a double sense: hypothetical models of integrated societies, as Lukes argued; and operative ideals, present in existing societies as beliefs that influence actions, as Richter argued. That double meaning of the term "ideal" is comparable to Durkheim's discussion of religion as an ideal world "from a double point of view:" it "does not exist except in thought" and man "attributes a higher sort of dignity" to it than to the real world.[39] He went on to discuss the formation of the ideal world as necessary for and a natural product of social life:

> For a society to become conscious of itself and maintain at the necessary degree of intensity the sentiments which it thus attains, it must assemble and concentrate itself. Now this concentration

brings about an exaltation of the mental life which takes form in a group of ideal conceptions where is portrayed the new life thus awakened.... A society can neither create itself nor recreate itself without at the same time creating an ideal.... Therefore when some oppose the ideal society to the real society, like two antagonists which would lead us in opposite directions, they materialize and oppose abstractions. The ideal society is not outside of the real society; it is a part of it.[40]

Durkheim also argued that only the ideal world could form the basis of religion, and not

the real society, such as it is and acts before our very eyes, with the legal and moral organization which it has laboriously fashioned during the course of history. This is full of defects and imperfections. In it, evil goes beside the good, injustice often reigns supreme, and the truth is often obscured by error. How could anything so crudely organized inspire the sentiments of love, the ardent enthusiasm and the spirit of abnegation which all religions claim of their followers?[41]

It would be consistent with Durkheim's theory to argue that he also believed that the real society, crudely organized and full of defects and imperfections, could not form the basis of true social integration, and that in order for French society to recreate itself, which was his principal motivation, it was necessary to create an ideal. Durkheim's vision of the "normal" society can be considered that ideal society. Defining that ideal as common or general had the effect of establishing as close a relationship as possible between it and the real society, so that it inspired "the sentiments of love, the ardent enthusiasm and the spirit of abnegation" necessary for social cohesion. If this interpretation is accepted, then the "normal" society is not in fact the common or general state of society throughout history. Rather, it is a "collective representation" commonly held among the individual members of the society and believed by them to be an accurate picture of the actual state of the society, when instead it is an idealized version of the state of society, whose major function is the representation of deeply held social values. Just as the basis for religion can be found only in the ideal world, so the basis for social solidarity can be found only in the ideal view of society that Durkheim called "normal."

Ideas and the Maintenance of Social Order

In effect, what Durkheim described as the "normal society" was a myth—i.e., it was a generalized belief system that did not actually reflect the nature of reality. As such, it was comparable in a sense to what Plato described as the "noble lie" and to what Marx described as "false consciousness" or the "ruling class ideology." The difference, of course, was that Durkheim argued that these beliefs were spontaneously derived from the social relations of the society, while Plato and Marx held that they were deliberately imposed on society "from above," so to speak. It was also comparable to Comte's "positive philosophy," except that that too was imposed on the society through propaganda and force.

All of the theorists agreed that these ideas were used to defend and stabilize the existing socioeconomic and political structures, Comte arguing that the ideas themselves were "true" or "valid" and Marx arguing that they were "false" and imposed on society by the ruling class in order to defend its own interests. Durkheim's emphasis, in contrast, was on the existence and the effect of these ideas, rather than on whether they were valid or invalid. Consider the following passage:

> As a matter of fact, at every moment of history there is a dim perception, in the moral consciousness of societies, of the respective value of different social services, the relative reward due to each, and the consequent degree of comfort appropriate on the average to workers in each occupation. The different functions are graded in public opinion and a certain coefficient of well-being assigned to each, according to its place in the hierarchy. According to accepted ideas, for example, a certain way of living is considered the upper limit to which a workman may aspire in his efforts to improve his existence, and there is another limit below which he is not willingly permitted to fall unless he has seriously demeaned himself. Both differ for city and country workers, for the domestic servant and the day-laborer, for the business clerk and the official, etc. Likewise the man of wealth is reproved if he lives the life of a poor man, but also if he seeks the refinements of luxury overmuch. Economists may protest in vain; public feeling will always be scandalized if an individual spends too much wealth for wholly superfluous use, and it even seems that this severity relaxes only in times of moral disturbance. A genuine regimen exists, therefore, although not always legally

formulated, which fixes with relative precision the maximum degree of ease of living to which each social class may legitimately aspire.[42]

The idea that there is an "upper limit" of comfort to which an individual in a given social class might legitimately aspire would have the same effect that Marx attributed to the "ruling class ideology," since it justified the advantages of the ruling class and kept other groups "in their place." It also fit quite comfortably with Comte's "Positive philosophy," since that defended the advantages of those in the upper class and argued that those in the lower class must accept their place in society. Because Durkheim presented these ideas favorably, it might be argued that he, like Comte and in contrast to Marx, believed that the ideas themselves were "true." But note that the discussion of social class in that passage is generally limited by the phrase "for example." In that part of the passage, Durkheim was using the ideas that were characteristic of his own society to illustrate his meaning. But the two opening sentences of the passage that are not limited by the phrase "for example" claim only that ideas about "respective value," "relative rewards," and "consequent degree of comfort" exist in every society. He goes on to argue that these ideas will change over time but that regardless of their specific form they will have the effect of setting an end and a goal to the passions.

Durkheim did not seem to consider the possibility that these ideas might change so fundamentally that they would no longer be associated with the basic class system that existed in his own society, and he seemed to believe, like Comte, that those in the upper classes "deserved" greater rewards because of their more valuable services.[43] But the major argument that Durkheim made was not dependent on the validity of that point. His major argument concerned the existence in every society of ideas relating to the relative value of different occupations and the rewards appropriate for them, along with the effect those ideas had on limiting human desires. Thus, it applies even in societies, such as modern communist ones, in which there are reward systems very different from the one he described in his own society.

Durkheim stated that these ideas could never be imposed on a society through propaganda and force but must evolve spontaneously from the social relations of the society itself. But many Western analysts would argue that the ideas about rewards found in communist societies did not evolve spontaneously but were in fact imposed on the society by those in power. Later in his life, Durkheim recognized this possibility and modified his stance to say that the consensus would grow of itself once the seeds had been planted. The planting of the seeds, in Durkheim's view, was to take place in the schools:

> We have here a unique and irreplaceable opportunity to take hold of the child at a time when the gaps in our social organization have not yet been able to alter his nature profoundly, or to arouse in him feelings which make him partially unamenable to common life. This is virgin territory in which we can sow seeds that, once taken root, will grow by themselves.[44]

Thus, the focus of Durkheim's effort to reconstitute social solidarity in French society became the struggle to obtain the introduction of his sociology into the school curriculum, and his efforts to promote the restructuring of social relations through the abolition of inheritance and the institution of professional organizations became secondary. That effort met with success in France when sociology was introduced into the syllabus of the *écoles normales primaires* and made a requirement for entry into the higher grades of teaching and administration in primary education. Nizan has given a Marxist view of that process:

> . . . in reality everything occurred as though the founder of French sociology had written *The Division of Labor* in order to permit obscure administrators to draw up an education destined for school teachers. The introduction of Sociology into the Ecoles Normales consecrated the administrative victory of this official morality. These were the years when Durkheim was engaged in building up his work and propagating his teaching, with great obstinacy and great authoritarian rigour, while giving that work the venerable appearance of science. In the name of that appearance, in the name of that science, teachers taught children to respect the French nation, to justify class collaboration, to accept everything, to join in the cult of the Flag and bourgeois Democracy.[45]

Thus, in the end, Durkheim did what he had originally argued would never work—propagated his sociology throughout French society as part of an effort to construct a general consensus as the basis for a new social solidarity. That was exactly what Comte had wanted done with his "positive philosophy" (as well as what Hobbes had wanted done with his teachings in *Leviathan*), and Durkheim had criticized Comte on precisely that point. Like Comte, Durkheim maintained that he was merely "helping along" an otherwise inevitable historical process. The shift in Durkheim's thinking seems to be related to an increasing identification of the "normal" society as an operative ideal or social fact embedded in the culture and producing social solidarity. At the beginning of his career, Durkheim had argued that social solidarity derived either from the collective conscience (which sprang spontaneously from the social relations of mechanical societies) or from the organic relations of advanced societies. Durkheim's criticism of Comte was that teaching could have no effect on these sources. But at the end of his career, the focus had shifted to the "myth" of the normal society, which is a belief system. Belief systems can be directly addressed through teaching, and that is precisely what Durkheim set about to do.

Simmel's Description of Contemporary Societies

Simmel's image of society was intended to be a middle ground between those who, like Dilthey, claimed that society did not exist apart from the multitude of individuals who made it up and those who, like Comte and Durkheim, held that it was an entity in itself, having in some sense an existence independent of those individuals.[46] Simmel argued that there was a sense in which only the individuals really existed but that to reduce society to a subjective reality in the minds of those individuals was to make a mistake similar to atomism in the physical sciences:

> Color molecules, letters, particles of water indeed "exist"; but the painting, the book, the river are syntheses: they are units that do not exist in objective reality but only in the consciousness which constitutes them.... It is perfectly arbitrary to stop the reduction, which leads ultimately to real elements, at the individual. For this reduction is interminable.[47]

Society is like the painting, the book, and the river in the sense that if one seeks what is ultimately real, one must reduce it to its tangible elements. But such a reduction is useless and misleading, since society is not a "thing" but a process or an event. It consists not of the individuals who make up the society but of the numerous interacting reciprocal relationships among those individuals. In this sense, society can be compared to the life process—life cannot be understood by reducing it to its component parts; it must be seen as a functioning interrelationship among those parts. Although Simmel continued to use the word "society" in various contexts, he also recognized that that term tended to reify the phenomenon, and thus preferred the term "sociation process," or, more literally, "societization process." Another term which he used, although less frequently, was "social life." Each of these terms was meant to avoid the problems of reification and at the same time convey a sense of the relational or processual nature of the phenomenon being described.[48] Simmel, then, held that "society" consisted of reciprocal relationships. These relationships could be as simple as "two people who for a moment look at one another or who collide in front of a ticket window," but in general he reserved the term for "*permanent* interactions only":

> More specifically, the interactions we have in mind when we talk about "society" are crystallized as definable, consistent structures such as the state and the family, the guild and the church, social classes and organizations based on common interests. But in addition to those, there exists an immeasurable number of less conspicuous forms of relationships and kinds of interaction. Taken singly, they may appear negligible. But since in actuality they are inserted into the comprehensive and, as it were, official social formations, they alone produce society as we know it.... That people look at one another and are jealous of one another; that they exchange letters or dine together; that irrespective of all tangible interests they strike one another as pleasant or unpleasant; that gratitude for altruistic acts makes for inseparable union; that one asks another man after a certain street; and that people dress and adorn themselves for one another—the whole gamut of relations that play from one person to another and that may be momentary or permanent, conscious or unconscious, ephemeral or of grave consequence (and from which these illustrations are quite casually chosen), all these incessantly tie men together. Here are the interactions among the atoms of society. They account for all the toughness and elasticity, all the color and consistency of social life, that is so striking and yet so mysterious.[49]

These permanent patterns of social interactions are taken to define the groups or social circles to which the person belongs. The largest of these groups is the state,[50] but in modern society an individual may belong to a wide variety of different groups, having different roles and statuses in each of them:

> The modern person belongs first of all to his parental family, then to his family of procreation and thereby also to the family of his wife. Beyond this he belongs to his occupational group, which often involves him in several interest-groups. For example, in an occupation that embraces both supervisory and subordinate personnel, each person participates in the affairs of his particular business, department office, etc., each of which comprises higher and lower employees. Moreover, a person also participates in a group made up of similarly situated employees from several different firms. Then a person is likely to be aware of his citizenship, of the fact that he belongs to a particular social class. He is, moreover, a reserve-officer, he belongs to a few clubs and engages in a social life which puts him in touch with different social groups.[51]

The extent to which a group is tightly knit can be gauged by the extent to which it has a "code of honor" regulating the behavior of its members.[52] Individuals are frequently affiliated with groups that have conflicting codes on specific issues[53] or that represent interests that are opposed to each other.[54] But Simmel identified membership in groups having conflicting values or interests with the growth of human freedom and individuality. Simmel argued that groups are initially formed on the basis of propinquity (such as the family and the local community), but that later associations tend to be formed on the basis of "common interests."[55] Here, Simmel used the term "interest" in the broadest sense of having an interest in or being interested in a common purpose.[56] That included, but by no means was limited to, economic interests. The development from groups based on propinquity to those based on common interests is characteristic of both individuals and society in general. It is associated with the growth of human freedom because the second type of group formation is a matter of choice, while the first is not. It is associated with the development of individuality because one's identity or personality is ultimately rooted in the groups to which one belongs. In primitive cultures, and for young human beings, only one group exists, and one's identity is drawn entirely from that group. But when one belongs to several groups that are in conflict among themselves, one must resolve those conflicts in terms of the uniqueness of the self. Thus:

> Conflicting and integrating tendencies are mutually reinforcing. Conflicting tendencies can arise just because the individual has a core of inner unity. The ego can become more clearly conscious of this unity, the more he is confronted with the task of reconciling within himself a diversity of group-interests. [57]

An example of this process can be found in Simmel's discussion of women. [58] He argued that women historically have been totally defined by their membership in the marriage-family group. The total involvement in this one group has restricted the freedom and individuality of women. But in recent times the necessity for total involvement in the marriage-family group has lessened, and women have begun to associate with other women in groups. These new groups have many values and interests that conflict with those of the marriage-family group, and because of these conflicts women may be under many psychological stresses and even may be in danger of schizophrenic breaks. [59] But precisely because of these conflicts, a woman is also able to achieve a sense of herself as a person independent of both groups, and a greater degree of freedom because she can select from the conflicting codes of honor and the conflicting interests embodied in the two groups those which suit her best as an individual.

Like Comte and Durkheim, Simmel was interested in creating a definition for sociology that would constitute it as a separate and legitimate science. His definition focused on the study of the reciprocal relations that constituted "society," or the sociation process. The obvious objection to this definition was that these relations could be studied either as unique factual situations or in terms of their psychological motivations, but that neither of these constituted an adequate definition of sociology as a separate science. But Simmel argued that these relations formed patterns quite separate from the facts of the situation or from the psychological motivations of the individuals involved in it. These patterns could be discerned by abstracting on the basis of intuition from the concrete, factual relations between individuals. This process is no different from that used by scientists in other disciplines, all of whom abstract from the unique event to the general rule. Simmel expressed this abstraction in terms of the distinction between "form" and "content":

> I designate as the content—the materials, so to speak—of sociation everything that is present in individuals (the immediate concrete loci of all historical reality)—drive, interest, purpose, inclination, psychic state, movement—everything that is present in them in such a way as to engender or mediate effects upon others or to receive such effects. In themselves, these materials which fill life, these motivations which propel it, are not social. They are factors in sociation only when they transform the mere aggregation of isolated individuals into specific forms of being with and for one another, forms that are subsumed under the general concept of interaction. Sociation is the form (realized in innumerably different ways) in which individuals grow together into a unity and within which their interests are realized. And it is on the basis of their interests—sensuous or ideal, momentary or lasting, conscious or unconscious, causal or teleological—that individuals form such unities.[60]

Simmel argued that similar forms of sociation occurred in concrete situations that were extremely dissimilar in every other respect. These forms included superiority and subordination, competition, conflict, imitation, formation of parties, division of labor, art, fashion, ritual, and secrecy. All of these forms of interaction occur in the most diverse groups and organizations, where the facts of the situation and the motivations or interests for which the groups are formed have no similarity to one another. Simmel attempted to describe these forms but did not present any overall theory of society, since he regarded such a theory as premature.

Conflict in Contemporary Societies

Simmel maintained that both associative and dissociative forces were essential to social life in the same sense that the universe could not exist without both centripetal and centrifugal forces.[61] Centripetal forces in societies (those tending to bring them together) included such forms of sociation as authority and subordination, while centrifugal forces (those tending to pull them apart) included conflict. Simmel did not argue that conflictual relations were primary in society—rather, they were one of many types of relations that all were inevitably found in any society, none of which by itself could produce the social structure.[62] He saw conflict and peace as alternating states in human history and noted that there is a human tendency to "bestow on the change of these elements a teleological accent so that one of them is always the point of origin, which is objectively primary, while the other develops out of it."[63] But, he argued, this was not in fact the case:

> Both in the succession and in the simultaneity of social life, the two are so interwoven that in every state of peace the conditions of future conflict, and in every conflict the conditions of future peace, are formed. If one follows historical developments back in time from this standpoint, one cannot stop anywhere.... Nevertheless, we "feel" an inner difference into this sequence of the links of the chain: conflict appears as preliminary, with peace and its contents as the purpose of it. While from an objective viewpoint, the rhythm of the two elements pulsates evenly on the same level, our valuation articulates, as it were, iambic periods, with war as thesis and peace as arsis.[64]

The tendency to see conflict as a secondary or derived phenomenon is related to the tendency to see it as destructive of social unity. This is based on a misunderstanding of the term "unity." If unity is taken to mean "the consensus and concord of interacting individuals, as against their discords, separations, and disharmonies," then conflict certainly is disruptive of social unity. But unity can also refer to "the total group-synthesis of persons, energies, and forms, that is, the ultimate wholeness of that group, a wholeness which covers both strictly-speaking unitary relations and dualistic relations."[65] This broader unity is the unity of the phenomenon itself, as the subject of sociological study. It can be illustrated in the case of marriages:

> A certain amount of discord, inner divergence and outer controversy, is organically tied up with the very elements that ultimately hold the (marriage) together; it cannot be separated from the unity of the sociological structure. This is true not only in cases of evident marital failure but also in marriages characterized by a *modus vivendi* which is bearable or at least borne. Such marriages

are not "less" marriages by the amount of conflict they contain; rather, out of so many elements, among which there is that inseparable quantity of conflict, they have developed into the definite and characteristic units which they are.[66]

Similarly, societies are not "less" societies because they contain conflicts, but the conflicts they contain are an integral part of the phenomenon itself. In this sense, conflict is part of the unity of society.

A second and related confusion about the "unity" of society concerns the obviously damaging effect that conflict can have on individuals. There is a tendency to conclude that it must have the same effect on the social group as a whole.[67] Simmel goes on to describe the integrative functions of social conflict, which have been summarized in propositional form by Lewis Coser.[68] To understand the integrative functions, one must recall Simmel's distinction between form and content. Simmel had classified as content everything that might be thought of as the "causes" of the conflictual behavior—"drive, interest, purpose, inclination, psychic state, movement." These "motivations" of such behavior, he states, are not in themselves social, and are not the subject of sociological inquiry. He simply presumes that they exist, have always existed, and will always exist. What is the subject of sociological inquiry is the forms of interaction through which these motivations are expressed. Conflict is an inevitable and necessary form of social interaction because these motivations inevitably and necessarily exist. Specific forms of conflict are functional to society because they permit these motivations to be expressed without destroying the society itself. To say that conflict is functional to society is like saying that learning how to fight is essential to the preservation of a marriage.[69] To make this statement is to presume that the conflicts exist to begin with and are inevitable in every marriage. From this point of view one does not really explore the sources of those conflicts but examines the methods by which they can be played out and resolved without damaging the marriage. The absence of conflict in a marriage may not mean that a couple lives in complete harmony and understanding. More often it means that both partners have given up, don't care any more, and have settled into a stultifying and closed relationship. Like those who study marital conflict,

Simmel did not focus on the causes or sources of the conflictual behavior but rather focused on the forms by which the conflicts were expressed and the functional or dysfunctional effects those forms could have for society as a whole.

Human Nature and the Ideal Society in Simmel's Theory

The purpose of Simmel's theory was to describe and analyze the "forms" of sociation. In the categories of the present analysis, that comes under "description of contemporary societies," since those forms were part of all societies that actually existed at the time Simmel wrote (as well as, in his view, all societies that ever had existed or would exist). Despite the fact the Simmel included both associative and dissociative forces in his description of contemporary societies, he did not describe societies themselves in consensual terms. Rather, at the broadest level, he said societies were composed of multiple overlapping and conflicting groups. Simmel agreed that such conflict was disruptive of the "consensus and concord of interacting individuals," but he maintained that it was part of the unity of the society itself. Thus, Simmel described contemporary societies in terms of conflict, not consensus.

Simmel's analysis of the causes or sources of the conflict was limited to general statements about "conflicts of interests" and to vague references to "hostile impulses" and "needs for hating and fighting." Because this question was part of what he called the "content" of conflict, it was not the focus of his concern. Nevertheless, those vague references and general statements make clear that he considered at least one source of the conflict to be human nature itself. That view was associated with the view that conflict is an inevitable part of all societies. Accordingly, Simmel never implies that any type of consensual society—even a hypothetical ideal one—can exist. Rather, to the extent that an ideal society appears in Simmel's theory, it is described in conflictual terms. It is a society in which the process of differentiation into conflicting interest groups is highly advanced, so that the maximum potential for individualization and freedom are achieved.

The Relation Between Form and Content

The form that Simmel's theory took is consistent with his assumptions that both human nature and contemporary societies are conflictual. Conflict is portrayed as an inevitable condition of humanity, so that no society, even a hypothetical ideal one, can be free from it. Consequently, the theory concentrated on describing and analyzing real societies. Simmel also avoided all moral assessments in his descriptions of conflict—there is no implication in his theory that some parties may be "right" while others are "wrong." Thus, his theory took on the nonevaluative, "objective" stance of sociological conflict theories.

Durkheim's description of human nature as "dualistic" might suggest that he should be classified as falling in between the sociological consensus and conservative positions, much as Comte is. But Durkheim identified the "consensual" side of human nature with the social forces that were exerted against the conflictual impulses of the individual side of human nature, so that his position was effectively the same as describing human nature as conflictual but societies as consensual. Accordingly, his theory took the form of a sociological consensus theory. The theory focused on describing and analyzing a hypothetical ideal society—the "normal" society—and presented real, contemporary societies only as part of the description of the processes by which they could be transformed into the hypothetical ideal. It portrayed real societies as being deficient in their social control mechanisms, so that the transformation to the ideal could be accomplished solely by strengthening those mechanisms. Socioeconomic inequality was defended by Durkheim's theory as a reflection of human inequality, and changes in the socioeconomic system were said to be necessary only to the extent that they affected the social control mechanisms. The ideal ("normal") society was portrayed as "full of tension," because its conflicts were merely controlled, not resolved. In contrast, to the extent that Comte described humans as naturally consensual (and his theory took the form of a conservative theory), both real and ideal societies were said to reflect the natural tendency for people to organize themselves hierarchically, so that those societies lacked conflict rather than controlled it. Such a "conflict-free" society does not appear in Durkheim's theory.

General Similarities and Differences

There are several points at which the theories of Durkheim and Simmel can be compared for similarities and differences. One similarity is that both argued that the analysis of the motivations of particular behaviors was not the proper subject matter of sociology. Simmel had referred to such motivations as "content," but Durkheim had taken a similar stance when he refused to analyze the motivations of particular suicides. He argued instead that it was the *rate* of suicide that was a social fact and had to be explained sociologically. Where Simmel used sociological methods to analyze patterns of interaction, Durkheim used them to analyze rates of behavior.

Despite the fact that Durkheim refused to analyze the motivations of particular behaviors, his theories implied causes of those behaviors, something that Simmel's theories did not do. In particular, Durkheim portrayed conflict as a function of the insatiable desires that were a part of human nature. Such an argument fell into the realm of the "content" of conflict, rather than its "form," and by entering that realm, Durkheim eliminated from consideration in his theory a number of sources of conflict that can be included in Simmel's more general formulation. First, Durkheim's theory excluded the idea that there might be aggressive instincts per se as a part of human nature, as has been argued by some anthropologists.[70] For Durkheim, fighting was a function of inadequately limited appetites seeking some desirable ends, rather than fighting for fighting's sake alone. Second, Durkheim excluded from his theory conflict over scarce resources necessary for survival, focusing on human desires that are "beyond the indispensable minimum which satisfies nature when instinctive."[71] He did not deny that this type of conflict existed, but he treated it as an unimportant, residual category. Finally, Durkheim did not believe that there could be, in any given society, any true conflicts of values. Despite the fact that he recognized that the increasing division of labor would intensify the "centripetal forces on moral beliefs," Durkheim, in Warner's words, held that "ethical choices were unambiguous in principle (if, indeed, arduous to work through) only because he believed in the immanent harmony of social life, because at the deepest level he did not believe in the necessity of tragic choices."[72] If any of these types of conflict—instinctive conflict, conflict over scarce resources necessary for survival, and value conflict—can be shown to be a general form of conflict in human societies, it would be a substantial problem for Durkheim's theory. Such conflict would be anomic, because it is not productive of social change or individual freedom, but it also would be normal, because it is general. Because of this contradiction, Durkheim could not consider that these represented genuine sources of social conflict.

In contrast, the "content," or specific motivations of conflict, were unimportant to Simmel's theory, so these sources of conflict can be accepted or rejected without damage to it. At the same time, Simmel had no concept that corresponded to Durkheim's concept of anomie. Anomic conflict, according to Durkheim, was all conflict beyond that which was "normal" or necessary for social change and individual freedom. Durkheim argued that anomic conflict was pathological in the sense of being unusual or atypical. Simmel made no comparable distinction between "normal" and "pathological" conflict and no argument about which types of conflict are typical and which unusual.

All of this is related to the fact that Simmel did not present an overall theory of society, while Durkheim did. Simmel regarded such a theory as premature. What he presented instead was a large number of propositions about the various social forms. For example, in the case of conflict, he described the types of conflict, the degrees of combativeness or violence of conflict and the processes of determining those degrees, the methods and motivations for terminating conflict, and the effects of conflict on the organization of groups and on the integration of the social whole. But because these propositions were not woven into an overall theory, one or another of them can be rejected without rejecting the entire work. This is not the case with Durkheim's theory, where the rejection of a relatively minor point can cause serious problems for the overall theory. The same point can be made in comparing Simmel's work to that of Marx. Turner has contrasted some of the propositions about conflict made by Simmel and Marx, several of which are directly contradictory.[73] For example, Simmel argued that as goals become more clear-cut, conflict tends to become instrumental, with compromise more likely and violence less likely. Marx argued the opposite—that as classes become aware of their true interests, they tend to polarize, so that compromise becomes impossible and violence inevitable. Simmel's point could be rejected (if research demonstrated that Marx was correct) without jeopardizing the rest of his work, since this is merely one observation among many. But if Simmel's point is accepted and Marx's rejected, then Marx's entire theory of history must be reexamined.

The difference between Durkheim's and Simmel's work is also related to the specific type of theory that Durkheim presented. Durkheim's purpose in theorizing was to discover and explain the sources of social solidarity. As Parsons stated, "'Solidarity' cannot be treated as a component for Durkheim's purposes because it is his dependent variable; he is concerned with the conditions on which it depends."[74] Durkheim's theory is not intended to be a description of societies or social phenomena as they exist but, rather, an analysis of these phenomena as independent variables in terms of their relationship to the dependent variable, social solidarity. Thus, Durkheim presents social conflict as being generally destructive of social solidarity, but also as having specific effects that contribute to it. In addition, he argues that the conditions that permit conflict to emerge in society also permit the emergence of individual freedom and social change, both of which are necessary for social solidarity.

In contrast, Simmel's primary purpose was the description of societies and social phenomena as they exist. His description included those elements of conflict that are a part of every society, just as elements of conflict are a part of every marriage. He agreed entirely that such conflict was destructive of social unity if one meant by that "the consensus and concord of interacting individuals," but he regarded it as part of the unity of the phenomenon itself. Simmel also regarded consensus and solidarity as part of that unity, but he did not argue that either consensus or conflict should be the primary focus of sociological theory, or that either was causally prior to the other. Unlike Durkheim, Simmel was not a social reformer and was not primarily concerned with improving his and other societies. He was an academic, an acute observer of social phenomena, who believed that such observations were necessary before any overall theory such as Durkheim's could even be attempted.

Thus, to a great extent, the two theorists simply went off in quite different directions. Durkheim would not have been interested in Simmel's descriptions of the types and degrees of conflict, the methods of terminating it, and so on, because they had no relation to his primary concern—the establishment of social solidarity.[75] Like uncorrelated variables in a multiple regression equation, these phenomena simply "dropped out" of Durkheim's theory, and in a very real sense they were meaningless to him. Simmel, in contrast, would have regarded Durkheim's theory as "premature." He believed that it was necessary to accurately describe microsociological phenomena before any attempt were made to tie them together into a macrosociological theory.

Consensus and Conflict in Contemporary Societies

In spite of the differences in the general purposes of the theories, it is still possible to compare their descriptions of consensus and conflict in contemporary societies. One similarity between the two theories lies in their descriptions of the integrative functions of socially disruptive behavior. As Coser has said about Durkheim's theory: "One has only to replace 'crime,' which may sometimes be a form of conflict, with 'conflict' generally, to arrive at Simmel's meaning of the integrative function of antagonistic behavior."[76] The difference between the two, though, was that Durkheim's theory was concerned with the integrative functions only at the societal level, while Simmel's theory was concerned with all levels of groups, including the state as the most comprehensive group. In his concern for the establishment of social solidarity, Durkheim described society as a single group, while Simmel described it as numerous interlocking and overlapping groups. Durkheim argued that societies developed common values and represented common interests, while Simmel argued that at every level, groups were formed on the basis of common interests and developed "codes of honor," and that the interests and "codes" of different groups often conflicted with each other. Because Durkheim described society as a single group, his theory could not accommodate the types of conflicts of values and interests that were described in Simmel's theory.

Durkheim's theory has been criticized on this point. For example, Piaget argued that Durkheim's theory of pedagogy ignores the fact that children form social groups among themselves, apart from their relations to adults. These groups evolve a great variety of rules to which the child adheres, and constitute "child societies" which are in many ways parallel to the adult societies that Durkheim discussed. Piaget stated:

> Durkheim thinks of children as knowing no other society than adult society or the societies created by adults (schools), so that he entirely ignores the existence of spontaneously formed children's societies, and of the facts relating to mutual respect. Consequently, elastic though Durkheim's pedagogy may be in principle, it simply leads, for lack of being sufficiently informed on the subject of child sociology, to a defence of the methods of authority.[77]

Piaget argued that "the child ties himself down to all sorts of rules in every sphere of his activity, and especially in that of play," so that "alongside of the social relations between children and adults there exist social relations that apply distinctly to the groups which children form among themselves."[78] Because Durkheim ignored these other social relations, Durkheim's theory of the socialization of children was extremely conservative. Piaget described it as follows:

> All authority comes from Society with a big S ('la' société); the schoolmaster is the priest who acts as an intermediary between society and the child; everything therefore rests with the master, and rules are a sort of revelation which the adult dispenses to the child.[79]

These children's groups, as described by Piaget, are directly comparable to the groups described by Simmel. They are formed because of an interest in a common purpose and develop "codes of honor" regulating the behavior of individual members. In addition to being a member of the general community (as represented in the school) and of children's societies, each child is also a member of a particular family. The family also functions as a group regulating the behavior of the child, often in ways that conflict with the regulations of both children's societies and schools. These, then, are the interlocking and overlapping groups of which each child is a member, and whose values and interests compete and conflict with each other, as described in Simmel's theory.

Lukes has argued:

> [Durkheim] failed to consider the whole question of competing socializing influences upon the child, and the extent to which social contexts and institutions outside the school may affect its significance, militating against, and diminishing the potential coherence of, what is taught there. He never saw the school teacher as operating within an essentially conflictual situation, having to combat other equally or more powerful agencies of socialization. Indeed, there is something in the view that he was inviting the teacher to embrace an exposed position in a highly conflictual situation, on the basis of an ideology which concealed the conflicts of the real situation in which teacher and pupil were placed.[80]

To the extent that Durkheim's theory "concealed the conflicts of the real situation" of the child in school, it also concealed the conflicts of the real situation of individuals in society generally. Such concealment could only enhance the propsects of accomplishing Durkheim's major goal—the reestablishment of social solidarity. But as a theoretical description of an empirical situation, it must be considered inferior to Simmel's approach. Durkheim acknowledged as much in a footnote, where he stated:

> To simplify the exposition, we hold that the individual appears only in one society. In fact, we take part in several groups and there are in us several collective consciences; but this complication changes nothing with regard to the relation that we are now establishing.[81]

Durkheim was establishing the relation between crime and social solidarity, which, as Coser pointed out above, is identical to Simmel's description of the integrative functions of conflict. But unlike Simmel, Durkheim did not develop the implications of the fact that "there are in us several collective consciences." Had he done so, he would have come to a formulation like Simmel's.

The fundamental difference between the theories of Durkheim and Simmel with respect to consensus and conflict can be illustrated by their descriptions of children and teachers. Durkheim described children as less socialized individuals who needed to be shaped and formed in accordance with societal conventions by the more socialized teachers, whereas Simmel would have described children and teachers as two groups in varying degrees of conflict with each other within the context of society. Durkheim identified teachers with the society itself and the demands they made on children with the demands of the collective conscience. In contrast, he attributed the demands that the children made on teachers to their lack of socialization. Thus, in the context of Durkheim's theory, the teachers' demands were accorded an inherent legitimacy, while the children's could be said to be "illegitimate." Piaget's criticism of Durkheim's theory can be paraphrased as asserting that the demands children make on teachers have an inherent "legitimacy" of their own and that it is not sufficient to treat those demands merely as evidence of lack of socialization. Simmel's theory, unlike either Durkheim's or Piaget's, would not assess the legitimacy of the demands of either party—rather, it would simply describe and analyze the conflict between them in terms that have nothing to do with legitimacy.

Durkheim extended the same evaluations of inherent legitimacy to the actions of the ruling groups of contemporary societies when he identified the law with the demands of the collective conscience. Consequently, Durkheim did not describe any conflict between ruler and ruled in contemporary societies. Rather, like the other consensus theorists before him, he attributed a fundamental legitimacy to the actions of the ruling groups and described the need to use force and other means to obtain conformity from other groups.

The major difference between the theories of Durkheim and Simmel with respect to their descriptions of conflict and consensus lies in their differing evaluations of the legitimacy of the demands that ruling groups make on other groups in the society. Durkheim described those demands as legitimate because they reflected the demands of the collective conscience of the society itself. Simmel did not evaluate the legitimacy of the demands. He merely described and analyzed the processes of interaction, including conflict, among the various groups in the society, including the ruling groups. Simmel and Durkheim did not make differing empirical assertions about the existence or extent of conflict in societies generally. Rather, they offered differing descriptions of the same empirical phenomena, those differing descriptions being based on differing evaluations of the actions of ruling groups. Thus, the difference between the theories of Durkheim and Simmel is not an empirical difference and cannot be resolved through empirical investigations.

Notes

1. This description is taken from Emile Durkheim, *The Division of Labor in Society* (New York: The Free Press, 1964).

2. Ibid., pp. 62–69.

3. Comte, *The Positive Philosophy,* Harriet Martineau, trans. (London: George Bell, 1896), 4:425.

4. Durkheim, *Division of Labor,* p. 80. See also pp. 171–73.

5. Ibid., p. 366.

6. Emile Durkheim, *Suicide* (New York: The Free Press, 1951).

7. Alvin W. Gouldner, "Introduction," in Emile Durkheim, *Socialism* (New York: Collier, 1962), pp. 26–29.

8. Durkheim, *Division of Labor,* pp. 383–84; Emile Durkheim, *Professional Ethics and Civic Morals* (Glencoe, Ill.: The Free Press, 1958), pp. 213–18; Durkheim, *Suicide,* pp. 373–86.

9. Durkheim, "Preface to the Second Edition," in *Division of Labor,* p. 1–38; Durkheim, *Suicide,* pp. 373–86.

10. Rousseau's description of human nature is presented in more detail in Ch. 6.

11. Emile Durkheim, *Montesquieu and Rousseau* (Ann Arbor: University of Michigan Press, 1960), pp. 80–81.

12. Durkheim, *Suicide,* p. 246. See also the statement on p. 248: "The awakening of conscience interrupted the state of equilibrium of the animal's dormant existence; only conscience, therefore, can furnish the means to re-establish it"; and Durkheim, *Montesquieu and Rousseau,* p. 90.

13. Durkheim, *Suicide,* p. 247.

14. Emile Durkheim, "The Dualism of Human Nature and Its Social Conditions," in Kurt H. Wolff, ed., *Essays on Sociology and Philosophy* (New York: Harper and Row, 1964), p. 337.

15. Durkheim, *Suicide,* p. 249.

16. Ibid., p. 250.

17. Durkheim, "Dualism," pp. 338–39.

18. Durkheim, *Suicide,* p. 247.

19. A different position was taken in Robert K. Merton's reformulation of anomie theory as seen in his *Social Theory and Social Structure* (New York: The Free Press, 1968), pp. 185–214. Merton argued that man's desires are culturally induced, instead of being an unchanging part of human nature. Strain results when the level of comfort permitted by society deviates excessively from the culturally induced desires of any given group.

20. Emile Du. heim, *The Rules of the Sociological Method* (New York: The Free Press, 1966), pp. 46–75.

21. Durkheim, *Suicide,* pp. 2–3.

22. Ibid., pp. 252–53.

23. Durkheim, *Division of Labor,* pp. 374–76, 384.

24. Durkheim, *Rules*, p. 64.

25. Steven Lukes, *Emile Durkheim, His Life and Work* (New York: Harper and Row, 1972), p. 29.

26. Emile Durkheim, *Moral Education: A Study in the Theory and Application of the Sociology of Education* (New York: The Free Press, 1961), p. 101.

27. Contribution to "Enquête sur l'impuissance parlementaire," *La Revue* (1897) 13:397, quoted in Lukes, *Emile Durkheim*, p. 313.

28. Durkheim, *Suicide*, p. 256. Durkheim's use of the term "normal" here appears to be a conscious contradiction of his other uses of the term. Anomie was not "normal" (i.e., general) in societies throughout history, although it was "normal" (i.e., general) among societies at that particular time.

29. Durkheim, *The Division of Labor*, pp. 203–4.

30. Ralf Dahrendorf, *Class and Class Conflict in Industrial Society* (Stanford, Calif.: Stanford University Press, 1959), pp. 161–62.

31. Lukes, *Emile Durkheim*, p. 30.

32. Melvin Richter, "Durkheim's Politics and Political Theory," in Wolff, ed., *Essays*, p. 191.

33. A.D. Lindsay, *The Modern Democratic State* (London: Oxford University Press, 1943), 1:47, quoted in Richter, "Durkheim's Politics," p. 191.

34. Durkheim, *Porfessional Ethics*, pp. 76–84.

35. Ibid., p. 89.

36. Ibid., p. 90.

37. Emile Durkheim, *L'Allemagne au-dessus de tout*, (Paris: Armand Colin, 1915), p. 44, cited in Richter, "Durkheim's Politics," p. 204.

38. Durkheim, *Professional Ethics*, pp. 98–99. See also Durkheim, *Division of Labor*, p. 28.

39. Emile Durkheim, *The Elementary Forms of the Religious Life* (London: George Allen and Unwin, 1976), p. 422.

40. Ibid.

41. Ibid., p. 420.

42. Durkheim, *Suicide*, p. 249.

43. See Beth Ensminger Vanfossen, *The Structure of Social Inequality* (Boston: Little, Brown, 1979), pp. 23–33 for a brief review of the long debate over whether the unequal distribution of rewards reflects the functional importance of different social roles.

44. Durkheim, *Moral Education*, p. 236.

45. P. Nizan, *Les Chiens de garde* (Paris, 1932), pp. 97–98, quoted in Lukes, *Emile Durkheim*, p. 357. See also Richter, "Durkheim's Politics," p. 172.

46. Lewis A. Coser, *Masters of Sociological Thought* (New York: Harcourt Brace Jovanovich, 1971), p. 194.

47. Georg Simmel, *The Sociology of Georg Simmel*, Kurt Wolff, ed. (New York: The Free Press, 1950), pp. 6–7.

48. Georg Simmel, "The Persistence of the Social Group," Albion Small, trans., *American Journal of Sociology* (1898) 3:665–66.

49. Simmel, *The Sociology of Georg Simmel*, p. 9.

50. Georg Simmel, *Conflict and The Web of Group Affiliations* (New York: The Free Press, 1955), p. 163.

51. Ibid., p. 138.

52. Ibid., p. 163.

53. Ibid., pp. 164–65.

54. Ibid., pp. 156–57.

55. Ibid., pp. 128–29.

56. Ibid., p. 163; Georg Simmel, "The Problem of Sociology," in Kurt Wolff, ed., *Essays on Sociology, Philosophy and Aesthetics* (New York: Harper and Row, 1959), p. 315.

57. Simmel, *Conflict*, p. 142.

58. Ibid., pp. 180–84.

59. Ibid., p. 141.

60. Simmel, "The Problem of Sociology," p. 315.

61. Simmel, *Conflict*, p. 15.

62. Ibid., pp. 21, 25.

63. Ibid., pp. 107–8.

64. Ibid., p. 109.

65. Ibid., p. 17.

66. Ibid., p. 18.

67. Ibid., p. 17.

68. Lewis A. Coser, *The Functions of Social Conflict* (New York: The Free Press, 1956).

69. See George R. Bach and Peter Wyden, *The Intimate Enemy: How to Fight Fair in Love and Marriage* (New York: William Morrow, 1969).

70. E.g., Konrad Lorenz, *On Aggression* (New York: Bantam, 1969).

71. Durkheim, *Suicide*, p. 247.

72. Neil J. Smelser and R. Stephen Warner, *Sociological Theory: Historical and Formal* (Morristown: General Learning Press, 1976), p. 89.

73. Jonathan H. Turner, *The Structure of Sociological Theory*, rev. ed. (Homewood, Ill.: Dorsey Press, 1978), pp. 130–40.

74. Talcott Parsons, "Durkheim's Contribution to the Theory of Integration of Social Systems," in Parsons, *Sociological Theory and Modern Society* (New York: The Free Press, 1967), p. 14. See also pp. 33–34.

75. See Emile Durkheim, "Sociology and Its Scientific Field," in Wolff, *Essays*, p. 359.

76. Coser, *The Functions of Social Conflict*, p. 127; see also p. 123.

77. J. Piaget, *The Moral Judgment of the Child* (New York: The Free Press, 1965), p. 356.

78. Ibid., p. 361.

79. Ibid., p. 362.

80. Lukes, *Emile Durkheim*, p. 134.

81. Durkheim, *Division of Labor*, p. 105, n. 44.

– CHAPTER 8 –

Parsons and Dahrendorf

TALCOTT PARSONS and Ralf Dahrendorf are probably more strongly identified with consensus theories and conflict theories than any other modern sociologists. In fact, the use of the terms "consensus theory" and "conflict theory" in modern sociology seems to have originated, at least partially, in reference to their theories. Accordingly, a more detailed presentation is made of their theories than has been made of the theories described so far, as well as a more comprehensive comparison on the issues of consensus and conflict.

Parsons' Description of Human Nature

Parsons began his theorizing by examining the concept of social action in the theories of Alfred Marshall, Vilfredo Pareto, Emile Durkheim, and Max Weber.[1] He later commented that "judging by the secondary literature available at the time, they should be considered as diverse in points of view as any four thinkers one could have picked."[2] He found, however, a convergence of their conceptual schemes into a common frame of reference that drew from each of the three major theoretical traditions: utilitarianism, positivism, and idealism. That common frame of reference included the concept, from utilitarianism, that man is goal oriented, although Parsons argued that the utilitarians had taken this position to the extreme of arguing that man's actions were always attempts to maximize profits. In the positivist tradition Parsons found the concept that situational conditions, such as social, psychological, and biological factors, could have a deterministic impact on social action. Again, though, Parsons rejected the extreme position that all analysis of human action should be reduced to cause-and-effect relationships. Finally, from the idealist tradition Parsons took the notion that beliefs, values, norms, and other "ideas" could have a deterministic impact on human action, but here he rejected the extreme position that these ideas were somehow independent of the social life they regulated. Parsons argued that situational conditions and ideas had an impact on human action through the existence of alternative means through which the individual could accomplish his goals. Thus, the individual is rationally motivated and goal seeking but is constrained in the choice of means to accomplish those goals through situational conditions such as biological, psychological, and social factors, and through "ideas" such as values, norms, beliefs, and so on. Parsons identified this as a Hobbesian view of human nature, so that his theory of society was primarily a response to the "Hobbesian problem of order."[3]

Parsons' Description of Contemporary Societies and the Ideal Society

Having completed his analysis of human action, Parsons turned his attention to the social world in which man lives. He defined a "social system" as "a plurality of individual actors interacting with each other in a situation which has at least a physical or environmental aspect, actors who are motivated in terms of a tendency to the 'optimization of gratification' and whose relation to their situations, including each other, is defined and mediated in terms of a system of culturally structured and shared symbols."[4] That definition was based on his "voluntaristic theory of action," but as seen from the point of view of the interaction of actors, rather than the actions of a single actor. Parsons gave a number of examples of social systems, including kinship systems, business firms, professional associations, and religious organizations.[5] A society is a specific type of social system, one "which attains the highest level of self-sufficiency as a system in relation to its environments."[6]

Parsons argued that all social systems must perform four functions in order to persist: *pattern maintenance*, which refers to maintaining the stability of institutionalized values, beliefs, ideologies, and so on; *goal attainment*, which refers to the problem of selecting, ordering, and attaining collective goals; *adaptation*, which refers to "providing disposable facilities independent of their relevance to any particular goal" as a general precondition to goal attainment; and *integration*, which refers to "the mutual adjustments of 'units' or subsystems from the point of view of their 'contributions' to the effective functioning of the system as a whole.[7] He also defined four "structures" by which social systems carry out these four functions: *values*, which are "conceptions of desirable types of social systems" and take primacy in the pattern-maintenance function; *norms*, which are "value components specified to appropriate levels in the structure of a social system [and] also specific modes of orientation for acting under the functional and situational conditions of particular collectivities and roles," and take primacy in the integration function; *collectivities*, which are group systems with "definite statuses of membership" and "some differentiation among members in relation to their statuses and functions within the collectivity, so that some categories of members are expected to do certain things which are not expected of other members," having primacy for the goal-attainment function; and *roles*, which define "a class of individuals who, through reciprocal expectations, are involved in a particular collectivity," and take primacy in the adaptation function.[8] These four structural components may vary independently of each other in different social systems, but in any given social system these structures are institutionalized in stable patterns with respect to each other.[9]

Of particular importance is the role of the institutionalized value system, since it is the primary method of legitimating the society's normative order:

> We have stressed the importance of cultural legitimation of a society's normative order because it occupies a superordinate position. It operates in the first instance through the institutionalization of a value-system. . . . Its subvalues, which are specifications of general value patterns, become parts of every concrete norm that is integrated into the legitimate order. The system of norms governing loyalties, then, must integrate the rights and obligations of various collectivities and their members not only with each other, but also with the bases of legitimation of the order as a whole.[10]

Thus, the institutionalized value system has two interrelated functions. On the general level, it implies that the social system of which it is a part is a desirable type of social system, and on the individual level, it generates subvalues that integrate individuals and collectivities with each other through the system of norms.

Parsons' concepts can be illustrated using a social system other than a society. Parsons cites the Roman Catholic Church as one such social system.[11] Structurally, that church can be seen as a bounded collectivity of individuals—i.e., there are reasonably definite methods to determine who is and who is not a member. These individuals are distributed in roles within the church (i.e., layman, priest, bishop, pope, etc.) that have different behavioral expectations. The roles are organized in a hierarchical normative order that coordinates their activities and enables the attainment of collective goals (e.g., conducting worship services, building churches and schools, etc.). The normative order is "legitimized" in terms of an institutionalized value system (the divinity of Jesus, the primacy of Peter and his successors, etc.) that implies that the organization of the Roman Catholic church is a desirable type of social system. The interrelationships between the four structural components allow the accomplishment of the functions Parsons says are necessary for the persistence of the Catholic Church as a social system: pattern maintenance, goal attainment, adaptation, and integration.

Parsons spent considerable time analyzing American society as a social system. Structurally, he described it as a bounded collectivity whose membership is defined by citizenship and in which roles are organized into a hierarchical normative order, permitting the accomplishment of collective goals. The hierarchical normative order is justified and legitimized through an institutionalized value system, which Parsons describes as "instrumental activism":

> It is oriented to control the action situation in the interest of range and quality of adaptation, but with more economic than political emphasis. In goal definition it is highly indefinite and pluralistic, being committed to a rather general direction of progress or improvement, without any clearly defined terminal goal. Economic production is highly valued as the most immediate focus

of adaptive capacity. Beyond that, however, we value particularly technology and science as means to productivity, and the maximization of opportunity for individuals and subcollectivities (manifested above all in concern with health and education). Moreover, we have a special set of attitudes toward organization and authority which might be summed up as involving, on the one hand, a pragmatic acceptance of authority in the interest of limited specifically approved goals, but, on the other hand, an objection to any pretensions of generalized superiority of status.[12]

Parsons argued that "the core of a society as a social system is ... its integrative subsystem," which he called "the societal community."[13] The term "refers to that aspect of the total society as a system, which forms a *Gemeinschaft*, which is the focus of solidarity or mutual loyalty of its members, and which constitutes the consensual base underlying its political integration," and is associated with the group of people who are considered "full citizens" of the society.[14] The societal community is a "single, bounded collectivity" whose normative system is defined as "the system of legitimate order."[15]

Because Parsons stated that the societal community "constitutes the consensual base underlying [society's] political integration," it is important to examine the concept closely. First, the consensus specifically concerns what Parsons calls "societal values," i.e., "conceptions of desirable societies" that are "distinguished from others types of values—such as personal ones—in that the category of object evaluated is the social system...."[16] Second, the consensus on these values is a matter of degree:

Insofar as this set of values is in fact held in common and is institutionalized, it is descriptive of the society as an empirical entity. This institutionalization is a matter of degree, however; for members of a going society will, to some extent, differ in their values even at the requisite level, and they will, to a certain degree, fail to act in accordance with the values they hold.[17]

This statement indicates that there are two respects in which the degree of consensus can vary: the uniformity of content (the extent to which values differ) and the degree of commitment (the extent to which people fail to act in accordance with their values). Third, the degree of consensus, as described by Parsons, is a separate question from the degree of "inclusiveness" of the societal community. For example, in his article "Full Citizenship for the Negro American?" Parsons states:

> This membership (in the societal community) is central to what it means to be defined, in the case of our own nation, as "an American"—hence it gives a special justification for the word order in the title of the present [article]... that it is the Negro American, not vice versa. The Negro slave could have been, and certainly was called, an "American Negro"—he was resident in the United States and owned by American citizens, but was not part of the societal community in the present sense.[18]

Thus, the societal community does not necessarily include all people in a given territorial unit. Parsons described the original American societal community as consisting of white, Anglo-Saxon Protestants and stated that other groups, such as Jews, Catholics, and Negroes, have been slowly "included" in the societal community over the years. He said the process was only completed for Catholics in 1960 with the election of John Kennedy as president, and was not completed yet for Negroes.[19] While membership in the societal community implies at least some degree of consensus with the value system, exclusion from that community implies neither consensus nor dissensus. To the extent that groups are not members of the societal community, their beliefs are irrelevant to it. The nature of the ideal society in Parsons' theory is now clear—it is what he called the "fully integrated" society.[20] Such a society is characterized by a totally inclusive societal community, so that no social groups are excluded from it. In addition, the consensus on the social values is characterized both by uniformity of content and high degree of commitment. Parsons recognized that such a society was purely hypothetical and that although some societies could be "well integrated," none could ever be "fully integrated."

"Getting Results in Interaction"

Parsons' theory, as presented so far, was intended as a solution to the Hobbesian problem of how social order is possible. Parsons had rejected the solution attributed to Locke and Spencer, that there was a natural community of interests among men.[21]

Similarly, he rejected the solution proposed by Hobbes himself that societies were based on force, calling that solution "palpably unacceptable"[22] and stating that "I start with the view that repudiates the idea that any political system that rests *entirely* on self-interest, force, or a combination of them, can be stable over any considerable period of time."[23] Parsons' solution to this problem was to focus on the normative order and the value consensus that legitimizes it, stating, "Normative order at the societal level contains a 'solution' to the problem posed by Hobbes—of preventing human relations from degenerating into a 'war of all against all.' "[24] But because there are variations in the degree of consensus within the societal community, and there are groups in the society who are either excluded entirely from or only partially included in the societal community, the "solution" proposed by Parsons is not yet complete. It is still necessary to explain the persistence of order despite an incomplete consensus. Thus, Parsons described "ways of getting results in interaction" in order to explain the existence and persistence of social order despite these problems.

He began with a general "paradigm of modes by which one acting unit—let us call him 'ego'—can attempt to get results by bringing to bear on another unit, which we may call 'alter,' some kind of *communicative operation:* call it 'pressure' if that term is understood in a non-pejorative sense."[25] That pressure can be directed at either alter's situation or his intentions and can involve either positive or negative sanctions. Power and its limiting case, force, were described as negative sanctions directed at alter's situation.[26] Parsons defined power as "generalized capacity to secure the performance of binding obligations by units in a system of collective organization when the obligations are legitimized with reference to their bearing on collective goals and where in case of recalcitrance there is a presumption of enforcement by negative situational sanctions."[27] Elsewhere he offered a shorter definition of power as "the capacity of a social system to mobilize resources to attain collective goals."[28] Force is the coercive end point or limiting case of power, involving "the use of control of the situation in which 'alter'—the unit that is the object of 'ego's' action—is subjected to *physical* means to prevent him from doing something ego does not wish him to do, to 'punish' him for doing something that, from ego's point of view, he should not have done (which may in turn be intended to deter him from doing similar things in the future), or to demonstrate 'symbolically' the capacity of ego to control the situation, even apart from ego's specific expectations that alter may desire to do things that are undesirable from ego's point of view."[29] Parsons argued that, while power must not be seen as a "simple linear function of the command of physical force," power is based on force in exactly the same way that money systems are based on gold.[30] Power as a generalized medium for controlling actions is dependent primarily on normative elements, rather than overtly coercive ones, so that the resort to force is comparable to returning to the use of gold instead of paper money in the economy. If that happens, the power system, just like the monetary system, will have largely disintegrated:

> Seen in this light the threat of coercive measures, or compulsion, without legitimation or justification, should not properly be called the use of power at all, but is the limiting case where power, losing its symbolic character, merges into an intrinsic instrumentality of securing compliance with wishes, rather than obligations. The monetary parallel is the use of a monetary metal as an instrument of barter where as a commodity it ceases to be an institutionalized medium of exchange at all.[31]

Parsons argued that power was primarily based on influence, and not on force, where influence was defined as "generalized capacity to persuade through contingent acceptance." Parsons continued:

> We have defined 'persuasion' as an offer of good reasons why alter should, in his own interest, act in accord with ego's wishes. The contingent positive sanction attached to persuasion is *acceptance*, which is an attitudinal as distinct from a situational sanction. ...Persuasion will involve a normative reference defining the sense in which the reasons offered are 'good'; this reference may be called the *justification* of their acceptance by alter. The benefits alter then receives are those of acceptance and consequent freedom to act within the context of membership.[32]

Parsons concluded that "power... as a generalized societal medium, depends overwhelmingly on a consensual element, i.e., the ordered institutionalization and exercise of influence, linking the power system to the higher-order societal consensus at the value level."[33]

The Role of Power in Parsons' Theory

Parsons' conclusion certainly seems to be a strong and direct contradiction to the most fundamental assumptions of conflict theory, making it necessary to explore his meaning very closely. First, Parsons associates "power" with "legitimation," "justification," and "obligation," while "force" is associated with "wishes, rather than obligations." It is important to recognize that all these terms refer to the institutionalized values of the social system being discussed. Using the example of the Catholic church, the prohibition on the use of artificial methods of birth control is not merely the "wish" of the pope but an "obligation" that is "legitimized" and "justified" by the institutionalized values of the church. The point is that the demands of a particular normative order are "legitimate and justified obligations" only within the context of its particular institutionalized values, and there is no necessary relation between those values and what are usually thought of as "universal" or "absolute" values. In fact, sometimes those demands directly contradict what are usually considered moral values, such as was the case in Nazi Germany. The Third Reich was certainly a social system in Parsons' sense,[34] and its institutionalized values legitimated and justified the extermination of the Jews as an obligation to the state. The terms "legitimate and justified obligation" must therefore be understood in the context of an explanation of the existence and persistence of social order, whether that social order be found in the United States or in Nazi Germany, and must not be understood as referring to morality.

Second, when Parsons stated that "power... depends overwhelmingly on a consensual element," he was specifically referring to the absence of the use of overt physical force—i.e., the end point of power. The example of the Catholic church as a social system can illustrate his point, since that church exercises considerable power over its members while possessing (in the modern world) no capacity for overt physical force at all. In social systems that have the ability to use physical force, it is still unusual for that to be the primary means of exercising power:

> ... in most power systems, physical force is not the most important operative sanction but a "reserve" sanction available for

emergencies. In particular, it is not likely to be resorted to internally or even directly threatened in a stable power system, except
in minor instances like routine police functions in attempting to
control ordinary criminals. In certain type of crisis situations,
however, it may come to dominate the social scene.[35]

Even in social systems where there is a clear absence of a general
consensus of values, such as in prisons or unpopular dictatorships, power is still normally exercised without overt use of
force. The persistence of such power systems is explained by
what Parsons called the "confidence" in the system—i.e., the
expectation that superior force can be marshaled to overwhelm
any specific challenge to the system that might be mounted.[36]
Parsons also argued, however, that all power systems are ultimately "insolvent" in the sense that if all potential challenges to
the system were made simultaneously, the power system would
be defeated.[37] "Confidence" in the power system is part of what
Parsons referred to as the "penumbra of effect" of force, an effect
that extends "well beyond the direct effectiveness in the context
of deterrence or compulsion."[38] That effect is associated primarily
with the "demonstration of capacity to act," such as the use of
exemplary force.

The Role of Force in Parsons' Theory

The above discussion indicates that force and its penumbra of
effect emerges in Parsons' theory as a source of social order
separate from and in a reciprocal relationship with the institutionalized system of normative order. Parsons stated, for example, that force is "the means which, again independent of any
institutionalized system of order, can be assumed to be 'intrins-
ically' the most effective in the context of deterrence, when
means of effectiveness which *are* dependent on institutionalized
order are insecure or fail."[39] That is, to the extent that social order
is not based on normative elements, it can be based on force and
its penumbra of effect. That description would match the general
perception of repressive dictatorships, in which, it can be argued, the social order is based not on a consensus of values but
rather on the overt and potential uses of force. However, such an

argument does not contradict Parsons' general conclusion that "power... depends overwhelmingly on a consensual element,"[40] since Parsons used the term "consensual" with a very broad meaning. Specifically, it means that in the normal exercise of power, there is no necessity to resort to overt physical force, and thus the power system operates with the "consent" of the populace. That "consent" is based on "confidence" in the power system that any specific attempt to resist will be overwhelmed by force. This broad definition of the term "consensual" is implicit in Parsons' definition of power as essentially symbolic, while force is defined as the coercive end point of power.[41] Because the term "force" is limited to the end point, the term "power" encompasses all of what Parsons himself called the "penumbra" of force. That statement does not contradict Parsons' definition of power as involving "legitimation," since even in repressive dictatorships there is normally an institutionalized value system that legitimizes and justifies the existing normative order, and without that value system, the degeneration of the power system to overt force would probably be rapid and total. Thus, social order must be seen as deriving from two complementary sources: the institutionalized value system and the overt and potential uses of force.

The fact that force apparently plays a significant role in the maintenance of social order in repressive dictatorships would be explained in Parsons' theory by arguing that a substantial proportion of the population is either entirely excluded from or only partially integrated into the societal community. Parsons stated:

> A society must constitute a societal *community* that has an adequate level of integration or solidarity and a distinctive membership status. This does not preclude relations of control or symbiosis with population elements only partially integrated into the societal community, such as the Jews in the Diaspora, but there must be a core of more fully integrated members.[42]

In the case of a repressive dictatorship, the "core of more fully integrated members" consists of members of the ruling group, as well as those who are closely associated with or supporters of the ruling group. The institutionalized values of the social system are in fact a "consensus of values" among those individuals, and they constitute the societal community. To what extent the societal community is representative of the population in general, and what proportion of the population is subject to "relations of control" by the societal community, is another question entirely.

Consensus of Values vs. Institutionalized Value System

Parsons identified the "consensus of values" with the "institutionalized value system," stating, "It is the members' consensus on value orientations with respect to their own society, then, that defines the institutionalization of value patterns."[43] But the term "consensus of values" as used by Parsons is somewhat misleading. The term is normally taken to refer to a consensus among all the members of a society, but Parsons used it to refer to a consensus only among those who are members of the societal community—i.e., the "core of more fully integrated members" who can be considered "full citizens." The question of what proportion of the population is included in the societal community is in principle an empirical one, although it would be difficult to achieve an operational definition of membership in the societal community, given the fact that Parsons described it as a matter of degree. One could speculate, however, that in a well-integrated country, the proportion would be reasonably high, while in countries where unpopular dictatorships are imposed by force, the proportion would be quite low. But one of the major criteria that Parsons gives for membership in the societal community is agreement with the institutionalized values. Thus, the definition is somewhat circular: the societal community is said to define a consensus of values that are institutionalized in the social system, but membership in the societal community is partially determined by agreement with the institutionalized values. Because of these difficulties of definition, the concept of a "consensus of values" among a "societal community" is relatively unsatisfactory.

The significance of these values, however, is not that they are the consensus of values among a particular group within the population but that they are the values that are institutionalized in the social system. These are the values that legitimize and justify the normative order, without which no social order would be possible. In contrast to the concept of "consensus of values," the concept of "institutionalized values" is rather easily definable in every society. Parsons described "instrumental activism" as the institutionalized values of American society, and there is likely to be only minor disagreement with that description as long as it is not also maintained that these represent a consensus of values among the American people. The institutionalized values of other societies can be described with the same relative ease and with the same likelihood of at least a general agreement. These values function to legitimize and justify the normative order even when the societal community comprises only a small proportion of the population, as has been argued in the case of repressive dictatorships. In societies such as these, it seems inappropriate to use the term "consensus of values" to describe the institutionalized values, although Parsons' use of it is appropriate, given his definition. But as mentioned above, the term conveys the idea of a consensus among all (or nearly all) the people of a society, something that is decidedly not true in many societies.

The question of whether some form of consensus exists among all (or nearly all) the people of a society is quite relevant to any discussion of the consensus-conflict debate. But that question would be difficult to ask if the phrase "consensus of values" is taken to mean only a consensus among some subgroup of the population, with no indication of the proportion of the population included in the subgroup. Accordingly, the phrase "consensus of values" is reserved for the broader phenomenon of a *consensus among all (or nearly all) of the people of a society* in the remainder of the discussion of Parsons' theory. The use of that phrase is thus distinguished from Parsons' use, where it referred specifically to a consensus among those in the societal community. In contrast, the "institutionalized values" of a society, remaining with Parsons' definition, are considered to be those values that are embodied in the institutions of a society, that function to legitimize and justify the existing normative order, and on which social order in the society is principally based.

Those values represent a consensus only among the core of more fully integrated members of the society who can be considered full citizens (the societal community).

Parsons identified the consensus of values with the institutionalized values of the social system. But with the new definition of "consensus of values" given the above, such identification is appropriate only in the case of a well-integrated society. In that case, the societal community would incorporate virtually the entire population, so that the institutionalized values would represent a consensus among nearly all the people of the society. In a poorly integrated society, however, these two concepts would diverge, and the extent of the divergence between them would be measured by the degree of force needed to maintain social order.

The utility of distinguishing between "consensus of values" and "institutionalized values" in the descriptions of real (as opposed to fully integrated) societies can also be illustrated in the case of revolutions, where one social system is entirely replaced by another social system. Parsons' theory has frequently been criticized for its inability to describe such changes, and even his close collaborator Edward Shils has stated: "There is truth in this charge."[44] Consider the Iranian revolution in which supporters of the Ayatollah Khomeini overthrew the government of the Shah Reza Pahlevi. Immediately prior to the revolution, the institutionalized values of Iranian society were those values generally associated with the Shah (modernization and Westernization); after the revolution, the institutionalized values were those generally associated with the Ayatollah (traditionalism and militant Islam). In each case, these institutionalized values functioned to legitimize and justify the normative order present in Iranian society at the time, and their content can be defined relatively clearly in the same way that Parsons defined the content of the institutionalized values of American society. In each case, too, those values represented a consensus of values among a core of more fully integrated members. The question of whether there was a consensus of values among all (or nearly all) the people of Iran is much more complicated. There were certainly many who still supported the Shah and his family even after the revolution. Others opposed both the Shah and the Ayatollah and desired a moderate, pro-Western government; still others were separatists and wished to establish independent governments in various of the provinces; and still others were communists and wished to establish a pro-Soviet government. Iran at the time was not well integrated, and to state that there was a consensus of values in it would be misleading. It would be more appropriate to describe Iran as Parsons had described Germany during the Nazi regime. He maintained that it would be a mistake to consider either the monarchy of the Kaiser, the Weimar Republic, or the Nazi regime as the "true Germany," since Germany was not a fully integrated society.

> This lack of full integration... means that the underlying institutional foundations of national behavior are not as firm as they would be in a better integrated system.... The expectation may then be that not too radical an alteration in the *balance* of forces could have 'disproportionately' great effects on immediate behavior. This is, indeed, what happened in the shift from Weimar to the Nazi regime. The Germany of Weimar was not spurious—a 'deceitful mask' as many are now inclined to feel. That would be as serious an error as the previous one of supposing that it was the one 'true Germany' once the 'bad' monarchy had been eliminated.[45]

Germany had been organized into three very different social systems, where the societal communities of these three systems consisted of substantially different sets of people. Certainly the "core of more fully integrated members" in the Nazi social system was different from the "core" of the Weimar Republic, which was also different from the "core" of the Kaiser's monarchy. Parsons predicted the possibility of a fourth social system if there was "not too radical an alteration in the *balance* of forces." In fact, two new social systems eventually replaced the Nazi social system, at least one of which was completely different from any of the earlier three—the communist social system of the German Democratic Republic. Thus, within the short space of about forty years, one set of modern, educated European people was successively organized into four very different social systems—monarchic, democratic, fascist, and communist.

Society vs. Social System

Despite the fact that Parsons recognized that social systems could be replaced by other social systems, his theory described societies in terms of whatever social system happened to exist at the time, and the problem of social order was phrased in terms of the existence of those whose values deviated from the institutionalized values of that social system. Parsons' theory is like a picture of the society at a specific point in time. But if one views the same society over a period of time, the picture changes. For example, if one views Germany as a social system throughout the period of this century, then the set of people who are defined as a problem for social order keeps changing. At least some of those who are defined as the problem in one social system become the fully integrated core of the next social system.

By viewing societies *as social systems*, Parsons' perspective necessarily entails standing in the position of the dominant social group (the societal community) and phrasing the problem in terms of how that group can achieve order in a Hobbesian world:

> Hence the stable equilibrium of the interactive process is the fundamental point of reference for the analysis of social control just as it is for the theory of deviance. But our attention will be focused on one aspect of the interactive process, the forestalling of the kinds of deviant tendencies we have analyzed earlier in the chapter, and the processes by which, once under way, these processes can be counteracted and the system brought back, in the relevant respects, to the old equilibrium state. This latter is, of course, a theoretical point of reference. In empirical fact no social system is perfectly equilibrated and integrated.[46]

The same stance is assumed in the discussion of "ways to get results in social interaction." The term "ego" is used to describe the person who stands at the fully integrated core of a social system and attempts to get "alter" to conform to its normative order. The presumption must be that alter is not fully integrated into the social system, or there would be no problem with his behavior. There is no discussion of whether alter might be integrated into a conflicting social system and might be attempting to integrate ego into that. In general, the presumption is that all alters are to be treated as individuals whose organization is considered only in the context of ego's social system. Another example of Parsons' stance is his description of a strike as the situation in which a unit in a power system withdraws its cooperation and obstructs the process of collective goal attainment in order to gain a measure of control.[47] There is no question that this is an accurate and appropriate description of a strike, as long as one views the industry *as a social system*. In that case, the management of the industry is, in Parsons' words, the "leadership" of the collectivity, and labor is a unit within it. The strike is seen as a conflict between a *unit* of the collectivity, and the collectivity as a whole. The "leadership" of the collectivity is not seen merely as another unit in it, but rather as its fully integrated core, defining the value consensus, the normative order, the collective goal attainment, etc. There is no other way to view industry *as a social system* except to·stand in the position of the management and look outward at the rest of the organization.

Parsons took that same point of reference in his discussion of American society. Parsons described the original core of American society as white, Anglo-Saxon, and Protestant, and then described "the substantial disturbances and anxieties over the presence of such large 'foreign' groups in our midst...."[48] Clearly, his reference point is with that core, looking outward at the "foreigners," and this is appropriate as long as the society is viewed as a functioning social system. An alternative viewpoint would be to stand outside all of the groups, describing one dominant and a number of subordinate groups. Such an observer would describe the problems of integrating the subordinate groups into the dominant group, as did Parsons, but would describe many other things as well, such as attempts by subordinate groups to achieve their own goals.

Because he looked at societies as social systems, Parsons described the values held by members of the societies in terms of their relative deviations from the institutionalized values (the consensus of values among those in the societal community). The institutionalized values of a society can be compared to a "zero point" on a graph, where other values are defined in terms of a set of coordinates originating at that zero point. It might be inferred, although Parsons did not imply it, that the zero point is also approximately at the center of the value graph, but that will be the case only if the society is well integrated. Otherwise, the point can be literally anywhere on the graph. When social systems change, the zero point changes, and all values in society will be described in terms of a new set of coordinates. The only general statement that can be made is that the further the institutionalized values are from the approximate center of the value graph (i.e., whatever consensus of values there might be among all or nearly all of the population), the more social order must depend on force and its penumbra of effectiveness. If sufficient force is not available, the social system may be overthrown and replaced. Parsons' theory does not maintain that the institutionalized values of a social system necessarily represent or even approximate a consensus of values among all or nearly all of the people of that society. One would have to ascertain the degree to which social order depends on force and its penumbra of effectiveness to estimate the disparity between the institutionalized values and whatever consensus of values there might be. In those societies where considerable force is required to maintain order, it could be assumed either that no consensus of values exists at all or that the institutionalized values do not reflect the consensus that does exist.

Consensus and the Societal Community

Even in societies in which social order is not dependent to any extensive degree on force and its penumbra of effect, there is no implication in Parsons' theory that the institutionalized values are the result of a free expression of opinion by all members of the population about the nature of a desirable social system. Rather, the institutionalized values begin as a consensus among a subgroup of the population (the societal community), where that subgroup may be quite small compared to the entire population—e.g., the Bolsheviks during the Russian Revolution. But that subgroup becomes the dominant power group in the society, and extends its ideas outward to the rest of society through persuasion and ultimately through force, those being the two modes in Parsons' theory by which political power is exercised. The "inclusion" of other groups in the social system is not the result of their free expression of beliefs, but rather reflects the ability of the dominant power group to mold the beliefs and behaviors of other groups to conform to the social system's demands. While that ability is not unlimited, it is much more extensive than is often acknowledged, as the repeated reorganizations of German society in this century demonstrate.

The only time within the context of Parsons' theory at which the institutionalized values might actually represent a full and free consensus of opinion is when those values are being formulated in the original societal community. Even in highly integrated societies where there is a widespread consensus of values among disparate parts of the population, it might still be possible to identify the institutionalized values as properly the values of one particular subgroup of the population. That subgroup would normally be in some sense the lineal descendants of the original societal community, and there would still be a sense in which the institutionalized values represent a full and free consensus of opinion on desirable social systems, as opposed to a consensus that has been shaped and molded through persuasion and ultimately force. That is the true societal community—the "core" of *most* fully integrated members—of the social system.

In the case of the American social system, Parsons argued that the institutionalized values, as quoted above, were those of "instrumental activism," focusing on progress, economic production, technology and science, maximization of opportunity, and authority without pretensions of superiority. It appears that the "core" of most fully integrated members of the American social system is what Parsons called "the elite within the economy":

> ... given the nature of an industrial society, a relatively well-defined elite or leadership group should be expected to develop in the business world; it is out of the question that power should be diffused equally among an indefinite number of very small units, as the ideal of pure competition and a good deal of the ideology of business itself would have it.[49]

There is a sense in which this group is the lineal descendant of the original American societal community, being also predominantly upper-middle- and upper-class adult, white, Anglo-Saxon, Protestant males. As Parsons pointed out, there has been some shift in this group from property owners to professional executives, but otherwise the groups are remarkably similar. The individuals in this group might be expected to spontaneously and freely express the values of instrumental activism as descriptive of desirable social systems, independent of any attempts to persuade or force them to do so, because there is an immediate and obvious sense in which those values are personally beneficial to them.[50] But as one moves away from this group in a social structural sense, it is less apparent whether the values of instrumental activism are personally beneficial to other individuals and groups in society. The allegiance of those individuals and groups may then depend on the persuasive influence of those whose commitment to the values is more spontaneous. For individuals and groups who, in a social structural sense, are furthest from the "core," the values of instrumental activism may appear to be quite harmful to their interests. Those groups may ignore the persuasion of the more fully integrated members of society, who would then have to resort to force and its penumbra of effect to maintain social order.

Theory, Purpose, and Descriptions of Contemporary Societies

The above discussion has been an attempt to illuminate the implications of Parsons' view of societies as social systems and his consequent stance at the fully integrated core of those systems. The purpose was not to demonstrate that Parsons' perspective was somehow inadequate, but to argue that it is intimately related to his purpose in theorizing. The question he addressed was not to empirically describe existing social systems—in fact, he explicitly denied he was doing that[51]—or to describe how social systems change over time. Rather, he was concerned with how order could be achieved in a Hobbesian world. What he said about Durkheim was true also of himself: "'Solidarity' cannot be treated as a component for Durkheim's purposes because it is his dependent variable; he is concerned with the conditions on which it depends."[52] Parsons' theories can be viewed as similar to a multiple regression equation in which the dependent variable is social order. The choice of the independent variables (i.e., the topics that Parsons discussed) was determined by their effect on social order, and not by their existence as social phenomena. Only those aspects of the independent variables that contributed to or detracted from social order were discussed, while those that were irrelevant to it dropped out of the equation.

Despite the fact that they were not his primary focus of concern, Parsons' theories do contain a number of descriptions of contemporary societies. Parsons emphasized that the fully integrated society is a "limiting case" at one end of the spectrum of possible societies, while the Hobbesian state of war is the "limiting case" at the other end.[53] Neither of these societies ever exists in reality, so that, contrary to the views of Comte and Durkheim, Parsons believed that the "normal" state of society was at least somewhat "anomic." Parsons recognized that societies could exist that "rest *entirely* on self-interest, force, or a combination of them." He only insisted that such a political system could not be "stable over any considerable period of time."[54] He also recognized that the societal communities that were "familiar in our intellectual traditions" have been integrated primarily on the basis of the "command of political power and wealth" and argued that the "new societal community" must go beyond those factors and achieve integration on the basis of "value commitments and mechanisms of influence."[55] Elsewhere, Parsons discussed the present situation of Western societies more extensively:

> Western society has in all its recent history been relatively highly stratified, involving institutionalized positions of power, privilege, and prestige for certain elements. In the nature of the case the sentiments and symbols associated with these prestige elements have been integrated with those institutionalized in the society as a whole. . . . It is in the nature of a highly differentiated social structure that such privileged elements should be in a position to exercise influence on the power relations of the society through channels other than those open to the masses, through political intrigue, financial influence, and so on. Hence, with the progressive increase in the acuteness of a generalized state of anomie it is to be expected that such elements, which have been privileged in relation to a traditional social order, should, within the limits provided by the particular situation, develop forms of

activity, sometimes approaching conspiratorial patterns, which in these terms may be regarded as a defense of their vested interests.[56]

Finally, Parsons stated: "I believe that class conflict is endemic in our modern industrial type of society,"[57] and he discussed "the following principal aspects of the tendency to develop class conflict in our type of social system":

1. Our inherently competitive system produces winners and losers, with a tendency towards resentment on the part of the losers. "The extent to which the system is institutionalized in terms of genuine standards of fair competition is the critical problem...."
2. Discipline and authority are inevitable, but "the structuring in terms of an opposition of sentiments and interests between those in authority and those subject to it is endemic in such a system...."
3. "There does seem to be a general tendency for the strategically placed, the powerful, to exploit the weaker or less favorably placed...."
4. "There seem to be inherent tendencies for those who are structurally placed at notably different points in a differentiated social structure to develop different 'cultures'..."
5. "The differences in the situation of people placed at different points in the occupational system and of the consequences for family income and living conditions seem to lead to a notable differentiation of family type ... [and] under certain circumstances can become an important factor in pushing toward cumulative separation of classes and potential conflict between them...."
6. "Absolute equality of opportunity in the occupational system, which is, in a sense, the ideal type of norm for such a system, is in practice impossible...."[58]

Parsons' reservations about class conflict did not concern its existence as a social phenomenon but rather its role in the social process:

I do not, however, believe that the case has been made for believing that [class conflict] is the dominant feature of every [industrial] society and of its dynamic development. Its relation to other elements of tension, conflict, and dynamic change is a complex matter, about which we cannot attempt the Marxian order of generalization with certainty until our science is much further developed than it is today.[59]

Dahrendorf's Description of Contemporary Societies

Parsons did not reject the possibility of a class conflict theory of social change, and argued only that the case had not been made. Ten years after Parsons wrote those words, the English translation of Ralf Dahrendorf's *Class and Class Conflict in Industrial Society* was published, the explicit intention of which was to make the case to which Parsons had referred. Dahrendorf did not deny the relevance or validity of functional analyses such as that of Parsons, but he argued that there were sociological phenomena that such analyses could not explain. Specifically, he pointed to the workers' uprising in East Berlin in 1953, which he said could not be considered "functional" within the context of the East German social system:

> Evidently, the uprising of the 17th of June is neither due to nor productive of integration in East Germany society. It documents and produces not stability, but instability. It contributes to the disruption, not the maintenance, of the existing system. It testifies to dissensus rather than consensus. The integration model tells us little more than that there are certain "strains" in the "system." In fact, in order to cope with problems of this kind we have to replace the integration theory of society by a different and, in many ways, contradictory model.[60]

The contradictory model that he proposed was part of a general theory whose purpose was "the explanation of structure changes in terms of group conflict."[61] Dahrendorf continued: "This purpose is therefore neither purely descriptive nor related to problems of integration and coherence in or of society." Thus, although the "models of society" on which Parsons' and Dahrendorf's theories were based were seen as "contradictory," the theories themselves were conceived by Dahrendorf to be complementary, where the one explained social order in terms of consensus and the other explained social change in terms of conflict. The quotation by Parsons about the role of class conflict in the social process indicates that he believed that such a complementary theory was at least possible.

Dahrendorf began with an extensive critique of Marx's theories. He attributed to Marx the argument that history is a sequence of epochs, where in each epoch the social structure constitutes a system "in the full sense of the functional notion."[62] In particular, preindustrial society, in Marx's theory, could be said to be "well integrated" in the Parsonian sense, being based on a "system of norms and values which guaranteed and legitimated the order":

> The "distinctions of rank" in preindustrial societies of even the Eighteenth Century rested as much on a myth of tradition, an intricate system of age-old, often codified rights and duties, as on the comparatively crude gradations of property, power, and prestige.... Its claim to the legitimacy of the present was also a product of history or, perhaps, an ideology.... The power of the landlord was not based on his having money, land, or prestige, but on his being a landlord as his fathers had been for time immemorial. The conditions of the master craftsman, his journeymen and apprentices, and even that of the laborer resembled that of the landlord in their legitimation by the authority of tradition. In this sense, preindustrial society was what contemporary sociologists like to call, with a somewhat doubtful expression, a 'relatively static social order.'"[63]

Dahrendorf referred to the legitimated positions of rank in preindustrial society as "statuses." But beginning with the industrial revolution, there grew up in society two new strata for which there was no historical precedent, "no tradition of rank, no myth of legitimacy, no 'prestige of descent.' "[64] They were "characterized solely by the crude indices of possession and nonpossession, of domination and subjection," and were "intruders in a system of inherited values and messengers of a new system." It was these strata, the "bourgeoisie" and the "proletariat," that are described by the term "class," so that the term refers specifically to "unlegitimated" rank.[65] The creation of these classes as a result of the developing forces of production introduced anomie into the well-integrated, preindustrial society.[66]

Within each of the two classes, the individuals had generally similar life situations based on the fact that they were similarly located in the social structure—i.e., had a similar relationship to the means of production. That relationship determined the distribution of scarce resources, including property, prestige, and power. Consequently, the individuals of each class had common interests that were diametrically opposed to the common interests of those in the other class—one being in favor of maintaining the status quo, the other being in favor of changing it. These "classes in themselves" coalesced into "classes for themselves" as they began to come into conflict with each other as groups rather than merely as individuals. Marx believed that the necessary outcome of that conflict was revolutionary rather than evolutionary change, and the establishment of a new social system.

Dahrendorf then described a number of changes in society since Marx wrote.[67] First, he argued, the essential feature of modern society is that it is industrial, and capitalism is but one form of industrial society. Second, a number of developments had occurred which tended to diminish the level and change the nature of conflict in society, although they did not eliminate it. Capital has decomposed into ownership and control, and labor has decomposed into skilled and unskilled workers. In addition, there is a whole new class of white-collar workers and bureaucrats who are difficult to classify in a capital/labor dichotomy. Social mobility has increased tremendously, and there has been a process of increasing equalization among all groups in society. Finally, conflict between labor and capital has to a great extent been institutionalized in terms of common rules, negotiation procedures, etc., and the opposing party has been recognized as a legitimate interest group.

Dahrendorf went on to provide a sociological critique of Marx's theory. First, he accepted Marx's basic point that there are sources of social structural change that are not functional within the existing social system. Dahrendorf emphasized that these were *in addition to,* not instead of, the sources of change described in structural-functional theories.[68] Dahrendorf agreed with Marx that this nonfunctional source of structural change was conflict between aggregates of men, and that these conflicts are not random occurrences, as they appear in the theories of the functionalists, but are necessary outgrowths of the structure of societies.

Having accepted these basic assumptions of the Marxist approach, Dahrendorf then rejected a number of other assumptions.[69] Marx had argued that class conflict was the only source

of social structural change. Dahrendorf argued that class conflict
was only one form of social conflict, that various forms of social
conflict can result in social structural change, and that structural
change can result from other "endogenous" factors besides conflict within the social system, such as the separation of ownership from control, as well as from "exogenous" factors such as
invasion and conquest. Marx had also argued that revolutionary
upheaval was the normal and inevitable outcome of class conflict,
but Dahrendorf declared that there were many possible outcomes. In addition, Marx argued that classes were always mani-
festly antagonistic groups. Dahrendorf agreed that classes as
conflict groups cannot come into existence except in an antagonistic relationship with another class, but added that such a
statement says nothing about the intensity or violence of the
antagonism, which can be anything from a civil war to contract
negotiations. Marx had used the criterion of ownership of property as the determinant of social class, but Dahrendorf argued
that property ownership was only one form of the social relations
of "legitimate" authority. It was Dahrendorf's contention that
class is best defined in terms of the possession or lack of authority in any given social organization. He stated that there is a
general correlation between the possession of authority in social
organizations and the distribution of social rewards, but otherwise he abandoned the idea that classes are in any sense economic groups. Marx had also argued that those who possessed
economic power necessarily also possessed political power, but
Dahrendorf argued that the state is a separate social organization
from those of business and industry, and that the relationship
between them is empirical. Finally, Dahrendorf said that any
given individual could be defined as a member of a class according to his role within a particular social organization where,
depending on whether he does or does not possess authority, he
plays the role of either dominance or subjection. The two major
social organizations Dahrendorf discussed were the individual's
political organization (the state) and economic organization
(work), but the analysis applied equally to all other social organizations. Obviously, dominance in one social organization does
not imply dominance in any other, so no individual is uniquely a
member of one class or the other. Dahrendorf admitted that the

concept of class as he defined it was not very useful for descriptive purposes, but claimed that within the context of any given social organization it was useful as the fundamental category of a theory of structural change.

Conflict in Contemporary Societies

As his basic category in the theory, Dahrendorf took from Weber the term "imperatively coordinated association." Dahrendorf used this term to describe the same social organizations that Parsons described with the term "social systems," but emphasized authority relations in those organizations:

> "Social system" is a very general concept applicable to all types of organization; and we shall want to employ an equally general concept which differs from that of social system by emphasizing a different aspect of the same organizations....Imperative coordination, or authority, is a type of social organization.... It appears justifiable to use the term "association" in such a way as to imply the coordination of organized aggregates of roles by domination and subjection. The state, a church, an enterprise, but also a political party, a trade union, and a chess club are associations in this sense. In all of them, authority relations exist; for all of them, conflict analysis is therefore applicable.... In looking at social organizations not in terms of their integration and coherence but from the point of view of their structure of coercion and constraint, we regard them as [imperatively coordinated] associations rather than as social systems. Because social organizations are also associations, they generate conflicts of interest and become the birthplace of conflict groups. [70]

Parsons' theory focused on the commonalities present in social organizations, while Dahrendorf's focused on the potential for conflict inherent in the fact that authority is normally distributed dichotomously in them. Those who possess authority in an association constitute a "quasi-group" in that they share a position with identical latent interests. [71] Those who do not possess authority also constitute a "quasi-group." Whether these quasi-groups will be organized into interest groups sharing manifest interests depends on a variety of technical, political, social, and psychological conditions. Dahrendorf's theory described those conditions, as well as the factors that affected the intensity and the violence of the resulting class conflict and the effect of conflict on the radicalness and suddenness of structural change.[72]

Dahrendorf denied that conflict could be suppressed over any considerable length of time, and also that societies were possible in which conflicts were actually resolved.[73] However, he argued that conflicts could be "regulated" in a society so as to reduce the level of violence associated with them. There are three prerequisites for the effective regulation of conflict.[74] The first is the recognition that one is in a conflict situation by acknowledging that one's opponent has the right to make a case. This is to be distinguished from acknowledging that the case one's opponent is making is "right." The second prerequisite is the formation of interest groups. Citing Simmel and Coser, he argued that it is only by providing organized channels for the expression of grievances and hostilities that social life is able to continue. Without such channels, relations between antagonistic groups would be sundered. The third is the evolution of certain "rules of the game" that can provide a formal framework for the relations between the parties in conflict. The presence of these three prerequisites does not guarantee that conflict will be regulated, but Dahrendorf says that regulation is impossible without them.[75]

This process is quite similar to what Durkheim described as the evolution of regulations in organic societies. The difference, however, is that Durkheim argued that these rules applied to all people in the society, while Dahrendorf pointed out that different groups participate in the process of forming these rules to different degrees. To the extent that a group participates in the process of forming the rules, the regulation of conflict will be effective, since the group develops legitimate channels to pursue its values and interests, as well as to express its hostilities and grievances. For groups that do not participate in it, the process does not provide similar channels, so that conflicts involving these groups are unregulated.[76] Unregulated conflicts generally either are suppressed or are expressed in socially unacceptable ways defined as crime and other forms of social deviance.

In a later work, Dahrendorf stated that class conflict, and group conflict in general, was merely a special case of a more general response to the relations of constraint. The general response includes both individual competition and collective action, which he states are "in principle mutually convertible... [and] basically equivalent expressions of the same great social force, contest."[77] Dahrendorf argued that class conflict becomes necessary only when "large numbers of individuals cannot realize their interests by individual endeavor."[78] In other situations, such as where there is high social mobility, most individuals will not join in collective action, since there is no need for them to do so. However, even in the most open and mobile societies, some individuals must necessarily lose out in the competition, and will be unable to realize their interests individually. Those individuals will tend to coalesce into conflict groups, so that group conflict will be present to some degree in every society.

Dahrendorf conceded that his analysis of the substance of conflict between authority and subjects had been highly formal, limited to statements about structured interests in favor of maintaining versus changing the status quo.[79] To fill the gap, he introduced the concept of "life chances."[80] Dahrendorf defined the term "chance," following Weber, as the structurally determined probability of the occurence of certain events, in particular those events that bring about satisfaction of interests, wants, and needs.[81] Life chances, he stated,

> are (in principle) measurable possibilities to realize needs, wants, and interests in, or at times against, a given social context. They are the substratum of social structures, in which life chances are therefore organized. They are also the motive force of social processes, which are therefore about life chances.[82]

Life chances are functions of two elements: ligatures, which are allegiances, bonds, or linkages that anchor the person to a social position and role and give it meaning; and options, which are possibilities of choice or opportunity, alternatives for action within the social structure.[83] Life chances are a function of both elements, since "ligatures without options are oppressive, whereas options without bonds are meaningless."[84] Modernization has generally meant a tremendous expansion of life chances, but this has been mostly a function of the expansion of options at the price of the disruption of linkages. That disruption "is, of course, the prevailing theme of social analysis from Durkheim and Tönnies to Weber and Parsons."[85] But that social analysis focused only on the ligatures of society without any analysis of the options associated with those ligatures, and Dahrendorf held that the "immobility" of a society without options is as undesirable as the "anomie" of a society without ligatures.[86] Dahrendorf also argued that the "apparently inverse relation" between options and ligatures in the modern world was "an empirical rather than a logical condition," and that

> ... it is possible to have both choices and linkages, and that the growth of one does not necessarily mean the decline of the other. What we are aiming at here is of course that most complex of ideals (a version perhaps of that elusive value, public happiness), a liberal society that is not libertine, a structure of authority that is not authoritarian, a social order that is not informed by law-and-order hysteria, thus a world in which choices are more than invitation for endless *actes gratuites,* and bonds are more than painful restrictions of individual development.[87]

In fact, he considered that life chances had been continually expanding throughout human history in just such a way.

While Dahrendorf's earlier theory had addressed the questions of the intensity and violence of class conflict, the addition of the concept of life chances allowed him to address the questions of the substance and the direction of conflict.[88] Social conflict, he stated, is about life chances—i.e., options embedded in ligatures. It is about the struggle either to acquire more life chances or to defend the share of life chances one already has within the prevailing linkages. Social conflict becomes class conflict when these two positions are associated with the dichotomous distribution of authority within an imperatively coordinated association.

Dahrendorf seemed to imply that there was a necessary relationship between possession of authority in an imperatively coordinated association and increased numbers of life chances, but he did not make any substantive argument defending that implication. Much easier to defend would be the assertion that there is a general correlation between the two factors but no necessary relation. That would be similar to Dahrendorf's argument about the relation between authority and social rewards. Such a correlation would be quite high in the larger and more prominent associations, such as the state and industry, but might be small or nonexistent in obscure associations, such as a chess club. Where there is no relationship between possession of authority and number of life chances, the term "class conflict" becomes meaningless within the context of Dahrendorf's theory, and structural change in that association would develop from other endogenous or exogenous sources, or would not occur at all.[89]

The Relation Between Form and Content

Dahrendorf's place in the conflict tradition is apparent, but because he took his fundamental question from Marx, it might be thought that he belongs in the radical conflict branch with Plato, Rousseau, and Marx. But Dahrendorf rejects the basic assumption of that branch: the possibility of an nonantagonistic society. He argued that conflict is an attribute of all societies at all times, stating, "It seems to me necessary to emphasize in the strongest possible terms the assumption of the universality of conflict."[90] He goes on to associate conflict with life itself: "It appears that not only in social life, but wherever there is life, there is conflict. May we perhaps go so far as to say that conflict is a condition necessary for life to be possible at all?"[91] Thus, unlike the radicals, Dahrendorf seems to view human nature as inherently conflictual, so that his theory takes the form of a sociological conflict theory, comparable to those of Machiavelli and Simmel. Like their theories, Dahrendorf's theory primarily described and analyzed real societies, rather than hypothetical ideal ones. The "ideal" society was described in it as the "best" of existing societies, but it was not said to be consensual. The theory takes on the nonevaluative, "objective" character of sociological conflict theories in that there is no indication in the analyses which positions in the conflict are "legitimate" and which are "illegitimate."

Dahrendorf's view of the inevitability of conflict in societies was derived in part from the views of Karl Popper, who had attacked the "utopianism" of Plato and Marx in his work *The Open Society and Its Enemies*.[92] Popper's fundamental point can be summarized: "We cannot know, we can only guess." The problem with utopian views is that they leave no room for error, that they are not "open" to change as problems within them arise. Dahrendorf argued that every human institution produces unintended consequences that cannot be predicted, and therefore must be capable of responding creatively to unanticipated problems. Dahrendorf's view was a generalization of Marx's argument that at each of its stages the economic system produces its own contradictions, which then lead to the development of the next stage.[93] That, of course, was derived from Hegel's "dialectic," in which every thesis generates its own antithesis and is resolved through a synthesis, which then becomes the new thesis. A theory that describes new conflicts being generated out of the solutions to old conflicts is therefore called a "dialectical conflict" theory. Both Marx's and Dahrendorf's theories were dialectical conflict theories, but there was a major difference between the two. In Marx's theory, there was a stage of economic development that did not generate its own contradictions; that stage was communism. The dialectic itself was assumed to reach an end point with communism, since no new antithesis would arise requiring a new synthesis that would replace communism as a stage of economic development. It is this assumption that Dahrendorf rejects as "utopian." He argues, in contrast, that every type of society will generate unanticipated consequences. Therefore, the best societies are those that, like the American political system, build in a capacity to institutionalize conflict so as to minimize the necessity for violent upheaval in the processes of social change.[94]

Where the essential question for Parsons had been how societies achieve order, the essential question for Dahrendorf was, "How do open societies remain open, and how do others become that way?"[95] Open societies are societies with the capacity to change, and Dahrendorf regards that capacity as the necessary condition of liberty. What constitutes liberty depends on the world we live in, so that the liberty of tomorrow will look different from the liberty of today or yesterday. The new liberty, Dahrendorf says, will be "the politics of regulated conflict, and the socio-economics of maximizing individual life-chances."[96]

While Dahrendorf's theory took the form of a sociological conflict theory, Parsons' took the form of a sociological consensus theory. He assumed human nature was conflictual, just as Dahrendorf did, but he described contemporary societies as consensual. His theory therefore focused on the description and analysis of a hypothetical ideal (i.e., "fully integrated") society, rather than on the description and analysis of real societies. The theory was not concerned to any great extent with real societies, except to describe and analyze the process by which they could become more like the hypothetical ideal. No conflict was attributed to socioeconomic structures, so no changes in those structures were necessary as part of that process.

Parsons' theory follows the tradition of Hobbes, Comte, and Durkheim, but a number of developments resulted in substantial differences in their theories. Parsons stated that his work addressed the "Hobbesian problem of order," but in fact it addressed something quite different. Hobbes' problem can be phrased, "How is it possible to construct social order in a disorderly world?" Hobbes assumed that the world as it existed was disorderly, and his theory represented a "solution" to the "problem" of disorder. Parsons, in contrast, presumed that social order existed in the world, and he sought to explain it. Thus, he did not confront a problem that required a solution, but rather a question that required an answer: "Why does social order exist in a world that ought to be disorderly?" That might be called the "Parsonian question of order." Comte and Durkheim played transitional roles in this development by arguing that social order did not presently exist, but was "normal." Thus, their theories addressed both the Parsonian question of why order would be normal in a world that ought to be disorderly and the Hobbesian problem of how to construct order in a world that really is disorderly.

The Hobbesian solution to the problem of order was inherently tied to the existing socioeconomic system. Radical theorists, such as Plato, Rousseau, and Marx, had also addressed the problem of order in a disorderly world, but their solutions had required socioeconomic reorganizations. Hobbes' solution left socioeconomic arrangements alone, and changed political arrangements only to the extent that it gave the ruling groups absolute power. Thus, his solution had a certain appeal to powerful groups that the solutions of radical theorists would not have. The Hobbesian problem of order is more precisely stated, "How is it possible to construct social order in a disorderly world *with only minimal changes to the existing socioeconomic and political arrangements of societies?*" The emphasis on existing socioeconomic and political arrangements continued in the work of Comte and Durkheim, and in Parsons' theories it is transformed into the question: *"How do existing socioeconomic and political structures* create order in a world that ought to be disorderly?"

There was also a deemphasis, in the transition from Hobbes to Parsons, on the specific content of the ideas that were said to be the basis of social order. Hobbes had proposed the doctrines of *Leviathan* as the solution to the problem of order. Order would be achieved in society both because the doctrines were the rational way to govern (and thus would work best by themselves) and because individuals in society would recognize their rationality and would consent to them on that basis. Comte also had a specific content in his doctrine of "positivism," and he expected that the more rational groups in society would recognize its rationality and consent to it. Thus, both Hobbes and Comte stated that there was only one set of ideas that was rational (i.e., their own ideas) and that the consensus was to consist of all who agreed with those ideas. Durkheim, however, moved away from the position of Comte and Hobbes by making abstractions from the content of the ideas underlying in the social solidarity. In Durkheim's theory, what the ideas are is not really relevant, since they change in every society—the point is that they have similar effects in every society. But Durkheim did not fully free himself from the tradition of Comte and Hobbes: at the end of his life, he proposed his own ideas as the basis for the consensus. Like Durkheim, Parsons made abstractions from the content of the ideas underlying the social system, describing them merely as "consensus of values," and it might be argued that he had fully disengaged from the tradition of proposing a content for the consensus. However, it has been suggested that Parsons' theory, by describing the consensual bases of societies, is part of the process by which those same societies become even more consensual.[97] Thus, there is still a sense in which Parsons' ideas are regarded as somehow uniquely "correct," and in which the social consensus is at least partially based on those ideas.

Consensus and Conflict in Contemporary Societies

Having demonstrated that both theories take general forms that are consistent with their assumptions about human nature and contemporary societies, we turn to the question of the relationship between the two theories. Dahrendorf declared that his and Parsons' theories represented "two faces of society" in that they were equally valid but different perspectives on the same social phenomena; Parsons has made a basically similar statement.[98] But such statements, while interesting, do not precisely define the nature of the relationship between the two theories. I will argue here that the relationship between the two theories is a function of their different purposes in theorizing. Those different purposes are associated with different and broadly overlapping definitions of consensus and conflict, and of social order and social change.

I have already argued that Dahrendorf's purpose in theorizing was quite different from Parsons'. The problem that Dahrendorf addressed had originally been defined by Marx—to describe the processes of social change as a function of class conflict. The theory is often construed much more broadly than this, in such a way as to imply that it explains all social change, not merely change that results from class conflict, or that it explains social stability in addition to explaining social change. The problem that Parsons addressed had historical precedents going all the way back to Aristotle: to describe social order as a function of a value consensus. Parsons' theory is also construed much more broadly than this in many cases, to the point of implying that it explains all social order, or that it explains social change in addition to explaining social order.

Both theories are construed narrowly here. Parsons' theory is interpreted as a theory explaining social order as a function of value consensus, so that it does not explain social change directly (although implications about change can be derived from it) and does not explain the sources of social order other than the value consensus (although some of those sources, such as force, enter into the theory). It is because of this narrow interpretation that Parsons' theory could be compared to a multiple regression equation, with social order as the dependent variable. Similarly,

Dahrendorf's theory is interpreted as a theory explaining social change as a function of class conflict, so that it does not explain social stability (although implications about stability can be derived from it) and does not explain social change from sources other than class conflict. Dahrendorf's theory can also be compared to a multiple regression equation, except that his dependent variable is social change.

In Parsons' theory, the principal independent variable is value consensus, while in Dahrendorf's it is conflict. I have already said that Parsons used the term consensus to describe all forms of social relations up to, but not including, the overt use of force. Dahrendorf, in contrast, has been criticized for using an overly broad definition of "conflict," including all "contests, competitions, disputes, and tensions as well as... manifest clashes between social forces." Turner comments further that "when conflict can be *any* overt or covert state which hints of antagonism, then it is easy to 'document' the ubiquity of conflict."[99] Both theorists also used extremely broad definitions of their dependent variables: social order and social change. The social order described by Parsons' theory was not total immobility, while the social change in Dahrendorf's theory was not exclusively revolutionary upheaval. Both described the normal state of social organizations as evolutionary change. While Parsons emphasized the functionality of change after it occurred, Dahrendorf emphasized the dysfunctionality of the conditions that gave rise to the change. Functional theories have always denied that the functionality of the resulting change was the cause of that change—that is the old problem of "illegitimate teleology."[100] Dahrendorf's theory attempts to describe the cause of the change, so it does not necessarily contradict functional theories. In fact, Weingart argues that these changes are "functional" in Dahrendorf's theories in that they generate social change, so that in the end the two arguments are quite compatible.[101] That compatibility is illustrated by the fact that both theorists highly praise the American political system and regard it as generally reflective of their theories.

Thus, Parsons chose a comprehensive definition for the term "consensus" that included all types of relationships except the overt use of force, and built a theory of social order that included all social states except revolutionary upheaval. Dahrendorf chose a comprehensive definition for the term "conflict" that included all types of relationships except total and spontaneous agreement, and built a theory of social change that included all social states except total immobility. Each theory claimed to describe the vast majority of social states, leaving only a minimal number of residual cases outside the theory. That was because each theory "factored out" those aspects of the social relations and social states that were irrelevant to the theory. In the end, then, this is a very complicated case of the glass being half full or half empty. These two theories represent "two faces of society" just as two orthogonal regressions would represent the two faces of the same data.

Dahrendorf claimed that his theory represented a "better" solution to the "Hobbesian problem of order" than did Parsons' theory, having phrased that problem in its traditional form: How is society possible?[102] But Dahrendorf's theory did not directly address the problem that Hobbes addressed, nor did it directly address the question that Parsons addressed. Rather, it asked, following Marx: "How can social structural change be explained in terms of class conflict?" The theory that answered that question contained certain implications about the Parsonian question, but those implications were not the main focus of the theory. At least some of those implications reflected arguments already made in Parsons' theory about the use of force, although those arguments were made from a different standpoint and with a different emphasis. One could say about both theorists that each answered his own question better than the other one did, although it remains possible to challenge the adequacy of either theory as an answer to the question its originator asked.

Parsons' theory certainly was a superior answer to the question of how existing socioeconomic and political structures create order in a world that ought to be disorderly. That superiority was due not only to the fact that it was much more comprehensive than Dahrendorf's answer but also to its appropriate emphasis on normative elements in the creation of order. But to say that social order is based overwhelmingly on normative elements is not the same thing as saying that it is based overwhelmingly on "consensual" elements, unless one defines consensus as including all relationships short of physical force. In fact, in Parsons' theory, the effectiveness of normative elements depends both on whatever consensus of values there may be in the society and on the penumbra of effect of force. The degree to which the effectiveness of normative elements is dependent on one or the other is an empirical question in any given society. Thus, to say that social order depends overwhelmingly on normative elements says nothing about whether a consensus of values exists among all or nearly all the people in a society, and Parsons' theory does not assert the existence of such a consensus. It asserts only that a consensus must exist in the societal community, but it does not assert that the societal community must contain a majority of the population, or even that it must contain a large minority.

The limitation of Parsons' theory, of course, was in its approach to fundamental social change, which Dahrendorf's theory explained better. Such changes can be explained in Parsons' theory either as functional changes, which develop organically within the context of the existing social system, or as nonfunctional changes, which damage and destroy that system and can originate from outside it, as in the case of rebellions and revolutions. In both cases, the frame of reference for describing the fundamental social changes is the social system itself. While that may be appropriate for "functional" changes, it becomes complex and intuitively unsatisfying in the case of "nonfunctional" change; it is for these descriptions that Parsons' theory has received considerable criticism. The problem arises because the intent of Parsons' theory is to describe how social systems create order in societies. Therefore, all elements in the society are described in terms of their relationships to the social system. But in cases of rebellions or revolutions, it is more appropriate to describe all the elements of the society, including the social system, in terms of their relationships to each other. Then the social system becomes one element among a number that are in conflict with each other. That is more appropriate, because it is an unbiased description of the society. In contrast, Parsons' description is necessarily biased in favor of one of the parties to the conflict (the social system) and against the others, since it implies that the other conflicting parties must be integrated, in one way or another, into the existing social system. That is because the "function" of the system is to create "order" (i.e., eliminate the conflict) in the society. But it is only by describing the social system in the context of the society, rather than as the society itself, that a nonbiased description of the society can be presented and fundamental changes in the social system can be fully explained. It is this difference of perspective that is the major difference between Parsons' description of social systems and Dahrendorf's description of imperatively coordinated associations.

Parsons recognized this problem with his theoretical scheme when he discussed social developments in societies that he described as being poorly integrated, such as Germany and Japan around the time of World War II.[103] In those articles, he described the social systems in the context of the societies, rather than as the societies. That shift in perspective led Gouldner, among others, to argue that Parsons adopted a "conflict model" when he described empirical phenomena, as opposed to his "consensus model" in his general theoretical writings.[104] Parsons stayed within the perspective of his general theoretical scheme in his empirical articles only when they focused on well-integrated societies, such as the United States. In those societies, he said, the societal community contained the bulk of the population, so that the societies themselves were consensual. He then described the social system as the society rather than in the context of the society.

This difference in perspective was associated with differing evaluations of the actions of ruling groups. In both well- and poorly integrated societies, the actions of ruling groups are "legitimate" and "justifiable" within the context of the institutionalized values of the social system, but in well-integrated societies, those institutionalized values are identified with a consensus of values in the society itself. Thus, the actions of ruling groups can be characterized as having some "inherent legitimacy" in well-integrated societies within the context of Parsons' theory, whereas no such "inherent legitimacy" is attributed to ruling groups in poorly integrated societies. Accordingly, conflict in well-integrated societies, including conflict directed against the ruling groups, was characterized as being "inherently illegitimate" within the context of Parsons' theory, which then justified its suppression by force and other means. In contrast, Parsons described conflict against ruling groups in poorly integrated societies in terms that did not convey moral illegitimacy. In those descriptions, Parsons' writings took on the same objective, nonevaluative stance normally associated with the sociological conflict perspective—i.e., to a considerable extent he simply described and analyzed the conflict without implying whose position was "legitimate" and whose should be suppressed by force. That is the same perspective taken in Dahrendorf's theory in its description of all societies. By taking that perspective, however, Dahrendorf does not argue that all societies are poorly integrated. Rather, he does not differentiate between well- and poorly integrated societies. He simply takes the same objective, nonevaluative stance in describing the conflict in all societies, without any conclusion about whose position is "legitimate" and whose may be suppressed by force.

In each of the earlier comparisons between a consensus and a conflict theorist, it was found that the difference between the description of a society as consensual and description of the same society as conflictual lay in the theorists' evaluations of the actions of the ruling groups of that society, rather than in any empirical assertions about the existence or extent of conflict in the society. The same difference has been found with respect to the theories of Parsons and Dahrendorf. Parsons did not argue that there was no conflict in societies he said were consensual. Rather, he described the actions of ruling groups in those societies as being "legitimate" and justified the use of force and other means to suppress all conflict in the society, including conflict directed against the ruling groups.[105] Similarly, Parsons did not describe conflict in his discussion of "ego" and "alter." Rather, he took ego's demands as the point of reference and discussed how to "get results" from alter through "pressure" and "sanctions." Dahrendorf would describe the same empirical phenomena as conflict between authorities and subjects. Consequently, Parsons' description of a society as consensual does not empirically contradict Dahrendorf's description of the same society as conflictual. Rather, they are alternative descriptions of the same empirical phenomena based on differing stances on the legitimacy of the actions of the ruling groups in the society.

One can ask, of course, whether the actions of ruling groups in a well-integrated society really are justifiable, so that Parsons' theory expresses a larger truth than does Dahrendorf's. But the meaning of that question is not clear. In the context of Parsons' theory, the legitimacy of those actions is based on the argument that the institutionalized values represent a consensus of values among the bulk of the population. In principle that is an empirical assertion, but in practice it is difficult or impossible to test. Bensman, for example, argues:

> ... the *theory* of legitimacy is unprovable. That theory ultimately asserts that government rests on the *belief* in its underlying principles. This does not mean that some segments of a population do not believe in the principles of legitimacy of a government, or that governments do not make claims, promises, or justifications. But it does mean that there is no way to ascertain, before the fact, how much belief, or positive acceptance is necessary from how many members of its underlying population (and of what characteristics) to justify its legitimacy via belief. Ultimately it is not possible to separate "believers" from self-justifiers, expedient supporters, passive adapters, or the apathetic, the hopeless, the apolitical whose support is purchased by the gratification of material or ideal interests other than that of belief, or by "legitimacy of force" per se.... Since the *theory of legitimacy* is untestable in the absence of empirical situations of pure voluntarism, the attribution of legitimacy *as belief* to an empirical political order is indeterminable.[106]

Even if Parsons' theory says that a consensus of values exists in a particular society, considerably less is being asserted in the context of that theory than is often imagined. Parsons assumed that humans were naturally conflictual, so that there were no spontaneous and full agreements among them. Rather, consensus originates as a full and free agreement among a subgroup of the population, a subgroup that may be quite small. But that group achieves a dominance of power, and extends its ideas outward to the rest of society through persuasion and ultimately through force. A well-integrated society is not one where full and free agreements have spontaneously emerged among the bulk of the population, but rather one where the process of molding and shaping the ideas of the rest of the society by the group in power has been quite effective. The question of whether that process is "legitimate and justified" is separate from the question of how the process operates. A Marxist could agree entirely with Parsons' description of the process but describe it as the "ruling class ideology" generating "false consciousness" in the American society. Thus, the Marxist would describe as "illegitimate and unjustifiable" exactly the same empirical phenomenon that Parsons described as "legitimate and justifiable." The opposite situation could occur if the process were viewed in the context of Soviet society. Thus, the question of whether the actions of ruling groups in well-integrated societies are really "legitimate and justifiable" is a moral or evaluative question rather than an empirical one. That being so, the difference between the theories of Parsons and Dahrendorf with respect to their descriptions of contemporary societies as "consensual" or "conflictual" is, in the last analysis, not an empirical difference, and it cannot be resolved through empirical investigations.

Notes

1. Talcott Parsons, *Structure of Social Action* (New York: McGraw-Hill, 1937).

2. Talcott Parsons, "An Outline of the Social System," in Talcott Parsons, Edward Shils, Kasper D. Naegele, and Jesse R. Pitts, eds. *Theories of Society* (New York: The Free Press, 1965), p. 31.

3. Talcott Parsons, *The Social System* (New York: The Free Press, 1951), p. 36.

4. Ibid., pp. 5–6.

5. Talcott Parsons, *The System of Modern Societies* (Englewood Cliffs: Prentice-Hall, 1971), p. 10.

6. Ibid., p. 8. See also Talcott Parsons, *Societies: Evolutionary and Comparative Perspectives* (Englewood Cliffs: Prentice-Hall, 1966), ch. 2; reprinted as "The Concept of Society: The Components and Their Interrelations," in Talcott Parsons, *Politics and Social Structure* (New York: The Free Press, 1969), pp. 11–20.

7. Parsons, "An Outline of the Social System," pp. 38–40.

8. Ibid., pp. 42–44. See also Parsons, *The System of Modern Societies*, pp. 7–8.

9. Parsons, *The System of Modern Societies*, p. 8.

10. Ibid., p. 13.

11. Ibid., p. 10.

12. Talcott Parsons, " 'Voting' and the Equilibrium of the American Political System," in Eugene Burdick and Arthur Brodbeck, eds., *American Voting Behavior* (New York: The Free Press, 1959); reprinted in Parsons, *Politics and Social Structure*, p. 206. For a more extended discussion, see Talcott Parsons and Winston White, "The Link Between Char-

acter and Society," in S. M. Lipset and Leo Lowenthal, eds., *Culture and Society* (New York: The Free Press, 1961).

13. Parsons, *The System of Modern Societies*, p. 11.

14. Talcott Parsons, "Full Citizenship for the Negro American?" *Politics and Social Structure*, p. 253.

15. Parsons, *The System of Modern Societies*, pp. 11–12.

16. Talcott Parsons, "Durkheim's Contribution to the Theory of Integration of Social Systems," *Sociological Theory and Modern Society* (New York: The Free Press, 1967), p. 8.

17. Ibid. See also Parsons, *The System of Modern Societies*, p. 9.

18. Parsons, "Full Citizenship," p. 253. See also Jackson Toby, "Parsons' Theory of Societal Evolution," in Talcott Parsons, *The Evolution of Societies* (Englewood Cliffs: Prentice-Hall, 1977), pp. 18–19.

19. Parsons, "Full Citizenship," pp. 265–91.

20. See, for example, Parsons, "The Problem of Controlled Institutional Change," *Politics and Social Structure*, p. 132.

21. Parsons, "Durkheim's Contribution," p. 5.

22. Ibid.

23. Talcott Parsons, "Some Reflections on the Place of Force in Social Process," *Sociological Theory and Modern Society*, p. 265.

24. Parsons, *The Systems Of Modern Societies*, p. 12.

25. Talcott Parsons, "On the Concept of Influence," *Sociological Theory and Modern Society*, p. 361.

26. Ibid., p. 364.

27. Talcott Parsons, "On the Concept of Political Power," *Sociological Theory and Modern Society*, p. 308.

28. Parsons, " 'Voting' and the Equilibrium," p. 225.

29. Parsons, "Reflections on the Place of Force," p. 266.

30. Ibid., pp. 272–78.

31. Parsons, "On the Concept of Political Power," p. 331.

32. Parsons, "Reflections on the Place of Force," p. 149.

33. Talcott Parsons, "Evolutionary Universals in Society," *Sociological Theory and Modern Society*, p. 518.

34. Cf. Parsons' discussions of Nazi Germany in *Politics and Social Structure*, part II, especially "The Problem of Controlled Institutional Change," pp. 125–56.

35. Parsons, "Reflections on the Place of Force," p. 296.

36. Ibid., pp. 290–91.

37. Ibid., p. 288.

38. Ibid., pp. 294–95.

39. Parsons, "On the Concept of Political Power," p. 313.

40. Parsons, "Evolutionary Universals," p. 518.

41. Parsons, "On the Concept of Political Power," p. 308.

42. Parsons, "The Concept of Society," p. 19.

43. Parsons, *The System of Modern Societies*, p. 9.

44. Edward Shils, "The Calling of Sociology," in Parsons et al., *Theories of Society*, p. 1443.

45. Parsons, "Controlled Institutional Change," p. 132.

46. Parsons, *The Social System*, p. 298. See also Robert W. Friedrichs, *A Sociology of Sociology* (New York: The Free Press, 1970), p. 145: "Parsons stacked his entire deck—and all the games he would later play with it—the very moment he settled upon the focal

term 'system' as the characteristic concern of sociology. And, it is important to note, he did so in full awareness of its implications."

47. Parsons, "Reflections on the Place of Force," pp.276–77. See also p. 271, where he described this type of power as "counterpower."

48. Parsons, "Full Citizenship," p. 267.

49. Talcott Parsons, "The Distribution of Power in American Society," *Politics and Social Structure,* p. 193.

50. See Talcott Parsons, "Some Sociological Aspects of the Fascist Movement," *Politics and Social Structure,* p. 95, where he stated: "It is one of the most fundamental theorems of the theory of institutions that in proportion to the institutionalization of any pattern a self-interest in conformity with it develops. Self-interest and moral sentiments are not necessarily antithetical, but may, and often do motivate conduct in the same direction."

51. Parsons, *The Social System,* p. 204.

52. Parsons, "Durkheim's Contribution," p. 14. See also pp. 33—34.

53. E.g., Parsons, "A Controlled Institutional Change," p. 132, where he stated that "the conception of a completely integrated social system is a limiting case," and Parsons, "Order and Community in the International Social System," p. 297, where he stated, "I should regard the famous Hobbesian state of war as the limiting concept...."

54. Parsons, "Reflections on the Place of Force," p. 265.

55. Parsons, *The System of Modern Societies,* p. 121.

56. Parsons, "Some Sociological Aspects of the Fascist Movement," pp. 95–96.

57. Talcott Parsons, "Social Classes and Class Conflict in the Light of Recent Sociological Theory," *Essays in Sociological Theory,* rev. ed. (New York: The Free Press, 1954), p. 333.

58. Ibid., pp. 329–31.

59. Ibid., p. 333.

60. Ralf Dahrendorf, *Class and Class Conflict in Industrial Society* (Stanford, Calif.: Stanford University Press, 1959), p. 162.

61. Ibid., p. 237.

62. Ralf Dahrendorf, *Conflict After Class: New Perspectives on the Theory of Social and Political Conflict* (London: Longmans, Green, 1967), p. 3. Dahrendorf qualified that statement with the following footnote (ibid., pp. 26–27): "There seems to be an obvious difference between the functional system [and the "system"] of the Marxian 'epoch' in the fact that the former does not recognize the time dimension at all. The difference is deceptive; for in fact these are merely two aspects of the same notion, that of organism: at a given time, it has its structures and functions, over time it grows to its entelechy, but either way it remains closed, incapable of pointing beyond itself, i.e., incapable of change in the historical sense—with one (metaphorical) exception of death."

63. Dahrendorf, *Class and Class Conflict,* pp. 5–6.

64. Ibid., p. 6.

65. Dahrendorf stated that because of the strict distinction he defines between class and status, "one can predict with some confidence that the present study will be misunderstood." Ibid., p. ix.

66. Ibid., p. 30.

67. Ibid., pp. 36–71.

68. Ibid., p. 123.

69. Ibid., pp. 126–54. Dahrendorf summarized his modifications of Marx's theory on p. 245.

70. Ibid., pp. 167–68.

71. Ibid., pp. 173–89.

72. The theory is summarized in propositional form in ibid., pp. 237–40.

73. Dahrendorf, *Conflict After Class*, p. 19.

74. Dahrendorf, *Class and Class Conflict*, pp. 223–24.

75. Ibid., pp. 225–27.

76. Cf. Austin T. Turk, *Criminality and Legal Order* (Chicago: Rand McNally, 1969), p. 32: "For the groupings powerful enough to have some impact on the legal process, laws will be rather satisfactory regulative compromises. For those groupings who have lost out, or never really competed, in the struggle to control legal mechanisms, laws will be edicts. For them, to live in a legal order is to be dominated."

77. Dahrendorf, *Conflict After Class*, p. 19.

78. Ibid., p. 20.

79. See Peter Weingart, "Beyond Parsons? A Critique of Ralf Dahrendorf's Conflict Theory," *Social Forces* (December 1969), 48(2):151–65, for a strong criticism of Dahrendorf's failure to specify the content of the conflict.

80. Ralf Dahrendorf, *Life Chances* (London: Weidenfeld and Nicolson, 1979). David Lockwood, in "Some Remarks on 'The Social System,' " *British Journal of Sociology* (June 1956), 7:134–46, had argued in a somewhat similar way that the "substratum of social action" structures different *"Lebenschancen"* and that Parsons' theory had ignored that phenomenon.

81. *Life Chances*, pp. 63–67, 73.

82. Ibid., p. 53. See also p. 11.

83. Ibid., pp. 30–32, 74–84.

84. Ibid., p. 31.

85. Ibid.

86. Ibid., pp. 80–81.

87. Ibid., p. 33.

88. Ibid., pp. 53–62.

89. Cf. Jonathan H. Turner, *The Structure of Sociological Theory*, rev. ed. (Homewood, Ill.: Dorsey Press, 1978), pp. 151–54.

90. Dahrendorf, *Class and Class Conflict*, pp. 223–24.

91. Ibid., p. 208.

92. Karl Popper, *The Open Society and Its Enemies* (Princeton, N. J.: Princeton University Press, 1966). See Dahrendorf's description of Popper's influence on him in *Life Chances*, pp. 6–8, and *The New Liberty* (London: Routledge and Kegan Paul, 1975), pp. 4–5.

93. Dahrendorf, *The New Liberty*, pp. 5–6.

94. Dahrendorf, *Life Chances*, pp. 39–40.

95. Ibid., p. 53.

96. Dahrendorf, *The New Liberty*, p. 6.

97. Edward Shils, "The Calling of Sociology," in Parsons et al., *Theories of Society*, pp. 1405–48.

98. Dahrendorf, *Class and Class Conflict*, pp. 163–64; Talcott Parsons, *Structure and Process in Modern Society* (Glencoe, Ill.: The Free Press, 1960), p. 173.

99. Turner, *Structure of Sociological Theory*, p. 181.

100. Ibid., pp. 62–66, 105–10.

101. Weingart, "Beyond Parsons?" p. 157.

102. Dahrendorf, *Class and Class Conflict*, pp. 230–31; Ralf Dahrendorf, "In Praise of Thrasymachus," *Essays in the Theory of Society* (Stanford: Stanford University Press, 1968), pp. 129–41, 150.

103. Cf. the articles in Parsons, *Politics and Social Structure*, part 2.

104. Alvin W. Gouldner, *The Coming Crisis of Western Sociology* (New York: Avon 1970), pp. 341–70. For a discussion of this issue, see Irving M. Zeitlin, *Rethinking Sociology* (New York: Appleton-Century-Crofts, 1973), pp. 35–50.

105. Cf. C. Wright Mills, *The Sociological Imagination* (New York: Oxford University Press, 1959), pp. 35–40.

106. Joseph Bensman, "Max Weber's Concept of Legitimacy: An Evaluation," in Arthur J. Vidich and Ronald M. Glassman, eds., *Conflict and Control: Challenge to Legitimacy of Modern Governments* (Beverly Hills: Sage, 1979), pp. 43–44.

– Chapter 9 –

The Relation Between Consensus and Conflict Theories

IN THE preceding seven chapters, seven pairs of social theories have been presented and compared, one of each pair being classified as a consensus theory and the other as a conflict theory. The assumptions and/or assertions each theory makes with respect to the concepts of consensus and conflict (its content) and the way in which those assumptions and/or assertions are woven into a coherent argument (its form) were analyzed. The first section of this chapter generalizes the findings from those seven comparisons and presents, in a series of propositions, the general form and content of consensus and conflict theories. That generalization relies on the arguments made in the preceding seven chapters, so specific references to the relevant theories are not made here. The second part of this chapter is a discussion of the consensus-conflict debate, based on the propositional analysis.

The General Form and Content of Consensus and Conflict Theories

I. Types of Social Theories
  A. The principal difference between consensus and conflict theories concerns the terms they use to describe contemporary societies—societies that actually existed at the time the theories were written.

1. Consensus theories use the term "consensus" to describe at least some contemporary societies, although other contemporary societies may be described in terms of conflict. Past, future, or ideal societies may also be described in terms of consensus, but that is not the defining characteristic of a consensus theory.

2. Conflict theories use the term "conflict" to describe all contemporary societies. However, past, future, or ideal societies may be described in terms of consensus.

3. The selection of the term "consensus" or "conflict" to describe contemporary societies does not appear to be associated with any consistent empirical differences in the descriptions of those societies.

B. The description of human nature as consensual or conflictual cuts across consensus and conflict theories and divides each type into two branches.

1. Consensus theorists are divided into "conservatives" (Aristotle, Aquinas, and Locke), who describe human nature as consensual, and "sociological consensus theorists" (Hobbes, Durkheim, and Parsons), who describe human nature as conflictual. Comte falls in between these two branches, because he based his theory on both Aristotle (man's natural tendency to organize into hierarchical groups) and Hobbes ("the desire to command is almost always stronger than the willingness to obey").

2. Conflict theorists are divided into "radicals" (Plato, Rousseau, and Marx), who describe human nature as consensual, and "sociological conflict theorists" (Machiavelli, Simmel, and Dahrendorf), who describe human nature as conflictual. Augustine falls in between these two branches, because he argued that true human nature was consensual but that people were inevitably in conflict here on earth because human nature had been corrupted by sin.

3. The selection of the term "consensus" or "conflict" to describe human nature appears to be associated with substantive differences in assumptions, but those assumptions do not appear to be empirically testable at present.

C. The two groups of theorists can be divided along the two axes described above, as shown in table 1.

II. Problems and Solutions in Social Theories

A. The sociological consensus theorists and the radical theorists are confronted with a problem, because they describe human nature and society in opposite terms. Because the conservative

TABLE 1: Types of Social Theories

Human Nature		Contemporary Societies			
		Consensual (Consensus Theorists)		*Conflictual* (Conflict Theorists)	
Consensual	*Conservative:*	Aristotle Aquinas Locke	*Radical:*	Plato Rousseau Marx
Conflictual	*Sociological Consensus:*	Comte Hobbes Durkheim Parsons	*Sociological Conflict:*	Augustine Machiavelli Simmel Dahrendorf

theorists and the sociological conflict theorists describe human nature and society in the same terms, they do not confront a similar problem.

1. Sociological consensus theorists must explain why societies are or how they can be consensual when human nature is conflictual (the "Hobbesian problem of order").

2. Radical theorists must explain why societies are conflictual when human nature is consensual and how societies can become consensual (the radical problem).

3. The social consensus is not a problem for conservative theorists, because they argue that human beings are naturally consensual.

4. Social conflict is not a problem for sociological conflict theorists, because they maintain that human beings are naturally conflictual.

B. Central to the sociological consensus and the radical theories is a "solution" to the problem they have defined. Each such solution implies or describes a hypothetical state of society different from that of contemporary societies, in which the contradiction between human nature and society is in some way resolved. It also entails some indication of the way in which contemporary societies can or will be changed into the hypothetical society.

1. "Solutions" to the "Hobbesian problem of order" in the sociological consensus theories include Hobbes' "Leviathan," Comte's "Positive" society, Durkheim's "normal" society, and Parsons' "fully integrated" society. All of these societies were hypothetical, in that none was claimed to exist at the time the theorist was writing.

2. "Solutions" to the radical problem include Plato's "Republic," Augustine's "City of God," Rousseau's "social contract," and Marx's "communism." All of these were also hypothetical societies.

C. The nature of the solution to the contradiction between human nature and society depends on where the problem (i.e., the conflict) is said to lie.

1. The "problem" for the sociological consensus theorists lies in man's conflictual nature. Thus, the "solution" to the problem consists in strengthening social bonds (part of the consensual society) to control that nature.

2. The "problem" for the radicals lies in the conflictual nature of society, particularly its socioeconomic relations. Thus, the "solution" to the problem consists in changing those relations.

D. Each of the hypothetical states of society described by sociological consensus and radical theories is held to be "legitimate" in some fundamental sense—e.g., it is rational, historically inevitable, or culturally unique. Conflicts have been reduced to a minimal and residual level and are said to be "illegitimate" in some fundamental sense, so that they may "legitimately" be suppressed through force and other means. These societies are described as "consensual" despite the presence of residual illegitimate conflicts and the need to suppress them. Revolutions in each hypothetical society are theoretically impossible due to the low level of conflict. In addition, there are no theoretical sources of "undesirable" evolutionary change—change that would move the society away from its "legitimate" state. Because these societies are hypothetical, are considered consensual, and theoretically have no sources of revolutionary change and a limited range of possible evolutionary change, they may be described as "utopian."[1]

1. Sociological consensus theories assume that there will always be a great many conflicts between human beings because the source of those conflicts is in human nature. The hypothetical "utopian" society does not resolve the conflicts per se but rather strengthens social bonds to control their overt expression. It thereby eliminates the theoretical sources of revolution and of "undesirable" evolutionary change. These societies are described as consensual because the consensus is said to include all those who do not overtly express conflict, whether or not there is any full and free agreement.

2. In radical theories, the source of the conflict is said to be in socioeconomic relations, not in human nature, and the "utopian" societies are seen as resolving the conflicts by changing the relations. Thus, it is the conflicts themselves, not merely their overt expression, that are said to be reduced to a minimal and residual level. Once the socioeconomic relations have been changed, there are no theoretical sources for revolution or for "undesirable" evolutionary change. All those who do

not overtly express conflict are said to be in full and free agreement, so that the societies can be said to be consensual.

E. Conservative and sociological conflict theories do not describe any contradiction between human nature and society. Thus, they do not describe or imply any states of society other than those they say are real. There are no descriptions or implications of hypothetical states of society comparable to those found in sociological consensus and radical theories. To the extent that these theories identify an "ideal" society, it consists in the "best" form of real society, not in a hypothetical society. Revolutions and "undesirable" evolutionary changes are theoretically possible within these "best" societies, so that they cannot be described as "utopian."

III. Evaluations of Legitimacy in Contemporary Societies

A. The "utopian" societies of sociological consensus and radical theories are hypothetical ideals that were not held to exist at the time the theories were written. But contemporary societies are interpreted by comparing them with the hypothetical "utopian" societies. In particular, that comparison provides criteria for evaluating the "legitimacy" of the actions of groups who hold power in contemporary societies ("dominant power groups"), as well as of the actions of those in conflict with dominant power groups. The desirability of both revolutionary and evolutionary social changes in contemporary societies can also be assessed. A contemporary society is called consensual if its fundamental characteristics are consistent with the fundamental characteristics of the hypothetical "utopian" society. Conflicts in that contemporary society are then described as "illegitimate" in some fundamental sense, so that they may "legitimately" be suppressed by force and other means by the dominant power groups. The principal difference between a contemporary consensual society and the hypothetical utopian consensual society lies in the amount of illegitimate conflict each contains, with the contemporary society said to contain a great deal more. However, the contemporary consensual society, like the utopian one, is judged to contain little or no legitimate conflict. The higher levels of illegitimate conflict in contemporary consensual societies means that revolutions and undesirable evolutionary changes are possible but, like the conflict from which they spring, illegitimate.

1. In sociological consensus theories, the direction of desirable evolutionary change in consensual societies is that of strengthening social bonds to better control the conflictual human nature. That includes strengthening the control that dominant power groups have over other groups in the society.

But for any revolution to take place, the control of dominant power groups must first be weakened and ultimately be broken. Therefore, to the extent that the fundamental characteristics of a contemporary society are regarded as consistent with the fundamental characteristics of the utopian society, the sociological consensus theorist will oppose all revolutions and will also oppose all evolutionary changes that have the effect of weakening the control that dominant power groups have over the other groups in the society. The actions that dominant power groups take to defend and expand their control of such societies will be described by the sociological consensus theorist as legitimate, while the actions of those in conflict with dominant groups will be described as illegitimate. These contemporary societies will be described in consensual terms despite the existence of such illegitimate conflict and the need for dominant groups to use force and other means to suppress it.

2. In radical theories, all contemporary societies are described as conflictual, and new socioeconomic arrangements are proposed to resolve the conflicts. The radical theorist evaluates the actions of dominant groups in contemporary societies and the actions of those in conflict with the dominant groups in terms of the effect those actions have on the establishment of the new socioeconomic arrangements. In most radical theories, the actions of dominant groups are therefore described as illegitimate, while the actions of at least some of those in conflict with the dominant groups are described as legitimate. If the new socioeconomic arrangements are implemented in some contemporary societies, then the fundamental characteristics of those societies are consistent with the fundamental characteristics of the utopian society. The actions of those in conflict with the dominant groups in such societies are then described as illegitimate, while the actions of the dominant groups to suppress the conflict are described as legitimate. Those contemporary societies are said to be consensual despite the presence of illegitimate conflict and the need to suppress it by force or other means. Radical theories then describe human nature and at least some contemporary societies in consensual terms, so that they take on the form of a conservative consensus theory. Evaluations of legitimacy in societies with the new socioeconomic arrangements are identical to evaluations that conservatives make of "consensual" societies, as described next.

B. Conservative theories also provide criteria for evaluating the legitimacy of conflicts and the desirability of social changes in contemporary societies, but those criteria are associated with the "best" real societies rather than with a hypothetical "uto-pian" society. Consensual societies are portrayed as being dicho-tomously divided between those who participate in the consen-sus and those who do not. Because of their consensual natures, those who participate in the consensus are described as being capable of achieving a full and free agreement on what is legiti-mate and desirable in their society. Dominant groups in the society are among those who participate in the consensus, so that their actions are consistent with the full and free agreement. Those who do not participate are said to have no right to agree or disagree with the consensus, either because they do not share fully in man's consensual nature (i.e., are "irrational" and/or "selfish") or because they are not full members of the consensual society. The dominant groups may legitimately suppress con-flicts with this group by force and other means, and the society is described in consensual terms despite these conflicts and the need to suppress them. In practice, that means that all conflicts with dominant groups are held to be illegitimate, while all those who are not in conflict with dominant groups are held to be in full and free agreement with them. Entering into conflict with the dominant groups may be thought of as illegitimate in itself or may be taken as prima facie evidence that one belongs to the (irrational and selfish) groups that have no right to agree or disagree. The only legitimate social change is change approved of by the dominant groups. Revolutions and evolutionary changes not approved of by those groups are possible but, like the conflict from which they spring, illegitimate.

C. In contrast, sociological conflict theories do not assert that some parties to a conflict have legitimate positions while others have illegitimate positions. These theories may imply that all parties to a conflict have equally legitimate or equally illegiti-mate positions, or they may assert that the assessment of legiti-macy is beyond the scope of the theory. They may evaluate the desirability of social changes associated with those conflicts, but that evaluation is not based on a description of one position in the conflict as legitimate and others as illegitimate.

D. Evaluations of legitimacy in contemporary societies within all four types of theories are associated with overall evaluations of the contemporary societies themselves. Those overall evalua-tions can be inferred from comparisons between the contempo-rary societies and the "ideal" or "best" society, as presented in each theory.

1. In conservative descriptions of consensual societies and radical descriptions of reformed societies, all conflict is attrib-uted to deviant subgroups and none is attributed to any aspect of the society itself. The contemporary society corresponds

quite closely to the "ideal" or "best" society presented in the theory, so that a very positive evaluation can be inferred.

2. In sociological consensus descriptions, the contemporary consensual society is found to be deficient in its social control mechanisms when compared with the "ideal" society. However, it is similar to the "ideal" society in all other respects. Thus, the evaluation that can be inferred about the society is quite positive in general, but contains a significant negative aspect.

3. In radical descriptions, the socioeconomic arrangements of an unreformed society differ significantly from the socioeconomic arrangements of the "ideal" society. Conflict in the society is attributed to those socioeconomic arrangements, which are fundamental aspects of the society itself. Accordingly, the overall evaluation that can be inferred about the society is quite negative.

4. In sociological conflict descriptions, contemporary societies can be quite similar to the "best" society as presented in the theory. Thus, a positive evaluation about those societies might be inferred. However, even the "best" society is described in conflictual terms, from which a negative evaluation might be inferred. These theories are therefore associated with ambiguous evaluative inferences about contemporary societies or with an "objective," nonevaluative stance.

IV. The Relation Between Consensus and Conflict Theories

The consensus-conflict debate is centered on evaluations of contemporary (i.e., "real") societies and evaluations of the actions of dominant power groups and groups in conflict with dominant power groups in those societies. The evaluations are based on comparisons between the contemporary societies and the "ideal" or "best" society as presented in each theory. Because the absence of such evaluations constitutes a sociological conflict position, the other types of theories can be transformed into sociological conflict theories by removing the evaluations of legitimacy and illegitimacy. That does not change descriptions of the existence or extent of conflict in contemporary societies, or the analyses of social processes in those societies. However, what had previously been described as illegitimate conflict within a legitimate society or as legitimate conflict within an illegitimate society would now be described as conflict between dominant and minority power groups.

The Consensus-Conflict Debate

At least part of the confusion about the consensus-conflict debate stems from the fact that there are actually four different ways that it can be described—between conservative and radical theories, between sociological consensus and radical theories, between sociological consensus and sociological conflict theories, or between conservative and sociological conflict theories. Dahrendorf, for example, portrays the consensus-conflict debate as being between his own sociological conflict theory and Parsons' sociological consensus theory.[2] Others who seem to portray the debate in this way include Percy Cohen[3] and George Vold.[4] Radicals at times seem to portray consensus theories in terms of the conservative position rather than the sociological consensus position in their descriptions of the consensus-conflict debate. For example, Taylor et al. stated about consensus theories in criminology, "To insist that there is a consensus in society obviates all discussion of the possibility of fundamental conflicts of value and interest."[5] That statement does not seem to be consistent with the conflictual view of human nature found in Durkheim's and Parsons' theories, on which the dominant consensus theories in criminology are based. It seems more consistent with the consensual view of human nature found in Aristotle's theories. There do not seem to be any descriptions of the consensus-conflict debate as being between conservative and sociological conflict theories. Perhaps that is because those who adhere to the sociological conflict position can be expected to be familiar with sociological consensus theories as the dominant consensus position, while those who adhere to the conservative position may be unfamiliar with modern sociology in general and thus unaware that sociological conflict theories are distinct from the better-known radical theories.

By far the most frequent portrayal of the consensus-conflict debate is between the sociological consensus and radical positions. For example, Lenski maintains that consensus theorists "have been distrustful of man's basic nature and have emphasized the need for restraining social institutions," whereas "radicals have been distrustful of these restraining institutions and have taken an optimistic view of human nature."[6] That analysis directly reflects the dichotomous views of human nature and societies presented above in the descriptions of the sociological consensus and radical positions. In contrast, conservative consensus theorists cannot be said to be "distrustful of man's basic nature," and sociological conflict theorists cannot be said to "have taken an optimistic view of human nature." Roach et al. summarized the consensus and conflict theories into propositional form but included in "the conflict view" propositions such as "Stratification may be universal without being necessary or inevitable"; "Stratification impedes the optimal functioning of society and the individual"; and "The economic dimension is paramount in society."[7] These are all characteristic of the radical conflict position; none of them is held in sociological conflict theories. They then contrasted "the conflict view" with "the functional view," which is directly derived from what I have called sociological consensus theories. Horton described the consensus-conflict debate in terms that were generally sympathetic to conflict theories, but he described the "conflict perspective" as entailing a "utopian definition" of health, where the "implied ameliorative action" is "rupture of social control; radical transformation of existing patterns of interaction; revolutionary change of the social system."[8] Those views are associated only with radical conflict theories, not with sociological conflict theories. In contrast, Horton described the "order perspective" in terms of functionalism, citing Parsons and Merton as examples. Ossowski also analyzed the consensus-conflict debate in terms of functionalism and Marxism.[9] He demonstrated that both types of views have been found throughout history and have been applied to very diverse societies with very different social, economic, and political systems. He concluded that both are essentially analogies of the social and class structure and that modern societies are so complex that both types of views can be applied to most societies. The only common element is that the functionalist type of explanation has consistently been used to defend the status quo, while the Marxist type of explanation has consistently been used to justify fundamental change. Ossowski suggested that this is actually the purpose of the theories and pointed out "the fortunes of revolutionary ideologies"—that before the revolution, they portray the society as dichotomously divided, which justifies the need for the revolution itself, but after the revolution, they are transformed into functionalist-type justifications of the status quo. That is comparable to the analysis in the preceding section, in which I argued that radical theories portray the social structures of "unreformed" societies as fundamentally illegitimate, but then take on the conservative model once the societies have been "reformed" and so describe their structures as fundamentally legitimate.

The portrayal of the consensus-conflict debate as being between the sociological consensus and the radical positions may be partly a function of the fact that these two positions are better known among modern sociologists than the other two positions. And it is almost certainly related to the fact that these two types of theories, as pointed out in the above analysis, are in many ways mirror images of each other. One assumes that human nature is consensual and society is conflictual, while the other assumes that human nature is conflictual and society is consensual. Both describe conflict as a problem, and both propose hypothetical societies as a solution to that problem. In one theory, the solution is achieved by restraining the conflictual human nature, while in the other theory, it is achieved by reorganizing the conflictual social relations.

The failure to consider conservative consensus theories in most descriptions of the consensus-conflict debate is not surprising, because the position is not widely held among modern sociologists. But the failure to consider sociological conflict theories in those descriptions is quite surprising. Sociological conflict theories represent a strong and vibrant branch of modern sociology and have long been recognized as separate and distinct from radical theories. For example, in 1960, Martindale described the distinction between "conflict ideologies," such as Marxian socialism, and "sociological conflict theories," such as the work of Bagehot, Glumplowicz, Ratzenhofer, Sumner, Small, Oppenheimer, and Vold.[10] Martindale argued that conflict ideologies were "sets of ideas vindicating particular social positions and spurring particular action programs," while sociological conflict theory, "though some of its propositions coincide with those appearing in the [conflict] ideologies, is scientific, resting its hypotheses on the scientific standards of the discipline."[11]

More recently, Wallace and Wolf have described a similar distinction among conflict theorists:

> The first group of theorists believes the social scientist to have a moral obligation to engage in a critique of society. It refuses to separate—or to admit that one can really separate—analysis from judgment or fact from value. Theorists in this group also generally

believe that in principle a society could exist in which there were no longer grounds for social conflict. Therefore these theorists are frequently considered Utopian writers. The second group, by contrast, considers conflict to be an inevitable and permanent aspect of social life; and it also rejects the idea that social science's conclusions are necessarily value-laden. Instead, its proponents are interested in establishing a social science with the same canon of objectivity as informs the natural sciences.[12]

They include in the first group modern Marxists, the Frankfurt School theorists, and C. Wright Mills, while the second group includes Ralf Dahrendorf, Lewis Coser, and Randall Collins. The predominant influence on the first group, they state, is Karl Marx, while the predominant influence on the second group is Max Weber and "analytic" conflict theorists such as Simmel and Park. Turner presents the theories of Marx and Simmel as "The Conflict Heritage," but then focuses on the conflict theories of Dahrendorf and Coser.[13] He sees the two branches of conflict theory as "dialectical" conflict (Dahrendorf) and "functional" conflict (Coser), and does not bother to discuss the contemporary theories that Martindale would have called "conflict ideologies" and Wallace and Wolf referred to as "utopian." Wrong stated that "conflict theory" arose in the 1950s largely as a countertendency to structural-functionalism, and was exemplified in the works of Mills, Barrington Moore, Jr., Dahrendorf, Reinhard Bendix, Lewis Coser, and himself. He said that

> [conflict theory] obviously had broad affinities with the Marxist tradition. Nevertheless, none of the writers I have mentioned considered himself a Marxist.... Most of them, including Mills, were more Weberian than Marxist.[14]

Atkinson analyzed the theories of Marx and Parsons and concluded with a comparison that is quite similar to the one presented in the above analysis:

> For Marx, the question became: how is conflict possible when man is rational and cooperative? For Parsons the question became: how is order possible when man is basically destructive and competitive? It should not be a source of surprise that each man arrived at similar solutions.... Simply, the individual was constrained away from his basic nature by the fabric of social relations and his location or social position within these relations, into which he was born and through which he learned to be social. In

a word, man had no choice but to live in order (for Parsons) or conflict (for Marx).[15]

He analyzed separately the theories of Max Weber, from which he derived the sociological conflict theories of Dahrendorf and John Rex.[16] Atkinson's analysis is consistent with that of Turk in criminology, who also maintains that his own and other criminological conflict theories are derived from Weber's theory and are distinct from the "Marxian," or radical, criminological theories.[17]

Although sociological conflict theories are often ignored in descriptions of the consensus-conflict debate, sociologists have taken positions consistent with those theories when they attempt to "resolve" the debate by reaching a synthesis between functionalism and Marxism. Dahrendorf's sociological conflict theory was an attempt at such a synthesis, in which the basic elements of both Marx's and Parsons' theories were incorporated.[18] Van den Berghe attempted a similar synthesis between the dialectic and functionalism, commenting: "While Dahrendorf's central concern is much the same as ours, and while he reaches a number of similar conclusions, his reformulations are slanted more in favor of the dialectic and against functionalism."[19] He criticized Dahrendorf's concept of class and the dichotomous nature of conflict, suggesting instead a pluralist model and a "more general theory of group conflict, where authority would not occupy a privileged position, but would rather be one of many desirable 'goods.'..."[20]

Lenski attempted a synthesis of functionalism and Marxism on the basis of an extensive review of historical evidence, and concluded that both human nature and contemporary societies should be regarded as conflictual.[21] Those, of course, are the fundamental assumptions of sociological conflict theories. Lenski also found that the degree to which systems of inequality are maintained by coercion tends to be greater in societies with substantial economic surplus and less in societies with little economic surplus; that in general conflict is one of the chief consequences of inequality; that necessities of life tend to be acquired through hard work and other "legitimate" means, while the surplus tends to be acquired more often through force, fraud, or inheritance; that inequality must be seen as inevitable rather than as a function of the specific socioeconomic system; that law tends to function as an instrument of oppression and exploitation in agrarian societies, but in other types of societies is more related to the common good than to the good of a privileged minority; and that the question of whether the concept of class is a heuristic device or real groupings of people is an empirical question, but in general it is merely heuristic.[22] Some of these findings were inconsistent with functionalism, others were inconsistent with Marxism; but all can be incorporated without serious problem into a sociological conflict theory.

Finally, Vanfossen also attempted a synthesis of Marxist and functionalist positions, and arrived at what she called "basically a conflict model with systemic assumptions." Her first assumption was that

> human beings, when given a choice, will tend to act in terms of their own interests or the interests of the group with which they identify....What is defined by them to be in their interests is varied. It may be consistent with major value themes already extant in the culture—themes that are disseminated by religious precepts, major ideologies, or educational emphases and that provide world images, as Weber noted....But...definitions of self-interest or group interest usually include the acquisition of or control over scarce and valued goods and services.[23]

Her other assumptions were that in modern societies, "the economic institution (as compared to the state, the educational system, or the church) sets the basic form that social stratification will take"; that the other principal source of power is the political institution; and that "the other major institutions—the family, religion, education, communications media, law—primarily play supportive roles...."

Each of these attempts at a synthesis took the form of a sociological conflict theory, in that each described both human nature and contemporary societies in conflictual terms. Each focused on the description and analysis of real, contemporary societies and did not contain any descriptions of hypothetical societies in which the "problem" of conflict was somehow "solved." None contained assessments of the legitimacy of contemporary societies, or of the actions of dominant groups and of groups in conflict with dominant groups within contemporary societies.

The fact that a number of separate attempts to reach a "synthesis" between functionalism and Marxism have each resulted in positions that are consistent with sociological conflict theories suggests that the sociological conflict approach might be able to resolve some of the fundamental controversies between the sociological consensus and radical theories. That suggestion can also be derived from the conclusion of the propositional analysis that begins this chapter, i.e., that a sociological conflict theory would be able to "absorb" the descriptive and analytical content of both sociological consensus and radical theories while leaving out their contradictory assessments of legitimacy. Dahrendorf seems to have intended his theory of social change to be such an abstraction from the radical theory of Marx. He attempted to absorb from Marx's theory those elements that described the processes of social change, while leaving out those elements that assessed the legitimacy of the various positions in the conflicts. Dahrendorf erred, however, when he identified theories of social change with conflict theory itself and identified theories of social order with consensus theory. In fact, theories of social order are possible within the sociological conflict framework. Simmel's theory does not contain a complete theory of order or change, but contains many elements of both. And Machiavelli's *The Prince* is a complete theory of social order, describing the means by which the prince could construct a consensus in his society and thus achieve a stable and prosperous regime. His theory is reminiscent in many ways of Parsons' theory, except, of course, that Parsons' is much more modern and complex. Yet there is no essential contradiction between the processes that Machiavelli described and those that Parsons described. The major difference between the two theories is that Parsons described the processes as legitimate and justifiable in some fundamental sense, while Machiavelli described them as being fundamentally illegitimate though necessary and beneficial in the end. Machiavelli's theory seems to stand in much the same relationship to Parsons' theory as Dahrendorf's does to Marx's— i.e., it describes the same processes, but does not make the same assessments of legitimacy.

There are a number of areas of theoretical controversy between sociological consensus and radical theories that become either empirical questions or matters of terminology within the sociological conflict framework. Fundamental to that framework is Simmel's concept of multiple group affiliations: the individual is said to be a member of many different groups each of which shares common values and interests, but different groups to which the same individual belongs may have conflicting values and interests. The term "group" here is comparable to what Dahrendorf called a "quasi-group"—i.e., it denotes a set of individuals who are in structurally similar positions so that they share values and interests. The term does not necessarily imply that those individuals have organized themselves into an interest group to pursue and defend those values and interests. Simmel used the term in this way when, for example, he described women as a "group."

One area of theoretical controversy between sociological consensus and radical theories is the question of whether societies are characterized primarily by consensus or by conflict. Within the context of the sociological conflict framework, consensus and conflict are reciprocal terms in that every consensus implies conflict and every conflict implies consensus. There is no consensus that cannot be subdivided into conflicts: the American supraparty consensus can be subdivided into Democrats and Republicans, the Republicans can be subdivided into conservatives and moderates, and so on. Each individual is described in terms of multiple group affiliations, so that at each level there is said to be a consensus within the full group but conflict between the subgroups. Conversely, every conflict implies a consensus, since, as Dahrendorf stated, "there can be no conflict, unless this conflict occurs within a context of meaning, i.e., some kind of coherent 'system.'"[24] Sociological conflict theories do not simply describe the conflict but also describe the consensus, as Simmel's work makes clear. Dahrendorf's theory focused on a particular set of conflicts within a particular type of consensus—those between authorities and subjects in an imperatively coordinated association—because Dahrendorf said those conflicts led to social structural change in the association. But he did not imply that there was only conflict in those associations, or that conflict was their predominant characteristic.

To a considerable extent, the controversy between sociological consensus and radical theories on this point is a matter of terminology. Sociological consensus theories define consensus as the absence of overt conflict, while radical theories define it as the presence of full and free agreements. Sociological conflict theories would not use the term "consensus" but can describe in the same society groups based on full and free agreements as well as much larger and more encompassing groups based on the absence of overt conflicts. Beyond that, the controversy between sociological consensus and radical theories concerns the long-range capabilities of particular societies to deal with conflict. Parsons, for example, portrayed Western democracies as capable of subsuming the vast majority of conflicts under a value consensus, so that only a small number of conflicts had to be controlled through the overt and potential use of force. Marx, in contrast, argued that the dominant conflicts in those societies would inevitably break through the ruling ideologies, resulting in revolutionary overthrow of their governments. Within sociological conflict theories, it is an empirical question with respect to any particular society whether Parsons or Marx is more accurate.

A second question on which there is controversy between sociological consensus and radical theories is whether behavior is determined primarily by values or by interests. Parsons' theory conceded that interests were largely in conflict, but argued that commonly held values could override the conflicting interests and create social order. Marx argued that interests ultimately determined values and were the primary determinants of behavior. Simmel, like Marx, used the term "interests" to describe the sources of human behavior, but he did not limit that term to economic interests, as Marx did. Rather, his was a much more general formulation: interests in a common purpose. That common purpose could include but was by no means limited to economic purposes. In fact, Simmel maintained that those whose common purpose was a "noble cause" or a "supra-individual claim" had a tendency to enter into the most merciless and radical conflicts. Simmel also talked about "codes of honor" that develop as a group increases its social solidarity. Thus, Simmel's theory incorporated both values and interests as sources of human behavior.

The terms "values" and "interests" are often used in ways that imply that they are mutually exclusive, but in fact both can be subsumed under the term "benefits." The benefits associated with interests are normally direct and apparent, but at least some benefits to some people will always be said to be associated with values. The term "interests" may be used to imply that the intended beneficiaries of one's actions are either oneself or a very small group with whom one is identified—those who are closely related to or associated with oneself or who are quite similar to oneself in social characteristics. In contrast, the term "values" is often used to imply that the intended beneficiaries of one's actions are a much larger and more diverse group—for example, the entire human race, an entire nation, or an entire social class. The term "values" may also imply that the intended beneficiaries do not include oneself, as, for example, when an upper-class person struggles to benefit the lower class. The consensus-conflict debate has to a certain extent been a debate over whether the primary determinants of human behavior are "values" or "interests"—i.e., whether the intended beneficiaries of human action are more often large and diverse groups, or more immediate groups centered about the self.

To a certain extent, consensus theories (particularly of the conservative type) have maintained that as one rises up the social ladder, the determinants of human behavior shift from interests to values—i.e., the intended beneficiaries of one's actions become increasingly broader and more diverse groups. There may in fact be some basis for this argument, particularly when one considers Maslow's description of the "hierarchy of needs" as the basis of human motivation.[25] When the lower-order needs are not met, particularly physiological and safety needs, then one's focus is necessarily limited, and the primary beneficiary of one's actions will generally be oneself. When those needs are to some extent fulfilled, one addresses the needs for love, but the intended beneficiaries of one's actions will still be very restricted: oneself and those whom one loves. It is only when one moves into the higher-order needs, such as the needs for esteem and for self-actualization, that the intended beneficiaries of one's actions can expand very broadly beyond one's immediate group. Thus, it is only as one moves into the upper classes of most societies that a broader focus can be possible.

On the other hand, conflict theories (particularly of the radical type) have generally argued that the true beneficiaries of the actions of those in the upper class are not large and diverse groups but rather small and uniform groups that include the upper class itself. There may be some basis for this argument as well. As Durkheim pointed out, human nature is such that there is no point at which even lower-order needs are completely fulfilled. No matter how much one has, it is always possible to want more. As one seeks esteem and self-actualization, one may simultaneously be insuring that the physiological and safety needs of oneself and those one loves are increasingly protected. In addition, as social distance increases, knowledge of other groups diminishes, and it becomes more likely that one's beliefs about what will benefit other groups are wrong. For example, a hard-core capitalist may believe that unregulated free enterprise is in the best interests of all social groups. He may base that belief on his own immediate experience, where it clearly benefits his own social group, but he may have a genuine lack of familiarity with the groups that are socially distant from him. Because of that lack of familiarity, he may project his own experience onto them, and arrive at the sincerely held conviction that all groups will benefit from the dismantling of government regulations. Whether such dismantling actually will help all groups in the society is an extremely difficult question to answer, but it is clear that it will directly help some groups. Because his own group is among those who will clearly and directly be helped by the dismantling of government regulations, those who believe that such a change will harm other groups may be inclined to believe that the person's motives are insincere and that he is merely out for his own gain. So while the person would describe his motives in terms of values, others might describe them in terms of interests. A comparable scenario can be constructed for the case of a hard-core socialist who believes that the nationalization of all business and industry would be in the best interests of all social groups.

When considered in this way, the controversy about whether values or interests are the primary determinants of human behavior becomes both a matter of terminology and an empirical question. Both terms may be used to describe human behavior, as long as excessively narrow definitions are avoided. For example, the above discussion can be subsumed under Vanfossen's general assumption that "human beings, when given a choice, will tend to act in terms of their own interests or the interests of the group with which they identify." One need merely keep in mind that the term "interests" is not limited to economic interests but includes a wide variety of "benefits"; that the group with which one identifies can be a very broad and diverse group, as large as the entire human race; and that, despite one's intentions, one's actions may not have the expected beneficial effects.[26] Whether a particular individual is motivated to benefit only himself and a few others who are similar to himself, or is motivated to benefit a large number of people many of whom are quite different from himself, is then an empirical question. Within the sociological conflict framework, general statements can be presented that relate social position to type of motivation, but those statements must be supported by empirical investigations. In contrast, sociological consensus and radical theories are based in part on assumptions about the primary motivations for human behavior, assumptions that at present have not been empirically verified. It was because of the need for such assumptions that Simmel regarded macrosociological theories as "premature."

A third point of controversy between sociological consensus and radical theories concerns the size of the dominant power group in a society. Sociological consensus theories describe the dominant power group as incorporating the large majority of people in a society, while radical theories portray it as quite small. Within the sociological conflict framework, each individual can be described in terms of multiple group affiliations, where some of the values and interests of these groups may be in conflict while others are in agreement. Because values and interests are derived from social structural position, conflicts between groups on values and interests will tend to increase as the social distance between groups increases. Thus, groups that are quite distant from each other in terms of their social structural location will be more likely to have conflicting values and interests than will groups that are quite close to each other in social structural location. The term "dominant power group" can then be used to describe any number of concentric groups, all having the same core but including more and more people who have less and less in common with the core without at the same time entering into overt conflict with it. The core of the set of concentric groups is what Marxist theorists would call the "ruling class," while the entire set of concentric groups is what Parsons called the "social system."

The sociological conflict formulation differs from the Marxist formulation in that it implies that the probability of conflict between the ruling class and those groups who are closest to the ruling class in social distance is quite small, since most of their values and interests are similar. In Marxist theories, the ruling class is said to be in fundamental conflict with all other social groups because of their structural location with respect to the ownership of the means of production. The sociological conflict formulation also differs from the sociological consensus formulation in that it implies that there is a high probability of overt conflict between the core of most fully integrated members and those groups in the social system who are at the greatest social distance from the core. Many of the values and interests of the socially distant groups are in conflict with the values and interests of the core and similar to the values and interests of groups outside the social system who are already in overt conflict with it. These groups are held in "consensus" almost exclusively by the potential use of force, a fact which is not at all apparent in sociological consensus theories.

While the controversy about the size of the dominant power group is to some extent a matter of terminology, the process by which that group achieves and retains dominance in a society is a matter for empirical investigations. Once the moral evaluations of legitimacy and illegitimacy have been dispensed with, the analytical content of both radical and sociological consensus theories on that subject can be absorbed into a sociological conflict framework and empirically tested for adequacy. For example, Marx's analysis of the process can be tested and compared with Parsons' analysis. To a considerable extent, that is what is done when a synthesis between the two types of theories is attempted. Thus, the synthesis itself, as described above, will fall into the sociological conflict framework. The present state of empirical investigations may not permit a conclusive resolution of the issue of which (if either) of the two analyses is valid, but it is only by abstracting from the moral evaluations of legitimacy that the two theories can be empirically compared.

A fourth area of controversy between sociological consensus and radical theories is the question of whether conflicts can be reduced primarily through restraining human behavior or through reorganizing social structures. Sociological consensus theorists argue that the solution to the problem of conflict lies in strengthening social bonds to control human behavior, since they view the problem as located in the conflictual human nature. Radicals, in contrast, view the problem as located in the conflictual social structure and therefore argue that the solution lies in reorganizing that structure. Sociological conflict theorists state that both human nature and society are conflictual. That means that there can be no possible society in which conflicts are fully controlled, as implied in sociological consensus theories, or fully resolved, as implied in radical theories. Thus, within the context of sociological conflict theories, the "problem" of conflict cannot be "solved." Rather, conflict must be viewed as a continuing presence in societies, where the best that can be done is to "manage" it effectively in order to reduce the negative effects that are associated with it.[27] The description of both human nature and societies as conflictual implies that those negative effects might be reduced both through strengthening social bonds (as recommended by Machiavelli) and through reorganizing social structures (as recommended in Dahrendorf's discussion of conflict regulation). But these recommendations are merely to alleviate some of the negative effects of conflict—no "solution" is promised to the "problem" of conflict as in sociological consensus and radical theories. Thus, sociological conflict theories may be less attractive to those who have become accustomed to dealing with theories that imply a happier ending to the story of society. Nevertheless, the implications of sociological conflict theories may be more realistic than the implications of the more optimistic theories.

In general, sociological conflict theories may be less attractive than sociological consensus or radical theories, not only because they are more pessimistic, but because they imply less about the world. In each of the four areas of theoretical controversy described above, the sociological conflict position provides literally no useful implications. It merely provides a theoretical framework in which the controversy can be empirically described and analyzed. The solution to the controversy must depend on the empirical description and analysis, not on any logical implications of the theory itself. That has led some theorists to criticize sociological conflict theories as "trivial" or "tautological."[28]

But that same "trivial" and "tautological" aspect of sociological conflict theories can also be seen as a major advantage. Conflict is an aspect of all past and present human societies, but whether it should be attributed to human nature or to social organizations is not known at present. Both sociological consensus and radical theories take a position on that question and attribute the conflict to one of those phenomena and not to the other. They then develop full-scale social theories based on those positions. Sociological conflict theories can also be described as taking a hard-and-fast position on that question, or they can be described as taking a "tentative" position based on the present state of empirical knowledge. The sociological conflict position is appropriate as a tentative position because it relegates most of the controversy to the area of empirical investigations, rather than resolving it through theoretical assumptions, and because it is open to the entire range of policy implications, which can then be empirically tested for their effectiveness. It is also appropriate as a tentative position because it can be developed into either the sociological consensus or the radical position if future empirical investigations warrant. Thus, if empirical investigations find conclusive evidence that humans are naturally consensual and that conflict is exclusively derived from social organizations, sociological conflict theories could simply drop human nature as a source of conflict. Sociological consensus theories could not do that because they are based on the assumption that human nature is the *sole* source of conflict and that social organizations themselves do not generate conflict, although they may fail to control it. Conversely, if empirical investigations find conclusive evidence that humans are naturally conflictual and that variations in social organizations do not affect the incidence of those conflicts (although they may affect their overt expression), sociological conflict theories could simply drop societies as a source of conflict. That could not be done with radical theories, however, because they are based on the assumption that social organization is the *sole* source of human conflict and that humans themselves are naturally consensual. Thus, the assertion that sociological conflict theories are "trivial" or "tautological" may be in some respects accurate, but at the same time it may not be a criticism. It may be, as Schumacher has said, that "less is more."[29]

Like other discussions of consensus and conflict theories, this discussion has demonstrated that the areas of agreement among them are more extensive than the areas of disagreement. It can be asked why the consensus-conflict debate has generated such intense emotion when the two types of theories have so much in common. Certainly at least some of that emotion is derived from the fact that the two types of theories support and defend opposite political positions. But beyond their political implications, it is possible that the consensus-conflict debate is itself a manifestation of the tendency for any consensus to divide itself into conflicting parts. One of Coser's propositions, extracted from Simmel's theory, was that "the closer the relationship, the more intense the conflict."[30] The vast areas of agreement between consensus and conflict theories are evidence of a very close relationship, so that the intensity of the consensus-conflict debate may be a function of the very closeness of that relationship. One is tempted to speculate that if the consensus-conflict debate had not developed in sociology there would have been some comparable conflict around which passions and hostility would have been generated and which would have expressed what Simmel called the "inborn need for hating and fighting."

Notes

1. This analysis is not too controversial when applied to the hypothetical societies described by the earlier theorists examined in this work—Plato's "Republic," Augustine's "City of God," Hobbes' "Leviathan," Rousseau's "social contract," and Comte's "Positive" society. Once established, those hypothetical societies contained no theoretical sources of evolutionary or revolutionary change whereby they could return to a less desirable state—i.e., they were all described as having achieved a state of equilibrium. It was precisely that characteristic that led their authors to propose them as "solutions" to the problem of conflict in society.

A similar point can be made about the more modern theories, despite likely objections from those theories' adherents. Radicals might point out that Marx and Engels rejected the "utopian" socialism of their predecessors. But Marx and Engels did not object to the projection of a nonantagonistic future by those "utopian" socialists, only to their "unscientific" method of thinking. They argued that their own "scientific" socialism would replace the "utopian" socialism of the past, but they retained an essentially utopian view of the future. In particular, the ideal communist society that they proposed meets the four criteria in the analysis: it is hypothetical, is consensual, has no sources of revolutionary change once class conflict has been eliminated, and has no sources of evolutionary change whereby it might be transformed into a noncommunist society. Communism, as hypothesized by Marx and Engels, achieves a state of equilibrium and thus is a "solution" to the problem of conflict. Official descriptions of present-day communist societies reflect that same theoretical limitation on the possibilities of social change—revolutionary change is said to be impossible, and evolutionary change is said to be possible only in the direction of the fully communist state. Thus, it is appropriate to describe the ideal communist society as a "utopia." See Martin G. Plattel, *Utopia and Critical Thinking* (Pittsburgh: Duquesne University Press, 1972), p. 34; Judith Shklar, "The Political Theory of Utopia: From Melancholy to Nostalgia," Frank E. Manuel, ed., *Utopias and Utopian Thought* (Boston: Beacon Press, 1966), p. 103; and Thomas Molnar, *Utopia— The Perennial Heresy* (New York: Sheed and Ward, 1967), pp. 36–42.

Many mainstream sociologists might object to applying the analysis to Durkheim's and Parsons' theories. It must be kept in mind that the analysis refers to the hypothetical ideal society in those theories—i.e., the "normal" society and the "fully integrated" society—and not to descriptions of real societies. Both of those hypothetical ideals are described as being in a state of equilibrium, and neither theory contains elements by which societies would be removed from that state once it was achieved. Durkheim's "normal" society does contain elements of conflict, but only enough to create the possibilities for evolutionary (but not revolutionary) social change consistent with its remaining in its "normal" state. Although Durkheim maintained that "normal" societies that existed in earlier historical periods had in fact become "anomic," his theory does not indicate how that could have happened if those societies were truly "normal." One must assume that those societies were somewhat anomic to begin with. Parsons acknowledged that the "fully integrated" society was purely hypothetical, but it similarly lacked any theoretical elements by which it could ever become only partially integrated. Again, it is this characteristic of achieving an equilibrium that makes these societies appropriate as "solutions" to the problem of conflict in society. See Ralf Dahrendorf, "Out of Utopia: Toward a Reorientation of Sociological Analysis," *American Journal of Sociology* (September 1958), 64(2):115–27.

2. Ralf Dahrendorf, *Class and Class Conflict in Industrial Society* (Stanford, Calif.: Stanford University Press, 1959), pp. 157–65.

3. Percy S. Cohen, *Modern Social Theory* (New York: Basic Books, 1968), pp. 166–72.

4. George B. Vold, *Theoretical Criminology* (New York: Oxford University Press, 1958), pp. 218–19; 2d ed. prepared by Thomas J. Bernard (1979), pp. 296–97.

5. Ian Taylor, Paul Walton, and Jock Young, *The New Criminology* (New York: Harper and Row, 1973), p. 31.

6. Gerhard Lenski, *Power and Privilege* (New York: McGraw-Hill, 1966), p. 22.

7. Jack L. Roach, Llewellyn Gross, and O. R. Gursslin, *Social Stratification in the United States* (Englewood Cliffs: Prentice-Hall, 1969), p. 55.

8. John Horton, "Order and Conflict Theories of Social Problems as Competing Ideologies," *American Journal of Sociology* (May 1966), 71(6):705–6.

9. Stanislaw Ossowski, *Class Structure in the Social Consciousness* (New York: The Free Press, 1963).

10. Don Martindale, *The Nature and Types of Sociological Theory* (Boston: Houghton Mifflin, 1960), p. 200.

11. Ibid., p. 176.

12. Ruth A. Wallace and Alison Wolf, *Contemporary Sociological Theory* (Englewood Cliffs: Prentice-Hall, 1980), p. 77.

13. Jonathan H. Turner, *The Structure of Sociological Theory*, rev. ed. (Homewood, Ill.: Dorsey Press, 1978), pp. 121–97.

14. Dennis Wrong, "Oversocialized Man: Postscript 1975," in *Skeptical Sociology* (New York: Columbia University Press, 1976), pp. 47–48.

15. Dick Atkinson, *Orthodox Consensus and Radical Alternative* (London: Heineman, 1971), p. 109.

16. Ibid., pp. 66–104.

17. Austin T. Turk, "Class, Conflict, and Criminalization," *Sociological Focus* (August 1977), 10(3):209–20. See also Thomas J. Bernard, "The Distinction Between Conflict and Radical Criminology," *Journal of Criminal Law and Criminology* (Spring 1981), 72(1):362–79.

18. Dahrendorf, *Class and Class Conflict*.

19. Pierre van den Berghe, "Dialectic and Functionalism: Toward a Theoretical Synthesis," *American Sociological Review* (October 1963), 28:695–705.

20. Ibid., p. 701.

21. Lenski, *Power and Privilege*, p. 441.

22. Ibid., pp. 441–43.

23. Beth Ensminger Vanfossen, *The Structure of Social Inequality* (Boston: Little, Brown, 1979), pp. 52–54.

24. Dahrendorf, *Class and Class Conflict*, p. 154.

25. A. H. Maslow, "A Theory of Human Motivation," *Psychological Review*, (1943), 50:370–96.

26. See the discussion in Andrew Hopkins, "On the Sociology of Criminal Law," *Social Problems*, (April 1975), 22:608–19.

27. For a more comprehensive discussion of this perspective, see Paul Wehr, *Conflict Regulation* (Boulder, Colo.: Westview Press, 1979). The book is based on the proposition that "conflict is a natural process common to all societies, with predictable dynamics and amenable to constructive regulation" (p. 8).

28. Hopkins, "Sociology of Criminal Law," p. 614.

29. E. F. Schumacher, *Small is Beautiful: A Study of Economics As If People Mattered* (London: Blond and Briggs, 1974).

30. Lewis Coser, *The Functions of Social Conflict* (New York: The Free Press, 1956), pp. 67–72, citing George Simmel, *Conflict and The Web of Group Affiliations* (New York: The Free Press, 1955), pp. 33–35.

Chapter 10

Conclusion: Theory, Fact, and Value

THE PROBLEM examined in this work concerns the nature of the consensus-conflict debate. Consensus and conflict theories are often portrayed as making contradictory empirical assertions, and it has also been argued that they represent competing value imperatives or complementary heuristic principles. In order to ascertain the exact nature of the debate itself, fourteen theories that can be classified as either consensus or conflict theories were selected and examined. The assumptions and assertions each theory makes about consensus and conflict (the content) were analyzed, as was the structure in which those assumptions and assertions are woven into a coherent argument (the form). On the basis of the descriptions of the specific form and content of each of the theories, the general form and content of consensus and conflict theories was delineated and the relationship between the different types of theories was presented. The conclusion of the analysis was that the general form of each theory is substantially determined by the content of its assumptions and assertions about human nature and contemporary societies. The interrelation between form and content enables each theory to assert a coherent argument that can describe and explain a wide variety of empirical situations. While the theories do not differ substantially in their empirical assertions or descriptions, they differ dramatically in the evaluations they imply about the actions of dominant groups in contemporary societies, as well as the actions of those in conflict with the dominant groups. Those evaluations are based on differing descriptions of the ideal society, rather than different empirical assertions about real societies. Consequently, the examination concludes that the consensus-conflict debate is not an empirical debate and cannot be resolved through empirical investigations.

Certainly specific theories of each type may be verifiable or falsifiable by empirical data. For example, Simmel and Marx made contradictory predictions about the effect that awareness of true interests has on the violence of conflict.[1] The data so far seem to be consistent with Simmel's theory and inconsistent with Marx's. But such a finding will not, in general, convince radical theorists that the sociological conflict position is the correct one. Rather, radicals will adjust Marx's theory to incorporate this empirical finding within the same radical framework. That is, they would retain the view that human nature is consensual although contemporary societies are conflictual, and continue to seek methods of reorganizing societies so that man's consensual nature can be expressed. Such endeavors are what Kuhn calls "normal science" within the context of a paradigm.[2]

This work has been addressed primarily to sociologists. The earlier theories of the social philosophers were included because they are sometimes cited to support positions in the contemporary sociological debate, with the historic stature of the theorist being used to lend credence to the position being espoused. The attempt to confront the consensus-conflict debate in sociology and to build an effective case for a solution to it is enhanced by showing that the proposed solution is consistent with the earlier theories. In addition, considering the earlier social philosophers provides some distance from which the controversy can be viewed. The relations between the types of theories is demonstrated first for the social philosophers, where the arguments may generate less resistance among modern sociologists. Thus, the inclusion of the social philosophers was in part a way of leading into what I saw as a controversial analysis.

On the other hand, the inclusion of the social philosophers indicates that the analysis is applicable beyond the field of sociology, especially in the fields of political science, philosophy, and theology. The field of political science includes contemporary followers of each of the social philosophers examined here.[3] In addition, there are Platonists and Aristotelians in contemporary philosophy and Augustinians and Thomists in contemporary theology. One can also find the basic assumptions of a radical theory in contemporary theology, as illustrated by the following quotation from Tillich:

First: *Esse qua esse bonum est*. This Latin phrase is a basic dogma of Christianity. It means "Being as being is good," or in the biblical mythological form: God saw everything that he had created, and behold, it was good. The second statement is the universal fall— fall meaning the transition from this essential goodness into existential estrangement from oneself, which happens in every living being and in every time. The third statement refers to the possibility of salvation. We should remember that salvation is derived from *salvus* or *salus* in Latin, which means "healed" or "whole," as opposed to disruptiveness.[4]

One can easily see the basic radical framework in this statement—the consensual description of human nature, the conflictual description of all contemporary societies, and the possibility of a consensual society in which true human nature is expressed. To the extent that theories in fields such as political science, theology, and philosophy are based on assumptions or assertions about human nature and contemporary societies, they can be expected to take the general forms described in the previous chapters.

The method of analysis used here may be applicable to other chronic controversies besides the consensus-conflict debate, both in sociology and in other fields. Its application would entail analyzing the fundamental assumptions and/or assertions underlying the different positions in the controversy, along with the manner in which they are organized into a coherent theory that can describe and interpret a wide variety of empirical situations. One would then be able to ascertain the relationships among the various positions in the controversy. That method has been referred to as the analysis of the relationship between form and content. While Simmel used those terms in his analysis of social relations, I have used them here in the analysis of social theories. I am suggesting that the analysis of the relationship between form and content in social theories may be a general analytic technique that has significance beyond its utility in analyzing the consensus-conflict debate.

This book has focused its attention on the effects that descriptions of human nature and contemporary societies have on the form of the theory that follows from them. It seems appropriate at this point to ask whether human nature and contemporary societies *really are* consensual or conflictual. As presented here, the questions of whether human nature should be described as consensual or conflictual appears to be more substantive than the question of whether contemporary societies should be described as consensual or conflictual. On the one hand, human beings are said to be like bees in a hive, made for life in societies. On the other, they are said to be naturally aggressive, so that the war of all against all is just beneath the surface.

Similarly contrasting views of human nature can be found in fields other than sociology. For example, Freud argued that aggressive instincts were the most fundamental of man's natural drives and that they could be controlled only through repression.[5] Erikson believed quite the opposite:

> ... in the sequence of significant experiences the healthy child, if halfway properly guided, merely obeys and on the whole can be trusted to obey inner laws of development, namely those laws which in his prenatal period had formed one organ after another and which now create a succession of potentialities for significant interaction with those around him.[6]

Those contrasting descriptions of human nature determine in part the general form that each theory takes, and the controversy between the two theories can be traced in part to those descriptions. A similar controversy can be found in the field of anthropology. Lorenz and Ardrey have argued that there are instinctive drives for aggression and territorial space,[7] while Leakey has portrayed humans as naturally pacific and cooperative.[8] The debate between these two positions has been as sharp in anthropology as it has been in sociology,[9] and the theoretical implications of the two positions are similar to their implications in sociology and social philosophy.

The fact that no resolution of the question has been achieved in psychology and anthropology, which focus more directly on human nature than sociology does, makes the assumption of one or the other position in sociology highly questionable. Thus, the sociological conflict position has an advantage, since (as was discussed at the end of chapter 9) it can be regarded as a tentative position pending further empirical evidence. In addition, the sociological conflict position seems to have some merit in itself because of the concept of multiple group affiliations. Individuals are described as being consensual within groups but conflictual between groups, where groups occur and overlap at all levels of interaction. The consensus within groups is to a great extent generated by the conflict between groups. That more complex view seems to incorporate elements of both views of human nature—while man is made for life in groups, the war of group against group is always just beneath the surface.

I have argued that the description of contemporary societies is a matter of terminology that is not based on any differentiating empirical assertions. Is "society" the social system that organizes it, or is it all the interlocking and overlapping groups, including the social system as the dominant and, at times, the most comprehensive group? Is the "consensus" the presence of full and free agreements, or is it merely the absence of overt conflict? The way that "society" and "consensus" are defined will determine whether at least some contemporary societies can be said to be consensual. The choice of these definitions is the prerogative of each author and is not subject to empirical verification or falsification. However, the choice of terms is also related to whether the society in question is described as being in some sense "legitimate." Thus, the choice of terminology ultimately boils down to what types of societies, if any, can be said to be "legitimate." That, of course, is a question about which there is an immense literature, and no attempt will be made here to summarize the arguments of the various positions.[10] However, I have argued that the evaluations of legitimacy in some theories are not based on the assertion of different sets of empirical facts than are the evaluations of illegitimacy in other theories. The same sets of empirical facts have been used to support both evaluations. Thus, I have argued that the evaluation of legitimacy itself is not an empirical matter and cannot be resolved through empirical investigations. Rather, it must be considered a pure value judgment. This can be taken as an example of "Hume's Law," which states that moral conclusions cannot be deduced from factual premises.[11]

The claims that sociological conflict theorists have made for a value-free sociology must be considered against this background. Collins, for example, states:

> Conflict theory is intrinsically more detached from value judgments than is systems theory. To be able to recognize competing

interests as a matter of *fact*, without trying to squeeze some of them out of existence as unrealistic, deviant, or just plain evil, is the essence of a detached position. It is for this reason that I argue for conflict theory as the basis of a scientific sociology, precisely because it moves farthest from the implicit value judgments that underlie most other approaches. Conflict theorists have come in a variety of political shades, ranging from anarchists and revolutionary sociologists through welfare-state liberals to conservative nationalists. They have hardly been averse to arguing for their political values, but it is not so difficult to separate their value judgments from their causal analyses, and it is to the best of them—Max Weber, above all—that we owe the ideal of detachment from ideology in social science.[12]

I have argued that sociological conflict theories provide objective and value-neutral descriptions of contemporary societies. That neutrality was originally achieved because of a balance in the theory between conflictual descriptions of contemporary societies, from which negative evaluations of those societies could be inferred, and the projection of an ideal society that was the "best" of existing societies rather than a hypothetical "utopian" society, from which positive evaluations of contemporary societies could be inferred. Other theorists have argued that all scientists express values in such things as the selection of the problem to be examined, the preference for some hypotheses over others, and the choice of conceptual schemes.[13] That is as true for a sociological conflict theorist as it is for any other theorist. But I have made a different argument: that conservative, sociological consensus, and radical theories are in fact *based on* value judgments about the legitimacy of contemporary societies and that sociological conflict theories are not based on such value judgments. In that sense, sociological conflict theories are value free. I also argued that when the value judgments are removed from the other types of theories, they take on the form of sociological conflict theories. Because of that, only sociological conflict theories have the potential to be scientific.

Because they are based on value judgments, conservative, sociological consensus, and radical theories meet certain human needs that sociological conflict theories do not meet. Osgood, Suci, and Tennenbaum argued that one of the most important and consistent dimensions of meaning is an "evaluative" dimen-

sion that structures things on a "good-bad" continuum.[14] Kluckhohn and Strodtbeck argued that there are a "limited number of
common human problems for which all peoples at all times must
find solutions."[15] Included among those problems are the character of innate human nature and the modality of human relationships.[16] With the exception of sociological conflict theories,
the different types of theories allow people to structure questions
about human nature and human relationships on a "good-bad"
continuum. Radical theories imply that present human relationships are "bad," while individuals themselves are "good." Sociological consensus theories imply that contemporary human relationships are "good" even though individuals themselves are
"bad." The current unpopularity of conservative theories seems
to be related to their portrayal of some individuals and some
human relationships as "good," while others are portrayed as
"bad." Such a portrayal offends the egalitarian sensibilities of
many modern theorists, who prefer to describe all individuals in
the same theoretical terms. Earlier conservative theorists, as well
as modern conservatives, did not hold to such egalitarian values,
so the conservative theories were quite satisfying to them.[17] The
general unpopularity of sociological conflict theories seems to be
related to the fact that they are not conducive to structuring
things on a "good-bad" dimension. Early sociological conflict
theories implied that everything was "bad" and only minimally
differentiated between what was "worse" and what was "not so
bad." Later theories portrayed things in nonevaluative, "objective" terms that did not imply anything about what was "good"
or "bad." Thus, these theories are not satisfying to those who
believe that one of the purposes of a social theory is to distribute
social phenomena on an evaluative dimension.

The popularity of sociological consensus and radical theories may also be due in part to the clarity with which they
embody beliefs about social needs. Those who adhere to consensus theories generally believe that stability and order are the
primary social needs, and they may defend those theories in part
on the basis that their dissemination in society will contribute to
achieving that state. For example, Shils defended Parsons' consensus theory in part because he said it would further the process
of constructing the consensus it described and would lead to an

even greater appreciation for the individual and his welfare and stronger personal attachments among the members of society.[18] He criticized conflict theories in part because he said that they would lead to an increase in the socially harmful phenomena that they described, such as deception, manipulation, coercion, and pursuit of selfish individual interests. Radical theorists, on the other hand, have generally viewed change as the primary social need, and they have been criticized for ignoring descriptive and analytical accuracy in their concern to construct theories that contribute to the change process.

The problem with both consensus and radical theories is that by denying that conflict is "legitimate" in at least some societies, they deny that their opponents have the right to make a case. As Dahrendorf has pointed out, that does not lead to an absence of conflict but rather to its expression through unregulated and often violent means. Parsons' and Shils' description of a consensual American society is certainly appealing, but it denied legitimacy to those who had fundamental conflicts with the American social system. Those conflicts burst forth only a few years later in the violent riots of the late 1960s and early 1970s. Marx's vision of a communist society is also very appealing, but it too denies legitimacy to those who are in conflict with that society. Thus, violence has broken out in East Germany in 1953, in Hungary in 1956, in Czechoslovakia in 1968, and in Poland in 1970, 1976, and 1980. By denying that one's opponents have the right to make a case, one does not make conflict go away. One merely limits one's ability to deal with it in nonviolent ways.

To the extent that sociological conflict theories have embodied any beliefs about social needs, they have embodied the need for freedom. Burnham described Machiavellians as "defenders of freedom" and argued that it was only by exposing the true processes of politics that individuals could protect themselves from abuses of power by their political leaders. Simmel argued that the proliferation of conflict groups in society was associated with the growth of freedom and individuality. Dahrendorf contended that the institutionalized recognition of conflict was the necessary condition for liberty, and his major concern was how to achieve societal states that made liberty possible. Perhaps it is necessary to judge social theories in part on the basis of the social needs that they embody. But if that is so, then it could be argued that the social needs for both order and change should be subordinated to the social need for freedom.

In the last analysis, the preference for sociological conflict theories is itself a value preference, since it expresses a valuation of social theories that do not imply who is "right" and who is "wrong" when individuals and groups are in conflict with each other. That perspective is easier to maintain when one is not a party to the conflict oneself or when one does not identify with one of the parties to the conflict. Chomsky, for example, has argued that American scholars and journalists found it virtually impossible to describe American conflicts such as the Vietnam War in the same value-neutral terms they use to describe the conflicts of other nations.[19] Similarly, many people will find the sociological conflict perspective unacceptable in the description of common crimes, such as the conflict between a mugger and an elderly victim, or between a juvenile gang and the terrorized residents of a low-income housing project. In those conflicts, it may be felt that in order for a social theory to be "adequate" it must express "legitimacy" and "illegitimacy," who is "right" and who is "wrong," who is "victim" and who is "criminal." Sociological conflict theories of crime do not do so.[20] Rather, they provide value-neutral descriptions and analyses of those conflicts, just as they do with other conflicts in society. The preference for such "value-free" descriptions and analyses does not imply that one adheres to complete value-relativism, or that the actions of muggers and juvenile gangs are as "legitimate" as the actions of the people who are mugged and the police who arrest the gang members. Rather, by abstracting completely from the question of legitimacy, one expresses value preferences about the nature of social theories, not value preferences about human behavior. One may believe that social theories should be "value-free" without believing the same thing about oneself.

Notes

1. Jonathan H. Turner, *The Structure of Sociological Theory* (Homewood, Ill.: Dorsey Press, 1978), pp. 141–42.

2. Thomas S. Kuhn, *The Structure of Scientific Revolutions* (Chicago: University of Chicago Press, 1970), pp. 10–42.

3. See William T. Bluhm, *Theories of the Political System*, 3d ed. (Englewood Cliffs, N.J.: Prentice-Hall, 1978).

4. Paul Tillich, *Theology of Culture* (New York: Oxford University Press, 1959), pp. 118–19.

5. Sigmund Freud, *Civilization and Its Discontents* (New York: Norton, 1961).

6. Erik Erikson, *Childhood and Society* (New York: Norton, 1963), p. 67.

7. Konrad Lorenz, *On Aggression* (New York: Bantam, 1969); Robert Ardrey, *The Territorial Imperative* (New York: Dell, 1966).

8. Richard Leakey, *Origins* (New York: Dutton, 1977).

9. See, for example, Ashley Montagu, ed., *Man and Aggression* (New York: Oxford University Press, 1968); Roderic Gorney, *The Human Agenda* (New York: Bantam, 1973); and Anthony Storr, *Human Aggression* (New York: Atheneum, 1968). For the latest round in this continuing debate, see Derek Freeman, *Margaret Mead and Samoa: The Making and Unmaking of an Anthropological Myth* (Cambridge: Harvard University Press, 1983).

10. See, for example, Richard Barnet, "The Twilight of the Nation-State: A Crisis of Legitimacy," in R. P. Wolff, *The Rule of Law* (New York: Simon and Schuster, 1971); Jürgen Habermas, *Legitimation Crisis* (Boston: Beacon Press, 1973); G. Harries-Jenkins and J. Van Dorn, eds., *The Military and the Problem of Legitimacy* (Beverly Hills, Calif.: Sage, 1973); Arthur J. Vidich and Ronald M. Glassman, eds., *Conflict and Control: Challenge to Legitimacy of Modern Governments* (Beverly Hills, Calif.: Sage, 1979); and Bogdan Denitch, *Legitimation of Regimes* (Beverly Hills, Calif.: Sage, 1979).

11. J. L. Mackie, *Ethics: Inventing Right and Wrong* (New York: Penguin Books, 1977), p. 64.

12. Randall Collins, *Conflict Sociology—Toward an Explanatory Science* (New York: Academic Press, 1975), p. 21.

13. Alvin W. Gouldner, "Anti-Minotaur: The Myth of a Value-Free Sociology," *Social Problems* (Winter 1962), 9:199–213, See also similar statements by Gunnar Myrdal, *Value in Social Theory* (New York: Harper and Row, 1959); and Robert W. Friedrichs, *A Sociology of Sociology* (New York: The Free Press, 1970).

14. C. E. Osgood, G. Suci, and P. Tannenbaum, *The Measurement of Meaning* (Urbana: University of Illinois Press, 1957).

15. Florence R. Kluckhohn and Fred L. Strodtbeck, *Variations in Value Orientations* (Evanston, Ill.: Row, Peterson, 1961), p. 4.

16. Ibid., p. 11.

17. For an example of such a modern conservative theorist, see Edward Banfield, *The Unheavenly City* (Boston: Little, Brown, 1970).

18. Edward Shils, "The Calling of Sociology," in Talcott Parsons, Edward Shils, Kaspar D. Naegele, and Jesse R. Pitts, eds., *Theories of Society* (New York: The Free Press, 1961), 2:1405–48.

19. Noam Chomsky, *Towards a New Cold War: Essays on the Current Crisis and How We Got There* (New York: Pantheon, 1982).

20. Cf. George B. Vold, *Theoretical Criminology*, 2d ed. prepared by Thomas J. Bernard (New York: Oxford University Press, 1979), pp. 282–323; also Thomas J. Bernard, "The Distinction Between Conflict and Radical Criminology," *Journal of Criminal Law and Criminology* (Spring 1981), 72(1):362–79.

Index

301.01
B456C

AUTHOR

Bernard, Thomas J.

TITLE

~~Consensus-conflict debate.~~

301.01   Bernard, Thomas J.
B456C   Consensus-conflict debate.